Jordy Stone was born in a small beachside Australian town on the exquisite New South Wales central coast. While he loves the city and the energy that pours from every corner, he is a country boy at heart and is most at home on an empty beach or a meandering bush track. First and foremost, he is a husband, a father and a lover of the arts. Jordy comes from a family of writers and poets. Storytelling is in his blood. For many years, his creative outlet was song writing and live performance before turning his gaze to writing. Team sport and the game he loves will always be an integral part of his life, along with a good movie and the momentary escape it offers into another world. With his family, he's most often found on long beach walks or ocean swims where the seeds of each story begin. Side by side with his Labradors, he is a child of the salt water that runs through his veins.

For my wife and children – my life and inspiration.

For Mum and Dad – my bedrock in this world.

Jordy Stone

WHEN THE KNIVES RATTLE IN THE DRAWER

Based on a True Story

AUSTIN MACAULEY PUBLISHERS™
LONDON * CAMBRIDGE * NEW YORK * SHARJAH

Copyright © Jordy Stone 2023

The right of Jordy Stone to be identified as author of this work has been asserted by the author in accordance with sections 77 and 78 of the Copyright, Designs and Patents Act 1988.

All rights reserved. No part of this publication may be reproduced, stored in a retrieval system, or transmitted in any form or by any means, electronic, mechanical, photocopying, recording, or otherwise, without the prior permission of the publishers.

Any person who commits any unauthorised act in relation to this publication may be liable to criminal prosecution and civil claims for damages.

All of the events in this memoir are true to the best of author's memory. The views expressed in this memoir are solely those of the author.

A CIP catalogue record for this title is available from the British Library.

ISBN 9781398495791 (Paperback)
ISBN 9781398495807 (Hardback)
ISBN 9781398498273 (ePub e-book)
ISBN 9781398498266 (Audiobook)

www.austinmacauley.com

First Published 2023
Austin Macauley Publishers Ltd®
1 Canada Square
Canary Wharf
London
E14 5AA

Every step of this crazy journey was taken with my beautiful wife. From our first meeting as teenagers to the last word of this book and beyond, she has been my constant source of strength, inspiration and love. I knew she was the one from the second I met her and I am forever thankful for meeting my true soul mate, my best friend, my everything.

Table of Contents

Prologue	11
Chapter 1: Thresholds	12
Chapter 2: Stepping into Another World	19
Chapter 3: Contact	27
Chapter 4: Some Things Get Pushed Down Deep Inside	37
Chapter 5: The Upstairs	45
Chapter 6: 1817	54
Chapter 7: The Weird and the Wonderful	62
Chapter 8: The Second Time	74
Chapter 9: Five Is an Odd Number	85
Chapter 10: Nothing Is Ever Forgotten	96
Chapter 11: Your Dad Doesn't Love You	101
Chapter 12: Flying Paper Planes	107
Chapter 13: Light Versus the Darkness	122
Chapter 14: The Bar Mix	135
Chapter 15: When the Knives Rattle in the Drawer	147
Chapter 16: Three	158
Chapter 17: Finding the Strength to Be Happy	174
Chapter 18: Careful What You Wish For	181
Chapter 19: The Last Time	195
Chapter 20: Forgiveness Frees the Soul	219

Prologue

We had been married for 23 years and we played a simple game in the inner-city bars of Sydney. 20 Questions, ask anything you want. We were open, honest and flying above the average, suburban family life that was all we knew. Each night, after the questions were done, we went to the club. It was a world that I never knew existed, until that summer.

Desire, trust and love are woven into every sinew of our being. But just as they are built in to all of us, each person's journey is beautifully unique, agonisingly hard. Despite our best intentions, it's hard to understand certain journeys that we know nothing about. It's hard to challenge deep-rooted values when we haven't experienced certain things in life. Society sets the rules, ancient deep-rooted rules, but sometimes they are broken and people tread a different path.

As children, we are true to ourselves and we have not yet been moulded by what the world dictates that we should be or feel. But gradually, systematically we are beaten into shape. Early on we are told what is right and wrong, that the world is black and white. Many things are. But some are not. So many things depend on our own unique journey and it is up to us to be true to ourselves and our beliefs, finding our own sense of right. Every one of us is obliged to be honest, respectful, and kind. But we also owe it to ourselves to follow our hearts.

I was a broken person, but we're all broken in one way or another. Some of us are just better at covering over the cracks with lies, a bottle, possessions or whatever. But somehow my broken pieces gradually fitted back together to make a complete picture. There would always be cracks and fault lines but that was just part of being human. I was okay with that. Tess had been my glue for many years but she deserved better than that and I didn't need to be held together anymore

Just for a moment, forget what you were told. Open your mind and I'll tell you a story.

Chapter 1
Thresholds

I remember the sound of my mother's scream when my father told her that he was leaving. It was the sound of a heart breaking. She collapsed in the lounge room as he packed his clothes and golf clubs. I took my brother into his bedroom to play Lego. He was six. I was ten. I came back and held my mum tight as Dad walked back and forth to pack his things in the car.

It broke her. When the packing was done, my mother, brother and I stood on the small veranda of our rented house as he got the last of the beers that were left in the fridge. He told us he loved us and left. There was another woman waiting for him somewhere. Those moments were seared into my memory, my soul. My mother's broken sobs echoed through my life as I struggled to process the scars.

I never felt like I was a good enough husband or father, even though they were the only things I ever wanted to be. I did my best, although every man deceives himself with those words to some degree. This world has a way of clouding the mind, like a smoke machine spewing onto an empty stage. I felt inadequate, alone, much of the time. Lost.

Tess' question jolted me out of my daydream and I was comforted by the expectant smile across her face.

"What do you fear most?" she asked, as the summer breeze from the open pub window rippled through her hair. That question had haunted me, sitting at the periphery of each day. But the search to answer it would also unearth truths that would eventually liberate me.

"There are so many things to be afraid of in there, losing you more than anything. If things go wrong tonight, you know I love you right?" I meant it more than ever.

"I know you do. I love you too," she replied simply.

"People walking past wouldn't even know it's a club," I said to Tess, as my voice quivered slightly with raw excitement.

"Never mind what sort of club," she replied, staring intently across the silhouetted inner-city road.

Married couples from the country didn't come here, they didn't do this. But here we were in the pub across the road. It was seven forty-five pm. Deepest Desires opened at eight.

Tess and I sat in the bustling front bar of the aging, red brick pub in Surrey Hills. She sipped her vodka and orange while I nervously drank my beer. I could never stomach vodka after that one awful night when I was eighteen. But Tess loved it, even though she didn't drink that often and even then, it was mostly in moderation.

"You drank that quicker than the last one, if that's possible." She laughed as I put the glass down.

For the first time that night, a moment of contemplative silence settled over us as I joined her gaze through the window at the club across the street. It was nothing more than a plain brown terrace building, five metres wide and two storeys high. The unassuming façade was a rabbit hole, hiding a seductive world behind it. There was not a sign or word on the whole building, just a street number, eighty-four. I could just see the dimly lit door set back from the footpath and the silver number above it.

"At work last week, I checked the club out on Google Maps. It seemed so far away. It doesn't seem quite real sitting here looking at it," I said.

"No, it doesn't. It looks so plain. What question are we up to, we haven't got long," asked Tess.

"Nineteen, I still can't believe your last answer," I replied. We had decided that if we were going to do this, that we would put everything on the table. We played a simple game involving twenty questions each. Ask anything you want, nothing was off limits; fidelity, family, lust, trust and every other thing that mattered in a happy marriage. Just be honest.

"OK, nineteen," whispered Tess, not wanting to be heard by the group of young blokes sitting only two metres from our table.

"Nineteen."

"What do you think it will feel like to touch another woman?" Tess stared.

"Shit T. I don't know. How do I answer that?"

"Just be honest, rule two." She expected an answer.

"I don't know. I haven't really thought about it, I'm just taking this as it comes." I really didn't have an answer for her.

"You can't tell me you honestly haven't thought about it?" She knew me better than I knew myself.

"Okay, I have thought about it but I have no idea. It scares me. And then I think of you." It had filled my head for weeks.

"And what did you think?"

"Um." Just be honest, "What would it be like? Maybe it would feel like flying into outer space. Somewhere that I've never been before and then when we get to the middle of nowhere, I'll have to jump. Like leaving everything I ever knew and shoving my hand into a power point, like electricity. I don't know if I'll be able to breathe."

"Electricity?" Tess asked.

"I really don't think I would want to explain it, if it happened. As long as you're there and we stick to the rules, that's all that matters. How could anyone know what it would be like?" I was being as honest as I could.

"Well, you might find out in a few hours. No, I know exactly what you mean." Her fingertip sparked as she ran it across my hand.

"Would you really want to know? Outer space might not have been the best analogy. Strange, new. Frightening is what I meant. It could be fucking awesome." I really couldn't imagine being with anyone else but Tess.

"We're doing puns now?" Tess sipped her vodka and laughed.

"It wasn't a pun. So, what do you think it would be like?"

"Me?"

"Yeah, you. What do you think it would be like to touch another man?" I expected an answer too.

"It's not your question."

"If you ask, you have to answer too. What do you think it would be like?" It was my turn to stare expectantly.

"Well, it'd probably be like this rocket ship in outer space."

"Very funny."

"I was seventeen when we met, Ry. I remember when I first saw you at school." Tess took her turn to pause and think. These answers were as much for ourselves as they were for each other. "I never got a chance to be with anyone else, and I don't ever regret that. I have no clue what it would be like either. Strange, amazing maybe. We were so young."

"Yeah, we were just kids. Seems like a lifetime ago and just like yesterday at the same time."

"Feels like forever," Tess replied.

"Ease up. Okay, my last question, number twenty." I paused and looked at her beautiful smile. The rest of the world seemed to disappear in those hours. It was just us. "No matter what happens in there, will you promise to love me forever? Promise to never leave?" There would always be a part of me that was the broken little boy from a broken home wanting to be loved. He was asking question twenty.

"Of course. You're stuck with me forever. I promise." She reached across the table and squeezed my hand tight. "Last one. I didn't like my number twenty. I like yours better. Will you promise to love me forever too, no matter what happens in there?" For all of her strength and independence, part of her would always be a broken child too.

"You know that I will. Always." I couldn't help but wonder what her real question twenty was. Unfortunately, I would find out eventually.

We enjoyed the last comforting drops of our drinks, almost stalling to enjoy the normality of that moment. Then we stood. We looked at each and grinned. Tess seemed so calm but I am sure she was churning inside, just like me.

"Are you ready?" I asked.

"I think so," Tess replied. She paused. "Are you?" This was the moment when we both asked ourselves, as much as each other, if we were really doing this.

"We're here. I'm ready if you are. No regrets remember?" I meant every word.

It was as if neither of us was listening to the words, it was our souls that were speaking, something deep within us. Could we really do this? This was the moment when we needed to hear 'yes' from each other, confirmation that we really were taking this crazy, unbelievable journey. We were taking it together, and that's all that mattered. Then we started walking.

"I'm shaking," I said as the summer heat enveloped us. "I can't believe we are here." The electricity thundered inside me. I had never felt so alive and I wondered if Tess felt the same.

"Shaking alright. Maybe we should just run. This is madness," Tess said.

"Did you get the drinks?" I murmured, as I turned and saw the white plastic bag in her hand containing six beers and four double black vodkas.

"You take them," she replied. We walked through the old wooden door frame out onto the footpath, only forty metres from the club. "I can't believe we are doing this. It feels like a dream." Although a cliché, it was utterly true.

"Yeah, something like that," I replied. "It's been a pretty good dream so far. How good was today?"

"It was fun. So good to get away. I miss the kids but it was so good to have time to ourselves. Just us. Yeah, it was nice," she said, reassuring herself as much as me.

"Look, we're not going to be the first ones there," I mumbled as a professional looking couple strode confidently from the footpath to the front door. We had stopped walking as soon as we stepped out of the pub without even realising, just for a moment. But just as quickly, we were walking across the narrow road. Twenty metres.

Five hours earlier we had walked into the first quiet, well-worn Kings Cross pub at three pm. It was an Irish pub with a neatly drawn sign out the front: 4 cocktails for twenty-five dollars. We sat contentedly with two illusions and two strawberry daiquiris. It was a blur of questions, laughter, live music and fun as we meandered from one pub to the next. We had been together for twenty-three years but those moments felt new. We looked at each other, touched, like we had done at the very beginning.

It was 8:10pm, we were ten metres away. Twenty steps.

"I love you," I said, never meaning those words more in my life. Time seemed to slow down, almost stop.

"I love you too." There was a reassuring certainty in her voice. She meant it too. I wondered if we were getting there way too early. No one turned up on time for anything did they, especially in the city?

"No way. There are two couples there already," I whispered out of the corner of my mouth, lips hardly moving at all. Tess was silent and squeezed my hand tight. We joined the line, six of us now, and it became real.

"Hi, I'm Jen," said the attractive woman that had just walked across the street before us. "This is Mark." She gently brushed my arm as she offered her introductions and immediately, I felt at ease. Somehow the tightly wound fear of the unknown I had felt dissipated instantly. I looked at my beautiful Tess, holding her hand tighter than ever, and I knew we would be okay.

"I'm Ryan, this is Tess," I stated quietly. "It's great to meet you. How crazy is this? Lining up on the footpath to get into this place, I never thought we'd be here." Jen and Mark both smiled warmly.

"Crazy alright, but here we are," assured Mark. Both were immaculately groomed in professional dress, almost like they'd come straight from a law firm in the city. Mid-thirties, they were comfortable in their own skin. It was strange to immediately feel so at ease with a pair of total strangers.

Conscious of the conversation beginning, the nervous looking couple ahead of Jen and Mark turned to greet us and the same cordial introductions followed. He was tall, thick set, wearing dress pants and a white collared shirt. His shoes looked as they had been polished for the entire day. She was much shorter, with kind, anxious eyes. Late twenties maybe. She gave a curtailed smile and seemed relieved when the jet black, wooden door opened.

"Hi guys, welcome to Deepest Desires. I'm Mav. How are you tonight?" announced the lively doorman. He smiled widely through a thick, black beard. He was clearly someone who enjoyed their job. Instantly welcoming, he seemed larger than life and perfectly suited to the job.

Shiny Shoes fished for his wallet, while the rest of us listened intently, and he pulled out a glossy black card with seemingly nothing on it.

"Hi Mav, ah, we're members," and he handed the card to Mav.

"Cool, welcome back guys. It's gonna be a great night. Masquerade party."

"We've got our masks," replied the girl, nodding to the red designer bag in her hand.

"Did we need to bring masks?" I whispered in Tess' ear.

"I don't know, I hope not," she replied, giving a half smile and keeping her eye on the doorman.

"Ok, that's one hundred and twenty, plus the fifty-dollar key deposit. You'll get that back at the end of the night when you hand your locker key in," explained Mav. Shiny Shoes already had the cash in his hand, one hundred and seventy exactly. He looked like he knew the drill. They paid and disappeared into the building behind Mav. We still couldn't see inside.

"Okay, I'm really shaking now," whispered Tess.

Those moments, waiting to enter, were truly primal. I felt the raw sexual energy radiating from the walls. Everyone should have the chance to experience a moment like that, even just once. Everyone. Jen and Mark paid quickly and seemed eager to get inside.

"Thanks Mav, we'll see you in there," Jen said, turning to glance at us momentarily.

"We'll see you both inside, have a great night," Mark said courteously, and they too disappeared into the dream.

"Hey guys, welcome. Have you been to Deepest Desires before?" greeted Mav like a kid happy to see guests arriving at his own birthday party.

"Ah, no. First time. We came down from the central coast this morning. We love the city. It's been a big day already but, yeah, first time." I stumbled with the words, trying to assume an exterior that was as calm and cool as Mav. I could still feel my heart racing. Tess had not let go of my hand and I was thankful for that. For the first time, I could see the black curtain a metre and a half behind Mav and the red velvet wall just inside the door. Red velvet?

"Awesome, my cousin lives up there, but I don't get up there nearly as much as I'd like. Anyway, for your first night with us, it's one hundred and seventy plus a fifty-dollar locker deposit. You'll get the fifty back when you return your key. The one seventy will also get you a member's card which gets you a reduced entry fee if you decide to come back and visit us again. Cool?" asked Mav.

"Sounds great," I replied, handing over the cash. I had decided long ago that this would be a cash only night. I was not having a place like this on my credit card statement, that was for sure.

"Ah, names."

"Ryan and Tess. Tanner." Mav reached for a shelf near the door.

"There you go." Mav smiled reassuringly and handed me the same black card that Shiny Shoes and Mark had produced. I tucked it into the darkest recess of my wallet.

"Have a great night, you two," grinned Mav.

I turned to Tess and mouthed 'I love you'. She did the same. We took simultaneous deep breaths and then tentatively stepped over the threshold into a dream.

Chapter 2
Stepping into Another World

"I'm still shaking." Tess stopped after only a few small steps.

"Me too. Deep breaths," I replied.

"It looks more like someone's house than a club," was her first impression. "Way smaller than I thought." Inside the front door was an empty reception room, no bigger than an average master bedroom. It had leather bench seating running the length of two walls and heavy, black curtains covering the smallish window facing the road.

"So, we're really doing this?" asked Tess with a nervous grin.

"We could still run." I leaned close and kissed her cheek, swaying subtly to the music filling the air. "I don't think I've ever seen red velvet walls."

"Suits the place."

"They just work somehow with those dimmed down lights." I took a moment to examine the large abstract artwork to our right.

"You're dancing already." Tess' grin softened as Mav walked back into the club.

"I just feel like moving. Too much nervous energy." I loved to dance, always had. Besides paying to get in, Tess and I had not let go of each other's hand since leaving the pub and more than ever, we held on tight.

"It sounds like a crowd." I listened intently to the voices in the next room.

"Don't say that." Tess replied. The laughter and voices floated on the music into the front room.

Above the seating on the back wall I paused to digest the photo of a naked couple in bed, sheets covering just enough but still showing plenty. It was seductively beautiful. I tugged Tess' hand.

"Alright. Let's go."

"Okay, you first." She willed herself to start walking.

Another few steps and the doorway led to a second larger room, but still only the size of an average household lounge room. An L shaped cushioned lounge, big enough to fit about eight or 10 people, bordered two walls and in the middle of the room stood a stripper's pole. It rose about three metres to the ornately corniced ceilings of the elderly terrace building. In the opposite corner to the lounge was an oversized oscillating fan. Below the fan was a simple wooden table with an old school stereo, wired to the speakers around the club.

Next to the fan, on the wall to our right, was a set of stairs. I stared momentarily at the carved wooden railing. I knew what walking up those stairs would mean and the gravity of that choice really hit me for the first time.

"I wonder what's up there," I pondered aloud.

"Keep walking," whispered Tess. I took in every detail, every sound, during those few seconds walking across the middle of the room.

There were about six animated couples, each shooting subtle glances at the newbies who had just walked in. There was no sign of Jen, Dave or Shiny Shoes. A tall awkward looking guy sat close to his girl with a beautiful chocolate coloured complexion. They smiled and looked mid to late twenties maybe.

Next to them, mid conversation was an athletic looking bald guy and his stunning brunette partner. They really were an attractive couple, mid-thirties, and the only ones not to look up as we entered.

But one couple, standing near the fan, stood out most. Simply because they were in their underwear. He wore only briefs, highlighting his muscled legs and the extra few kilos around his waist. She stood confidently in dark maroon, laced panties and bra holding a large wine glass. They were deep in conversation with the couple on the end of the lounge, laughing and drinking. It could have been any normal conversation between two couples. Except it wasn't.

"Hi there, welcome to Deepest Desires, I'm Sara."

"Ah. Hi," I replied.

"Come on through." The room, filled with an indescribable energy, continued to buzz as we followed Sara through a door that led to a wide hallway, about four metres long. She stopped as soon as we left the main lounge.

"First time here?"

"Yeah, first time. We came down to Sydney today," Tess replied. We would find out later that she was a law student with a Japanese mother. I wondered what her mum would have thought of the mini skirt and Doc Martin boots she was wearing. I liked them.

"Awesome, looks like it should be a good night. Now if there's anything you need tonight, just ask. I'm here to help. You can drop your drinks off then head to the locker room straight ahead. When you're ready, I'll give you a quick tour hey?"

"Thanks, that'd be great," replied Tess, who looked horrified at the confronting medieval styled room on our left. If we needed a reminder that this was no ordinary club, then this was it.

"What is that?" I asked rhetorically.

"What is that?" repeated Tess.

I had heard nothing of Sara's last few sentences while I was trying to make sense of what I was looking at. The hallway wall had been cut out, about two metres by two metres, and been replaced by bars next to the door that showed the adjoining room. It was the size of a small bedroom with sets of handcuffs hanging on the back wall. On the left was a large wooden cabinet with exquisite glass doors. Inside, neatly laid out on the shelves, were whips, paddles, canes and a vast array of things I had never seen before in my life.

Dominating the room was a two-metre-high wooden A frame tripod. Leather wrist straps hung from the top of the textured mahogany structure.

"I have never seen anything like that," I gasped.

"You should see your face." Tess laughed. I could only imagine the naïve, country boy reaction.

"The dungeon is a lot of fun," offered Sara, quietly amused.

"Looks like it," I stuttered, trying to sound casual as I studied the contents of the cabinet.

"Let's get your drinks in the fridge and then you can head to the locker room. After that, I'll take you and any other new couples for a tour. Sound good?"

"Yeah, thank you." Sara began walking down the hallway. A tour? We certainly hadn't ever been to a club that involved a tour.

"Wow, we now live lives that involve a dungeon," I whispered proudly to Tess as she followed Sara. Things were changing. "This is wild. I can't believe, shit, how was that." My imagination spun in over drive, processing the dungeon and those stairs.

"How about you calm down?" Tess whispered back.

"I'm cool." I wrestled the grin off my face

A few more steps along the hallway wall to our left, on the same side as the dungeon, was the bar, if you could call it a bar. It was more like a small school canteen opening in the wall starting at waist height, with a bench and two large fridges in the small room behind.

Mav was talking to a tattooed woman with long, flowing red hair. Instantly he turned to greet us, while she continued to look at her phone without looking up.

"I'll just grab your key and then give us your key number whenever you need a drink," said Mav with a broad, schoolboy cheeky smile. "Would you guys like a drink each now?"

"Yes please," I said before he had even had a chance to finish the question. Tess shot me a quick glance and nodded.

"Thank you," she said as she placed the plain white plastic bag on the counter.

"Double blacks, nice. Enjoy your night," approved the tattooed woman as she finally looked up from the phone. She handed us a drink each and a key.

"This way. Sorry, I didn't catch your names," Sara smiled warmly.

"Ryan, ah, I'm Ryan and this is Tess," I spoke loudly over the music as we continued from the bar. We walked down five concrete steps and saw a toilet door on the left, below another staircase heading upstairs. On the staircase was the same DD logo that was on the key with a curvaceous silhouetted woman in the middle of the design.

The stairs opened out into a small back lounge area with high ceilings and a round high table and chair set which hosted two more couples, mid to late thirties. A third couple sat on the adjacent lounge, obviously enjoying the conversation. They looked up to briefly to check us out.

"Hi there," greeted the woman, draped in a smart red dress. She reminded me of a Latin flamenco dancer. He just smiled at Tess before returning to the chat.

"Hi." I gave half a wave as we followed Sara through another door, down two more stairs and then turned left into the locker room.

"Here, we are. You've got your key so just leave your jacket and anything else you want in the locker and we'll have a look around as soon as you're ready." Sara disappeared from the doorway with the same youthful, warm smile.

The locker room had about twenty lockers, each around twenty by fifty centimetres, on the side wall. There was a small step to our left, leading up to a platform spanning the width of the room. On it, there were two chairs and a large counter in front of a mirror that covered the entire wall. While Tess found our locker, I stopped for a moment and looked into the mirror. I took a memory snapshot of Tess' curved body as she leaned down to open the locker. It was the first of many that night.

Tess looked stunning in her knee length strapless black dress. It suited her, understated and elegant. She had an air of effortless class and she was beautiful, without really knowing it. Her indigenous skin, hardly dark enough for anyone to notice, gleamed under the soft lighting as she tucked her denim jacket and handbag away. Her deep brown eyes, evidence of her ancestry, looked at me briefly in the mirror.

She was forty-one now, a year younger than me. She loved to run, and she had always remained active over the years we had been together. Two children had changed the curves I had first loved, but she was more attractive than ever to me. Athletic enough not to be considered petit, Tess had a sense of calm and quiet self-assurance. Others saw it too and I still noticed the approving eyes of strangers fall upon her when we walked into a room.

I looked down at my slim fit dress pants and tan brown dress shoes before taking off my jacket and throwing it into the locker. My wallet, hotel key and phone went in next. I wouldn't be needing any of that.

We were ready.

"Evening. A locker room in a club," announced a woman's voice. She was followed by a smiling partner holding a beer. About our age, they looked nervously around the room and seemed a little out of place like us.

"Evening." I replied.

"Hi mate. Sorry to interrupt, Sara just pointed us this way," he said, almost apologetically.

"All good. First time I've seen a locker room in a club too. I guess the whole night is a first for us." I returned her smile as Tess shut the locker. It's strange how we can sometimes take so much from such a short conversation. They seemed instantly warm, nervous and honest, just like us. I don't know why I was surprised but I felt at ease, just like I had felt with Jen and Mark at the front door on the footpath.

"Did you see the masks?" asked Tess, nodding towards the pile in the corner of the bench beneath the mirror.

"Yeah. Might grab one later." I was already headed towards the door. "We'll see you inside," I said as the couple wrestled with their locker key. We rounded the door and walked up the short corridor to see Sara standing next to the round table beside the stairs.

"Ok, let's have a quick look around and then you can get in there and mingle." She turned and walked towards the front of the building.

"Would either of you like another drink?" Thank goodness I thought.

"Yes please," I replied instantly. I had almost skulled the first one while Tess had hardly taken a sip of hers.

We made our way back past the dungeon, into the main lounge, and stood with two new couples who'd arrived before us. I didn't know whether to laugh or blush at the vacant stripper pole. Sara explained the laid back, be respectful and enjoy your night kind of vibe that was expected in the club. Listening so intently over the music, I hardly realised that I had already followed her up four of the stairs that led to the second story.

"The bedrooms," was all I said to Tess. I had scoured the website enough times before coming to know what was at the top of the stairs.

"Good work Sherlock."

Seeing those stairs on the website was one thing but being there and walking up them was another thing altogether.

"This is intense. What if there's someone up there?" I continued.

"Can you shut up?"

I felt more alive than ever, charged with the energy of the city that day. That, combined with the sexual energy of this whole place, was off the scale. I jumped a step and grabbed Tess' hand. It was at the same time frightening and more exciting than I could have ever imagined. But by far the best thing about the whole crazy adventure was that I was doing it with my beautiful girl. We were setting each other free, for one night anyway, and doing this thing together. Sara turned left from the hallway at the top of the stairs.

"This is one of our two queen bedrooms, no blankets I'm afraid. Switch for the ceiling fan." I had stopped listening to Sara on the fourth step. I looked at the ornate black metal bed, sheet only, and the dark red, painted walls that matched the velvet down stairs. Two fashionable side tables held wicker baskets of condoms and packets with the word 'dam' written on them.

"What's a dam," I whispered over Tess' shoulder without reply.

"Any guest is welcome to use any of the rooms. Just be respectful if anyone is there before you. Please remember that you can't just join a group and it's best that you are clear about things downstairs before you make your way up here."

Sara exited the room and headed for the next doorway up the hallway on the right.

"This is the second queen bed room. It's the only room with a lockable door." Sara paused outside the room as we caught up. The hallway was particularly wide with newly laid black carpet and two abstract paintings on our left. She then continued to the end of the hall to what looked like a larger bedroom.

"I can hear voices," I whispered again. I couldn't stay silent.

"Shhh."

"This is the king bedroom with full ensuite." She paused. "We might just leave it for you to see later." I stepped forward as Sara turned. Before following her, I caught the briefest glance of the four people on the bed, two couples. They were naked on top of the sheet. Each pair were embracing, kissing, as their hands explored. They seemed not to notice us at all.

"Fuck," I whispered inaudibly. I don't know what I was expecting but to see it was confronting. "Fuck."

"It looks like someone is having fun already," Sara said on her way down the hallway to the stairs.

"They are the front three bedrooms. We'll head to the back bedroom to have a quick look and then you can hang." I was taking constant, nervous sips of my beer and hurriedly caught up to Tess.

"That was something." Tess smiled awkwardly.

"Wow. They must have been here right on eight. I didn't even see them downstairs." I took a mental inventory of the couples we had seen so far.

"I haven't heard this song in ages." Tess assumed normality as we followed Sara back down the stairs, past the dark maroon lingerie. Through the lounge door, she stopped at the dungeon on the left.

"You've already seen the dungeon, there's a heap of toys in there. Once you get used to it it's a lot of fun." She continued past the bar where Mav and the tattooed girl danced, shooting smiles at us. Down the stairs, we passed the toilet door on the left, underneath the back staircase with the suggestive DD artwork.

"Nice artwork," I commented. "But she's on her own."

"She might like it like that," Tess suggested. Again, we were the last of the three couples following Sara up the stairs and I was still digesting the scene in the last bedroom we had visited.

"I wonder what's in this one."

"Really?" replied Tess, shaking her head at me.

"This is the spa room which is very popular with our guests. Towels are provided. It's drained every day after use and cleaned so you know that it is perfectly fine to use." For a second, I felt disappointed that I had forgot to bring my swimmers. But I quickly surmised that no one would be wearing clothes in this particular spa.

"No way am I getting in that," Tess turned and whispered as we entered the empty room.

"King bed again and a bit more room in here. Ensuite as well." Sara refolded a clean towel from a small table next to the spa.

"Does the spa get much use?" asked the eager, thirty something woman at the head of the line.

"Yeah, a lot. You'll love it." The group silently scanned the impressive back room and the leopard print back board of the huge bed. Sara carefully replaced the towel and walked back through the doorway towards the stairs.

"Okay, we'll head back down stairs and you guys can mingle." Back at the bar, she waited for the six of us to assemble.

"Well, that's the tour, short and sweet. The rest of the night is a choose your own adventure really. Just be respectful. You've met Mav already, that's Candy. I hope you enjoy the night and I'll be around if you have any questions." She seemed relaxed and genuine, not really what I was expecting.

I caught a glimpse of a woman's silky blonde hair in the main lounge and took an unconscious step forward. My eyes travelled the contours of her body before she turned to look at me and my gaze dropped to the floor.

Chapter 3
Contact

My chest pounded. I wiped the sweat from one palm onto my pants and squeezed Tess' hand with the other, mouthing the words 'what are we doing'. We stood anxiously for a moment, not sure of what to do, and Tess tugged my hand to start walking.

"What are we doing?" I repeated aloud but Tess rightfully assumed it as rhetorical. I consciously fought the grin off my face and revelled in the waves of excitement. We walked past the dungeon into the main lounge where Jen and Mark were standing, chatting away with two other couples.

"Hello again, so you've had your tour I see?" Both had drinks, a beer and some sort of mini champagne bottle that suited Jen perfectly. They motioned for us to come over and join the group near the lounge.

"Yes, ah that was just a bit wild. We weren't really expecting a tour and there were definitely a few surprises," I said as we both laughed and looked at each other innocently. Jen and Mark laughed with us, they seemed to understand exactly what I meant.

"This place is full of surprises," Jen said.

"Um, I just wasn't expecting to see other people, upstairs, you know? So early. But it was all good. They looked like they were having a good time, not that we were watching or anything." I took a large swig of beer, conscious of any misplaced words.

"They sure did," agreed Tess.

"So, this is your first time I'm guessing," asked Mark. "It's a lot to take in. You'll get used to it in no time."

"I'm not sure if you ever really get used to it but you'll love this place. Are you guys from the city?" Jen danced to the pulsing music as she asked the question.

"Ah, no. We love the city and come down a bit but we could never live away from the beach. I don't think there are many youth workers living near the beach in Sydney." The couple beside Mark turned to listen to my answer.

"Ryan and Tess, this is Katy and Michael." Mark stepped back as the guy on the end of the lounge stood up. A handshake for both seemed formal but sufficient at the time.

"Hi," was all I could muster.

"It's great to me you both. How was your tour?" asked Katy. They would have seen Sara showing us around. Everyone must have been aware of each new couple in the club and checked them out discreetly.

"It was, ah, informative." Confronting, amazing, even the tour was difficult to describe. "We've had an awesome afternoon in the city hanging out together. How's your night going?"

"Couldn't be better. We've met some really cool people already," Michael replied.

Katy looked late twenties with shoulder length, strawberry blonde hair. She was both attractive and confident without any pretension at all. Michael seemed quietly spoken and courteous. He was boyishly handsome, with short, spiked brown hair. He was clearly enjoying the night, and drank his beer as quickly as I did.

"We had dinner down at the harbour, it was beautiful," Katy said.

"Did you hear that?" asked Jen, kissing Mark on the cheek. "It's dinner before a big night out, right ladies?"

Very quickly, it felt as though Mark was right. We took a seat on the lounge and felt strangely at ease in the company of strangers. The drinks started to flow and people danced, we danced. Couples arrived intermittently and were immediately welcomed into conversations and connections around the club.

Everyone we had spoken to so far was so open, honest and seemingly average, just like us. There was no hint of the pretence, predication or sleaziness that I thought we might encounter. They seemed genuinely nice people who were both inquisitive and likeable. We discussed work, family, and hobbies. It was like talking to people we had known for far longer than an hour or two. The feeling of meeting new people, interwoven with the sexual anticipation of what might happen, was a truly magical drug.

Then the clothes started to disappear.

"They seem so relaxed about it," Tess observed.

"Yeah, they dress down and head back in without missing a beat. Same conversations, same dancing minus the kit," I replied.

"I like her lingerie. Suits her," Tess remarked. I liked it too.

"I read on the website to bring your best underwear, or something like that. Did you see the photos?" I asked Tess. A few subtle photos also hinted that patrons would be dressing down as the night progressed. I had bought some Calvin Klein briefs a few weeks before. They felt great but I wasn't sure that I had the guts to walk around in them in front of strangers.

"Yep, I saw the photos."

"It's only ten, can't believe we've been here for less than two hours." I was so busy taking everything in that time just melted away.

"Should we go the locker room and get changed?" I asked Tess as we danced in the breeze of the large fan near the stairs.

"Maybe we'll wait. Let's get another drink." Tess was never one to be hurried. "I'm kind of enjoying just dancing and hanging out." I was loving the music too, and the flirting. We would do things in our own time.

"After this drink, we'll go back to the locker room yeah?" Tess said eventually.

"Whenever you're ready. I'm thinking I might give that pole a go soon." Tess took it as a joke but I was serious. We looked at one another and burst out laughing.

"Let's go," Tess ordered. The locker room was empty and I sat on the table in front of the mirror with the fresh beer I had grabbed on the way.

"You know you look stunning? I don't know how I got so lucky." She played with her hair carefully as I watched.

"I don't," she replied. "C'mon, get it off. Have you got the key?" I opened the locker and began to undress. I wondered why women seemed so down on their own bodies. They were hard markers on themselves that was for sure and somehow, they looked straight past the beauty that looked at them in the mirror.

Shoes, socks, pants and shirt. I folded them neatly as always and placed them in the locker. I turned for a moment to look at myself in the mirror. Youth work was stressful and I carried the burden and sorrow of every kid that I worked with. Exercise was my shield, my therapy. My footy days had long finished but I was still up early every morning lifting weights, running or moving in some way. I loved feeling strong, feeling fit. In the mirror, I looked lean and muscled. I was surprisingly comfortable in my Calvin Kleins.

Tess unzipped her black dress and it slid down her body, landing at her bare feet on the floor. I paused for a moment. We had spent twenty-three years together. I was more in love with her than ever, so why do this? I tried to get it straight in my head. We were together so young and never really got to experience other people. We were each other's first love, first sexual experience. We were exploring, together. I think that we were setting each other free, just for one night, for one wild night.

"The lingerie is perfect Tess. You really do look great."

It seemed that there was an underlying honesty in dressing down to only underwear. Everyone there had one night to meet, connect and then maybe make the decision to walk up those stairs. It was kind of like, this is me and this is my body. Certain things were fast tracked in that environment, there was no time for bullshit. People had paid their hard earned to get in the door and they had come to play.

Tess checked the mirror again and made final adjustments to her laced bra and panties.

"Nice undies Cal," she complimented.

"Not as nice as yours. There'll be a line up out there." I wasn't joking.

"OK, is my hair alright," Tess asked, facing the mirror. She had spent forever straightening it that day and it looked better than alright.

"Are you ready," I asked, not for the first time that night.

"Ready." We grabbed our drinks and started walking.

"This just feels so strange, but at the same time it doesn't feel strange at all. It's kinda exciting."

"You just better make sure you don't get too excited," Tess replied.

Two couples stood near the back stairs, deep in conversation, underwear only. We had met both earlier in the night. They looked up briefly and smiled as we passed.

"This is some crazy shit T, but you can't help but love it," I beamed.

"Crazy alright."

We walked past the bar where Mav was leaning against a fridge, and we could hear a smacking sound coming from the dungeon. The bald, athletic guy and his partner that I had seen at the start of the night were standing in the wide hallway watching. In a few short steps, we were beside them. A blonde-haired woman, around our age, stood on the wooden A frame with hands grabbing the leather straps at the top, legs slightly apart to match the A. She was being smacked ever so gently on the behind by a smiling guy who seemed to enjoy the attentive audience.

"That's not really something you see every day." I didn't quite know what to say. They kept their eyes on the tasselled whip flying through the air.

"Yeah, it looks pretty tame. Might even give it a try. You?" the woman asked.

"Ah. Maybe. Not yet though," stalled Tess.

"I'll try it," I said quietly, immediately, in Tess' ear. It looked like fun and I had never had the smallest experience in BDSM. I felt strangely drawn to the room. "And I'll be hitting you harder than that Tess when it's my turn." Tess looked just as surprised as I was at the comment and the four of us laughed.

"We're just going to relax for a while. Sit down maybe." Tess continued walking into the main lounge and I took another quick glance before following. We were still getting used to the lack of clothing in the presence of strangers thing and we were happy to find a seat.

For the first time that night, the stripper pole was occupied. A beautiful woman with short blonde hair, around 30, gripped the bar high with both hands and swayed her hips with the music. Conversations bubbled, interwoven with the music, but all eyes were on her. As she slid down close to the ground her legs parted. It was seductive, sensual. But she didn't seem to be showing off. She was dancing, moving in a world of her own without judgement which is what everyone was doing there in their own way.

"Hi Tess, Ryan." We heard Katy's friendly voice as we sat down on the lounge nearest the door, discreetly scanning the room.

"Hi. We were just watching the action in the dungeon for a sec. How wild is that?" Tess replied, sitting next to Katy, with Michael beside her. I was on the end closest to the hallway door.

"She dances really well. Braver than me," I commented on the pole dancer that was only two metres in front of us. Every movement was natural, beautiful. The pole no longer seemed out of place. "Are you guys from Sydney," I asked.

"Close enough. Berowra, just north of the city. I commute into the city every day. Katy doesn't have to deal with the train ride though." The drinks had eased Michael out of his shell. He rested his hand on Katy's inner thigh. They looked relaxed.

"I'm in real estate. I definitely spend enough time in Sydney. I just drive when I have to instead of do the hours on the train." She smiled as she sipped her white wine.

"Cool. So, you sell properties in Sydney too?" asked Tess.

"Some. A lot of the property owners from home live in Sydney so I often see them here. Where are you two from?" Katy asked as she swayed subtly with the music. I was acutely aware of every movement.

"Central Coast, not too far. We're here until tomorrow. We've got Monday off too. It's so good to have time to ourselves. We do miss the kids but they're happy with their nan and we don't leave them that often. It's only one night." I always found it hard to be away from them, but making time for each other was a priority. Making time for other people? Now that was something very new.

"How old are your kids?" Michael seemed genuinely interested. Maybe he was doing the maths to try and work out how old we were. There were couples ranging from early twenties to late forties. Early forties didn't seem that old and we didn't look it.

"Twelve and ten, they're great ages," said Tess. "Boy and a girl. Such awesome kids. Do you have any?"

"Not yet. One day, won't we Babe?" Katy didn't turn to listen for an answer. She looked as though she had already decided it was happening.

We briefly looked at the dancer as she left the pole. She was seductive without trying, not unlike Tess. She reached and grabbed her drink from a tanned man at the opposite end of the lounge to us and sat beside him. Without thinking, I got up. Beer in hand, I stepped towards the pole. Since when had I become a pole dancer, in my underwear, in front of strangers? The group cheered instantly.

"Go Ryan, show us some moves." Tess put her drink on the floor and clapped, bent over laughing.

"Oh, here we go. Is he a dancer?" Katy joined Tess' joyful laughter.

"No, he's not."

I grabbed the pole with my left hand at waist height with my beer fastened tight to my right. I honestly loved to dance and for some inexplicable reason, I didn't feel out of place or foolish in that moment. My hips swayed involuntarily side to side in exact harmony with the driving tempo of the music. I let go and turned so that my back was touching the pole, still moving with the music, sliding up and down just a fraction.

"Yeah mate," someone yelled.

I spun to face the 'audience' again who continued to laugh and clap. All eyes were now on me, which was never my intention, and they were loving the impromptu performance. I reached high and grabbed the pole again and danced simply because I enjoyed it, not because anyone else was watching. It was only a minute or two before I threw my head back, laughing, and called for someone else to have a go.

"Loved it. Go you," encouraged Katy.

I sat back down next to Tess as Jen decided that she would step up to the pole. The group roared again as couples stood and danced around the room. I couldn't see or smell the electricity but I could feel it charging through my body. I had never felt more alive. Katy and Tess chatted away while I watched Jen dance freely around the pole.

"Ok, I'm keen to try it if you are," Katy said, standing up immediately. Her tight, red lingerie hugged her body and complimented her strawberry blonde hair perfectly.

"Alright, let's do it." Tess got up in unison with Michael. My heart nearly beat out of my chest as I instinctively stood. Do what? Fuck. I moved to the side as Katy led the way, followed by Tess. But instead of moving towards the stairs, Katy walked back through the door behind us and into the dungeon. Three of us followed, each with a drink in hand.

"I must have missed this part of the conversation. I guess things move fast when you're dancing at a stripper's pole," I said to Tess.

"Sounded like you were keen earlier."

"I don't even know what most of those things are," Katy said to Tess as they both giggled at the range of items in the large glass cabinet.

"Look at that whip, there would hardly be enough room to swing it in here." Katy was right, the room was only small and it felt decidedly intimate with four people standing in it.

"That one looks like a table tennis bat," said Michael, awkwardly looking over Katy's shoulder. He looked as excited as I felt. This was so new to both Tess and I. She smiled over her shoulder at me. She was clearly enjoying the adventure as much as I was.

"That one," decided Katy as she opened the cabinet and pulled out a black paddle, about thirty centimetres long, with short tassels hanging from the handle. "Ok Michael, how about you first." It was a demand as much as a question and he climbed onto the A frame dominating the room. Michael looked awkward on the tall wooden structure. He was about six feet with neatly cut, short brown hair. His perfectly aligned teeth hinted at braces earlier in life and the few extra kilos around his waist flattened when he reached up to grab the leather straps at the top.

"Don't hit too hard, you look like you're enjoying this a bit too much," he said playfully. But he had not even finished the sentence before Katy landed the first smack, straight on his behind. I was instantly disappointed that she barely swung the paddle at all, just a small movement of the wrist that amounted to nothing more than a tap.

"Three each," he called, suddenly appearing a whole lot braver. Katy delivered two more of the same gentle taps as we all laughed together. "Now your turn," he said, climbing off the frame, in his best tough guy voice. He didn't look like he had a mean bone in his body. Katy excitedly jumped onto the wooden structure.

She couldn't have been much more than thirty. As tall as Tess, she was slim and toned enough to suggest that she worked out regularly. She reminded me of an old TV show character, Scully from the X-files, every time I looked at her.

Michael raised the paddle threateningly and then landed it on Katy's curved bottom, even more softly than she had hit him. Her tensed limbs relaxed as she turned to look straight at him. I ran my hand up Tess' thigh and across her bum, tracing the panty line up and down.

"Two more Kate. Ready?" They were loving the game, and so were we. How could this be so hot, watching someone get hit? There was not the slightest hint of malice, just this feeling of the wild unknown.

Michael delivered two more love taps before Katy jumped off the ride. She beamed with anticipation as she looked at Tess and I.

"Your turn. Who's first?" asked Katy. Tess already had the paddle in her hand. We did not need to answer the question.

"Alright then, just take it easy," I told Tess. She hit the paddle hard on her palm and waited for me to mount the frame. "Be gentle." I never took my eyes off her. She looked at Katy and threw her head back laughing.

"Ok, here we go." She raised the paddle as high as Michael. But instead of the soft landing that he had ensured, Tess swung hard. Really hard. Did she just do that? Katy and Michael gasped simultaneously and then both burst out laughing. I couldn't help but laugh too. It hurt but it felt so good. How could pain feel so incredibly satisfying?

Tess was the most loyal, loving person I had ever met. The world was much more 'black and white' for her than it was for me. No grey. If she was going to do something, she was all in or not at all. She was all in now. I loved it.

"Whack," the second paddle strike landed harder than the first on the other cheek.

"Ouch, are you right?" I asked between bursts of laughter. That whole pleasure and pain thing was true.

"I'm having a great time. One more to go. Turn around," Tess ordered. She was beginning to get the idea of the dungeon. "Ready?" She paused momentarily as another couple stopped outside the dungeon, watching. We were now the show.

The third hit landed, slightly softer than the first two. I felt a strange, unexplainable disappointment as I stepped off the frame. But it didn't last long. My turn. I'd be gentle, I'd never hurt a hair on Tess' head in our lives and I wasn't about to start now.

"That looks like fun," commented our new audience member. "She looks like she knows how to use that paddle."

"First time mate. All those years of tennis I think." I grabbed my beer as Tess carefully mounted the frame, careful not to place her legs to far apart and finding a comfortable position for her hands above her head. I paused to look at her for a moment. Her strong thighs and beautiful skin, the athletic contours of her calves. She dipped her head, facing the opposite corner, as if to signal that she was ready.

I raised the paddle, tassels dangling around my wrist, and to my great surprise, I hit her hard. Not as hard as she had hit me, but hard.

"Sorry," I mumbled before I even knew that I had said it.

"Don't be sorry, is that all you've got?" She turned for a moment to stare me in the eye. She arched her back and moved her gorgeous behind from side to side for just a moment to the music, almost daring me to go again. The audience were fixated. Katy and Michael danced as they grinned at me. They were loving the show.

Speechless, I swung again. Harder. It must have hurt. Tess spun around and looked me hard in the eye again, grinning ever so slightly. Our forehands were definitely on a different level to Katy and Michael. They were clearly impressed.

"Last one. Ready?" I paused for a moment as she swayed with the beat. She looked unbridled, free.

"What are you waiting for," Tess urged before I swung for the third time, a little softer than the first two as Tess had done. She stepped off and kissed my neck.

"That was," words escaped me, "that was impossible to explain."

"How about the girls hit each other and the boys do the same?" suggested Katy. Michael suddenly looked nervous.

"Yeah, sure," was all he could muster. I'm not sure he was too keen after seeing Tess and I take our turns.

"I'll go first," said Katy as she immediately assumed the position. I passed Tess the paddle. She was gentle, softly landing the blows as Michael had done to begin with. Similarly, Michael and I played as the audience members continued through to the main lounge. Tess and Katy giggled like old friends, enjoying the growing connection, dancing the whole time.

"Did you want to go up?" was all I heard Katy say. Up where? Fuck. I quickly placed the paddle in the neatly arranged cabinet.

"Yeah, OK," Tess replied. My heart pounded as Katy rounded the door of the dungeon. Then we were walking.

Chapter 4
Some Things Get Pushed Down Deep Inside

"Why do you think that is?" Bill asked. I squirmed in the uncomfortable leather chair opposite him.

"Don't know. We both were badly damaged as children. It doesn't sound like much to say it. My dad left when I was ten years old. Tess' dad was an abusive alcoholic. Everyone has got things that they have to deal with. Sometimes it feels like I should just get over it. Toughen up. But no one really gets over that stuff. We push all that shit that we suffered as children down deep inside thinking that it's gone. But it never really leaves. It's there below the surface affecting everything we do, although most of the time we don't even know it's there."

"You think that's how other people feel too?"

"Maybe. I know that's how my dad was."

"Are you like your dad?" Bill was measured and deliberate with every question.

"Probably. I'm not quite sure what is it about dads? I am one and I love my kids more than anything on earth. I would walk in front of a bus in a second for them, I would do anything. But I haven't been able to beat my demons for them, or slow down with the drinking. Not so far. Fatherhood's far more complicated than I ever thought. The responsibility of my actions moulding a life, lives, never really dawned on me. I never really understood. I did my best. But I think all that stuff inside is still stopping me from being the man I want to be."

"Admitting those things is a good starting point Ryan. I don't think any father really measures up to their own expectations."

"I saw a Bruce Lee movie once that said you beat your demons or you pass them on to your children. What a huge responsibility. The same week I read a newspaper article from some psychiatrist saying that eighty percent of the clients he worked with were there dealing with the shit that their dads had caused. I remember hating the guy instantly. Eighty percent. How can that be right?"

"Do you think you're a good father?" Bill asked, looking up from his notebook.

"I really don't know. My dad did the best he could. Tess' dad probably did too. Me? I hope I am. I do know that I try my best and I hope Josh and Leyla know that. My under fifteens coach said that a great referee was one that people didn't even notice was on the field. He just let the game flow. People only noticed him when he made mistakes. Maybe that's the same for dads."

I thought of Tess as Bill recounted memories of his dad. Everyone loves their mum. I certainly did. They are amazing, wonderful people. They love their family and make sacrifices that no one could ever understand. Tess was an incredible mum. No one ever messed with her children. No one. But mums just didn't seem to cause the damage that dads did.

I did the best I could as a dad. But I always felt inadequate. It took many years before I realised that this was the same feeling that I felt with my friends, on the footy field and in every other part of my life. It took time before I realised that it wasn't about how other people felt about me, it was how I felt about myself.

My dad left us. Big deal. That happened in over a third of marriages. But the statistics didn't diminish the hurt one bit. Broken marriages break children and I felt broken my whole life. Tess was my rock and my children were my inspiration. But I was still broken and I never knew if I would feel complete.

"Maybe you should be a bit more forgiving of yourself Ryan," Bill said.

"I know I should. It's much easier to forgive other people than myself," I replied.

"Would you say that you're an unhappy person Ryan?" Bill asked.

"I have a great life and a beautiful family. I've got heaps of good mates and a job that matters."

"That doesn't answer the question."

"Yes."

What is it about dads? Maybe they bear a load that no one can ever understand, not even them. Men are supposed to be strong according to an eternity of evolution and then in the fifties women finally began the long journey towards the equality that they absolutely, completely deserved. The oppression and gender suppression that they had withstood for so long was beginning to erode and society began to shift. Men were called out for the shit they had perpetrated over millennia and rightful change had started.

Men who did unmentionable, unconscionable things were finally called to account. But through no one's fault, many good men seemed to lose sight of their identity and who they really were in a postmodern world. Those good men had lost sight of the most important parts of being a man. I had anyway.

"What was your dad like?" I stalled at Bill's question.

"I remember the sound of my mother's scream when my father told her that he was leaving. It was the sound of a heart breaking. She collapsed in the lounge room as he packed his clothes and golf clubs. I took my brother into his bedroom to play Lego. He was six. I came back and held my mum tight as Dad walked back and forth to pack his things in the car."

"That must have been devastating."

"It broke her. When the packing was done, my mother, brother and I stood on the small veranda of our rented house as he got the beers that were left in the fridge. He told us he loved us and left." Those hours were seared into my memory, my soul. My mother's broken sobs echoed through my life as I struggled to process the scars.

"He's a good man," I continued. "He loves me and my brother. He never spoke much about his childhood. Aunty Jan was the one who told us about their upbringing. His father was a 1950s abusive alcoholic. The pubs closed at 6pm, then he would come home and unleash on his family. Nan and Jan would hide but Dad, probably wanting his father's love, was directly in the firing line." I picked at the leather lounge, not looking at Bill.

"He played footy from about six. He was a good player. Pop never even watched him play but another coach from the club would always watch Dad's games. Dad told me eventually that this was most likely his real dad, who watched his games from a distance." It was something that I had never talked about. The alcoholic mongrel that beat Dad almost daily was not really his father and never acted like it.

"Did you see him much after he left?"

"Not at first. Months after Dad left, he picked up Luke and I to spend the night together at Nan's house. I was so looking forward to that day to see him again. Then an hour after getting to Nan's house, after not seeing his boys for months, he told us that he had to go and 'see a man about a dog'. He spent the whole night at the pub and as hard as I tried to stay awake, I didn't see him until the next morning."

My depression crept up on me over many years. It was like an unnoticeable ocean tide leaving the shore, vast and invisible. Most people didn't even see it. I was so very good at hiding it and I always felt like I had to be strong for my family. Being a good father and husband was the only thing that ever really mattered to me. Others may have seen glimpses, but I gave every ounce of strength I had to be a support to Tess, not a burden.

I put my moods down to stress. My work took a deep emotional toll and I had always absorbed the hurt that others had suffered, thinking that I could 'fix' them. Maybe that's why I became a youth worker. Maybe the subconscious drive to help children was rooted in the yearning to come to terms with my own childhood, to fix me. It didn't work.

"I want you to start on Edronax. Twenty milligrams to begin with and we'll see how that goes." Bill was an excellent psychologist. He understood me, often better than I understood myself. That was his job I guess. Beyond anything a psychologist could read in a textbook, he seemed to know me personally, to understand my unique journey. He unpacked the emotions and hurt with honesty and gentleness. It wasn't always what I wanted to hear but he was right. I had resisted suggestions from people for years to go and talk to someone. Australian men didn't do that.

"But this is not permanent right? When things get better then I can stop?"

"Yes, when things get better. It's your choice, but at this point in time, I think it will help. We can re-assess down the track."

The drive home was full of internal conflict. I didn't want to take medication; I never even touched a tablet for a headache. But if it helped me to be happy, happy for my family, then maybe it was worth a shot.

"Are you crying?" Tess asked as she walked in from work. She threw her nametag on the bedside table.

"Nope." My head was still in my hands as I sat on the edge of the bed.

"What's wrong? Work again?" I lifted my gaze just long enough for her to see the tears. She stepped close and put my head on her stomach, running her fingers through my hair.

"I hate it when you see me cry." The silent tears didn't stop.

"What's wrong?"

"I don't know. Sometimes the shit at work gets into my head. You remember that kid Jacob? He finally got his own place. A job. He was doing alright. Kim found him dead two weeks ago. He just didn't want to be here anymore."

"No. Ryan I am so sorry." She just held me. No one knows what to say in times like that and Tess never said too much.

"I think I know how he feels sometimes. Alone."

"You're not alone Ry. You're never alone. I love you so much." She didn't say that often. I don't think her dad ever told her those words. Not nearly enough anyway. I was silent. It wasn't like me. For minutes, she just held me.

"How did it go today?" asked Tess.

"I, ah. I got off work early. It was okay."

"What did he say?"

"He said I'm a nutter and that I need to take something called Edronax. I have to see the GP to get a script. Why is sitting on that chair, talking about shit that happened thirty years ago so tiring? It's exhausting."

"I'm proud of you for going. We're all nutters. Do you think it helped?"

"Well, I don't feel any better. I just want to forget about all that stuff. I just want, I don't know what I want. Not to feel like this maybe."

"But we don't forget. Things get pushed down deep inside but they have to come out somehow. Maybe that's why you've been feeling like this. It's all that stuff you went through."

"I'm going to do fajitas tonight. I need to defrost the meat." I had just spent an hour talking about it. I was done talking for now.

"What time are they coming over tonight?" Tess sat beside me.

"Six," I said as I got up and headed towards the kitchen.

"I'm going to have a quick shower." Tess disappeared into the ensuite as I detoured to get the poem I had discussed during my visit with Bill. I opened the middle pages of a plain notebook in the spare room bookcase and began to mouth the words.

'Never felt so desperate, so alone
In a world full of people, I'm on my own
Don't understand how I got here
I was never in control
Don't know how to heal my aching soul
Don't know how to stop feeling so alone

Turn the lights down, they hurt my eyes
I live in darkness, 'cause it's easier to hide
I'm driving blind and I'm waiting to crash
I'm drowning in an empty sea
I'm driving with no direction
Searching, aching to find me'

Why did I feel that way? I had a wonderful wife and children. A rewarding job with no financial hardships that were any different to any other average bloke. Maybe it was those things down deep inside, my mother's tears from that day. Maybe it was the tears that I never cried because I thought I had to be strong.

"Can you get that?" I called to Tess as the doorbell rang repeatedly.

"There she is. What's happening T? You got him in the kitchen again?" Tim's booming voice filled the house.

"Hi Tim. He loves it. Hey babe, love the dress." Tess hugged Meg, Tim's wife.

"Thanks T. This is for us tonight. Tim's driving, for once." She handed Tess a bottle of Sauvignon Blanc.

"Hi Tess, hi Ryno," yelled their kids, Jet and Ella, as they headed straight for the bedrooms to find Josh and Leyla.

"What's up bro? They got smashed last night. You watch it?" Classic Tim, straight to the footy.

"Hey mate. They were rubbish. How you been?"

"Good, good. Busy as. Took on a new offsider last week. Could hardly read a measuring tape, never mind get his head around the rest of it. He loves the blue and whites though so I might keep him for a bit longer."

"He better get used to losing then. How's the family?" Tim gave me the full summary of kids, work and life in a few short sentences.

"What about you? Looks like you've still been hitting the gym?"

"Yeah, a bit. Keeps me sane." I still didn't feel like talking, but there were no silences with Tim around. I downed the next beer. More questions, they were exhausting.

"Mate, is everything alright? You seem a million miles away. You okay?" Tim asked.

"All good, been a big day at work, I'll be happy to sit down and watch the game. You wanna beer?" Tim looked closely at me for a moment, he knew me well.

"Is a frog's arse watertight? Wil and Tam will be here in five." He went to turn on the TV as Tess grabbed two glasses from the cupboard. She poured a wine for herself and Meg as I retrieved the single beer in the fridge.

"Have you finished the whole six pack already? It's a bit early isn't it?" asked Tess.

"No. I was thirsty. This is for Tim. I'll put some more in the fridge for him, I was busy with dinner."

"That's not what I meant Ry. Anyway, he's driving. Just go easy yeah?" She managed half a smile.

"That's the door. I'll get it." Wil and Tam arrived with as much enthusiasm as Tim. Wil immediately wrapped his arms around me and squeezed tight. He was a hugger. He threw his keys into the bowl on the cabinet beside the door, containing all of our household keys.

"Watch out mate, you throw your keys in the bowl and things could get interesting." Tim laughed.

"You wish mate. Tam's out of your league. Who's playing?"

I turned to see the look on Tess' face in the kitchen, grinning and raising her eyebrows all at once.

I loved having friends over and I had always enjoyed cooking. Everyone was obviously enjoying the Mexican feast I had prepared but I felt far away. I couldn't help thinking of Jacob, and Bill, and the conversation just sounded like a mesh of distant voices. Noise that made it hard to think. I looked past the laughter trying to listen to the commentary coming from the footy game on the TV in the background.

"How's work Ryan?" asked Tam as the boys compared under twelves coaching stories.

"Ryan," Tess squeezed my leg and smiled, "Tam's talking to you."

"Sorry Tam, I'm a bit tired."

"How's work?" She repeated and I forced my stare away from the TV.

"Work's work. I'd much rather watch the footy. They're in." The attention turned to the game and I was happy to avoid any further questions for the moment.

"Are you sure you're okay? This is not like you." Tess leaned close as everyone took their plates to the kitchen." I can call the GP in the morning if you like."

"Anyone want another drink," I asked, trying not to look at Tess, and settling in to watch the game with the next beer.

"And that's how it's done boys. Twenty-two to ten. They were always gonna win that one, and I picked up a hundred on my multi," boasted Wil after the final whistle blew.

"Great game. Listen to the boys yelling in Josh's room," Tim said. "I gotta work early so we might get going Tano."

"That's a first," laughed Wil.

"Yeah, all good. I'm pretty stuffed. Been a big week," I replied.

"You look it." Tim only ever called it like he saw it.

"Sounds good, we'll see you at the game tomorrow. I'll tell Lachy to go easy on Josh and Jet. We're on top of the ladder you know?" Wil was every bit as competitive as I was.

"Yeah, you told me. We'll see how we go. Thanks for coming over you guys. We'll see you tomorrow."

"Next week Tess. Text me. Thanks for dinner Ryan, it was top shelf as always," Tam said.

The car lights disappeared into the distance as Tess shut the door and walked into the kitchen.

"How many beers have you had? You've got to drive in the morning."

"Just let me count them all up Tess, do you want a wine count too?" I could feel the edge to my voice and the slurred pronunciation.

"Tam asked if you were okay. That was pretty rude. She can see something's up."

"Tam can mind her own fuckin business." I didn't mean it. Tam was one of the kindest, most loyal friends we had. "And I'll call the GP myself, I don't need you to do it." I could feel the sadness deep inside twist into the anger that propelled each word.

"You're pissed and I'm done tonight. You can sleep in the spare room. I'll drive Josh if I have too." Tess shook her head and shut our bedroom door.

"Bullshit you will," I yelled and walked back to the fridge.

Chapter 5
The Upstairs

Tess and I locked eyes for a split second before leaving the dungeon and walking into the main lounge which was in full swing. Staying left, we followed Katy and Michael up the stairs, the gateway to a world that I knew nothing about. Each step was filled with wild, primal anticipation.

There was no feeling of guilt. No second thoughts. We were setting each other free, for that one night anyway, while still standing by each other's side. We were living life to the full and we were doing it together.

We stepped into the hallway of the second story. I could hear that the first queen room on our left was definitely occupied. The next room to our right had the door closed so we continued down the hall to the largest king bedroom. Empty. I looked at the neatly tucked sheet on the bed, which looked completely untouched, and the baskets on the bedside tables. The shower in the ensuite was opposite the door and was clearly visible. I paused for a moment and took a deep breath before stepping into the room.

Katy turned and looked at me at the same as Michael reached out and placed his hand on Tess' hip and kissed her. He was taller than me and Tess tilted her head upwards as she kissed him back. That was the last time I looked directly at them together.

Katy took my hand as I paused for a second. We walked around the bed to the far side and she lay down, pulling me down beside her. I propped my head up on my elbow to look at her strawberry blonde hair for a moment.

"This should do," she said simply as our eyes caught each other. We kissed softly, passionately.

"Is this okay," I asked. She kissed me again and didn't answer. Tess and Michael lay down on the bed, less than a metre away from us. The taste of a new kiss was intoxicating. My body charged with the energy pouring from Katy's touch. I wanted more.

I ran my fingers up Katy's inner thigh and traced my fingers around her petite breasts. Back down her stomach, my hand flattened as it slid inside her panties. She took a deep breath and let out a deep hard sigh as I touched her. I could hear Tess breathing just as heavily. She sounded like she was enjoying herself. She sounded happy and I knew she was safe. She was right next to me and a world away at the same time.

I touched slowly, carefully, and took my time. I kissed her cheek, her neck and down to her chest. Time stood still and I savoured the minutes that went by. I carefully edged Katy's panties down each leg, until she slid them off her feet and kicked them onto the floor.

"I'll get this." She sat up and undid her bra, revealing her small, perfectly shaped breasts. My tongue was on them even before she had laid back down. The smell of her perfume, of her, filled me and my hands caressed every part of her body. My lips travelled up her neck and back to her lips. I kissed her hard and our tongues danced, explored. She dug her nails forcefully into my flesh as time ceased to exist. There was only us and our naked bodies deep in space.

I could feel the wetness between her legs and she stroked hard between mine. I felt like exploding as her small hands gripped me and she writhed as my fingertip pressed that exact part of her body. Katy reached into the basket beside the bed and handed me a condom.

"Put this on." As she gave it to me and I paused, looking at the small packet. For a moment, I wanted my beer just to step a little bit further from earth and all the rules that were disintegrating around us.

"Thanks." I stood and rolled the rubber onto me, rechecking that it was on properly. Katy watched me carefully before I crawled back onto the bed on hands and knees, directly above her. I kissed her again and I knew that there was oxygen in space, this space anyway.

"I want you," she whispered ever so softly as she bit my ear.

"I want you too." Again, I felt the soft, wet flesh between her legs and gently pushed. She looked up and kissed me before shutting her eyes and pushing her head back hard onto the pillow. I continued slowly, completely inside her.

I could feel every muscle in unison as I began to withdraw and push again, harder. Each time, a little harder than the last, until our bodies collided in perfect, primal rhythm. Eventually, she reached up and grabbed the tensed flesh of my chest and then my back, pulling me into her.

"Lie on the bed," Katy demanded, pulling me down by the shoulders and pushing me beside her on my back. She manoeuvred herself on top of me and carefully guided me inside her. I reached up to her breasts as she began to push, every bit as hard as I had. Her strawberry blonde hair danced in the breeze of the ceiling fan and I struggled to believe that this beautiful stranger above me was real and not just a tantalising dream.

I moved my hands down to her hips as they washed over me in waves. My right palm explored the flat of her stomach and slowly lowered until my thumb rested between her legs. She instantly pushed forward onto it and wriggled slightly to position it exactly where it was needed.

"There," she said before resuming the thrust of her hips upon me and I was lost completely, nothing else existed at that moment. Again and again, she pushed, tensed, as she lay her palms flat on my chest. Soft sounds that I had never heard made it clear that she was close and she squeezed the muscles in her legs around me. But I wanted it to last. I wanted to taste her.

In one motion I sat up, turning her onto her back, and she beamed at me in surprise. On hands and knees again, I lightly mouthed her nipples with my teeth and ran my tongue over them, one after the other. I kissed a trail down her stomach to her naval and kept going until my tongue settled on that place between the soft folds of flesh.

She was quiet, except for the uncontrolled breaths moving her entire body, and she pushed herself onto my tongue. My senses exploded with the taste and smell, with the sound of someone new. Her inner thighs tightened around my head and we became the only two people in the room. It was only moments before her whole body convulsed and she let out quiet, lasting moans. I kept the same rhythm, teasing the inside of her leg with my fingertip, until she sank silent and still into the bed.

Katy pulled me by the hair up to her and kissed me gently. Again, her hand took me inside her in one motion and I felt her tight around me. My body refused to wait any longer and gave in to the ecstasy that exploded throughout every sinew in my body. I looked down at Katy for a moment, caught inside a beautiful dream, as every note of the symphony played out.

Eventually, I heard Michael say something to Tess and they laughed.

"I'm going to take a shower," he then said as he walked to the open ensuite facing the bed. The shower started and he stood, watching us, still half-erect. We lay on the bed for only a minute before Katy turned to Tess.

"Just the three of us now," she said as she touched Tess' hair. I rested my elbow on the pillow and propped my head up on my palm to see Tess' face. She smiled warmly at me before wriggling closer to Katy and they kissed. I was stunned. I had known her for a lifetime. I knew everything about her. But I didn't know this.

Katy reached behind to grab me and pulled me closer to her and Tess. My palm sailed down her back and hips, just connected enough to be a part of this wild encore.

How could I not have known? But I didn't. Tess and Katy kissed gently, touched, explored. Soft kisses became passionate, intimate, as they ran their hands through each other's hair, over every part of each other's body. I kissed Katy's shoulder and reached across to touch Tess, but they only had eyes for each other. Disbelief ran through my mind, infused with the most incredible electricity that I had ever felt. It looked so natural, so beautiful, and Tess looked happy.

Again, time stood still in the upstairs as our three bodies explored, connected. We did wild things, amazing things in that room with Katy while Michael looked on. It was unreserved, sanctioned lust.

Strangely, there was no jealousy, no feeling of unfaithfulness. We did it together, side by side, and it just worked. We allowed each other the freedom to disappear into a hidden world of our deepest sexual desires, fantasies, and it just worked. It was like a perfect wet dream that you wished were true, and it was. It was everything you secretly, hopelessly, held somewhere deep inside.

Eventually, we lay naked on the bed. Still. The music echoed from downstairs. The shower stopped and we then slowly gathered our undergarments from the floor and slipped them on. Katy sang to the song playing in the background. Tess' eyes met mine and we smiled. Once again, I mouthed 'I love you', and she did the same.

"I wasn't expecting that," I gushed to Tess. "That was…beyond words."

"Wasn't it," agreed Katy as Michael slid his briefs around his waist.

"I think we need a drink," suggested Tess as she quietly sang along with Katy. Their eyes met for a moment, both grinning like schoolgirls with a secret.

They headed for the door with Michael and I following behind. As we left the room, Katy ran her hand up Tess's thigh.

"That was incredible, Tess. All of it. I was thinking, maybe we should swap numbers," Katy suggested. The music got louder as we neared the stairs and I couldn't hear the rest of the conversation. I wasn't sure whether to feel embarrassed or triumphant as we walked down the stairs. The main lounge was pretty full now, with about eight or nine couples dancing, talking, and enjoying the night. They gave us a brief glance as we descended the twelve steps and continued to the hallway.

We had never talked about swapping numbers.

We waited at the bar for another couple who were talking to Mav. They were similar ages to Katy and Michael. She had a pink one-piece teddy on and he had blue briefs with pink flamingos to match. I couldn't help but like them. Tess turned to see me staring at her, smiling from ear to ear, but it wasn't because of the flamingos.

"What," she laughed. "What?" The flamingo couple headed towards the back lounge.

"Nothing, I'm just so stoked…to be first in line at the bar," I didn't really know what to say.

"Hello you four, looks like you're enjoying yourselves." Mav's tone was both suggestive and playful. He danced as he spoke. "What can I get you?"

"Ah, a lemon ruski and a JD and coke please. Number eight." Michael stepped forward and rapidly put his order in.

"What was that about numbers?" I put my hands on Tess' hips and a chin on her shoulder as Katy and Michael took their drinks. Tess kissed my cheek.

"A double black and a beer please. Twelve." Mav handed over the drinks and I took a long, satisfying swig. "I don't know. Katy just asked. I'm not sure." Mav chatted away about the city traffic to the tattooed girl.

"Let's head back to the lounge, yeah? We'll see who's on the pole now," suggested Tess. The four of us headed through the doorway back into the main lounge room. There was a seat on the end near the front door. Tess sat promptly and I squeezed in beside her.

"Hey you two. How's your night been?" Jen's bubbly voice rose above the music as she and Dave eagerly waited for the answer.

"It's been great, how about you?" Tess replied. Like old friends we chatted about the mundane, the normal. Those social connections had their own type of magic.

It was 1pm, five hours since we had arrived. How could it have possibly have been five hours? Time really was relative. It seemed like the blink of an eye since we had walked nervously through the door. We stayed for another hour talking, dancing, and laughing. It no longer felt strange. The feeling of connecting with other people was powerful, intoxicating. They were just like us. Average couples who spoke about their jobs, their family and the struggles of everyday life. And like us, they had somehow ended up here in this place, at this time, to share a truly incredible night.

"It's getting late, we should probably get going," Tess said eventually. We could have easily stayed but it had been a huge day, leaving the hotel at 2pm, and the first waves of weariness washed in.

"Yeah, I'm starting to get tired, it'll be good to get into bed," I replied. We stood and headed towards the locker room, past the now silent dungeon and Mav, still chatting away as energetically as he was at the start of the night.

"Ouch," Tess protested as I gently smacked her behind when she bent over to retrieve our clothes from the locker.

We dressed slowly while we finished our last drink. I glanced repeatedly at the mirror, taking in the final moments of the night. But also, to appreciate Tess, sliding the tight black dress up her wriggling body. We had revelled in the freedom we had given each other, armed with trust and love. It was out of this world. Our world anyway.

Soon enough we were walking, saying a few quick goodbyes in the back lounge and to Mav. We continued through to the front lounge where there were five couples left. Jen, Dave and many of the couples we had met that night had already gone. Katy immediately stepped towards the centre of the room and kissed Tess on the cheek and then did the same to me.

"We had a great night, it was awesome," Katy beamed.

"Yeah, I didn't really know what to expect but that was something special," Michael said in agreement. He kissed Tess then shook my hand. A handshake seemed a rather formal farewell after the experience we had shared.

"Awesome alright, it was great to meet you guys. I never thought we would be in the city doing…this. It was amazing. Thanks for the night." Suddenly I didn't want to leave.

"Yeah, it was. We had a great night too. Thanks." Tess smiled warmly at both of them as we headed for the door. "Bye."

"Bye, we might see you again some time," Katy added hopefully.

"Maybe, see ya," Tess concluded as I reached for the door handle and we stepped out onto the street. We both took deep breaths of the warm summer air and began walking. We only took five steps before I stopped and turned to take in the old Sydney building in the middle of the city.

We never did swap numbers. I think it was Tess' intuition more than anything that made the decision. It was a good call. No ties or promises for the future. No loose ends. Each night would be its own adventure, completely isolated from the past or the future. Just a wild adventure for that one moment in time. It was like throwing each other into the night like a paper plane, flying free in the wind.

"Did we just do that?" laughed Tess.

"Yeah, we just did that. Or was it just a dream?"

We walked back into the hotel and opened the curtains to show the nighttime city views over Hyde Park in all its glory. The lights shone like a symphony of colour. The beautiful food platter of fruits, cheeses, chocolates and dips lay on the bed where we had left it that afternoon. I grabbed the wooden platter and placed it on the kitchenette bench. Tess kicked off her shoes, slid out of her dress and lay arched on the end of the bed with her feet still on the floor. I turned and looked at her. Every curve was perfect and I traced the line of her panties and bra with my eyes. She propped herself up on her elbows and grinned seductively at me. The sexual energy filled the room, filled my mind. I was so hard it almost hurt.

"Are you tired," I asked as I walked over to stand directly in front of her. Tess sat up.

"Not at all. Are you?" She undid my brown leather belt.

"Not at all," I replied as I caressed her jawline, down her neck to her cleavage line, and then inside her bra. "This night just keeps getting better." She took both of my hands and pulled me onto the bed, on top of her. We kissed slowly, passionately, and once again time stopped.

Tess peeled her sexy black lingerie off and I quickly undressed so that we were both naked on the bed. The city lights shone from the window canvas. I touched every part of her. Gently. Deliberately. Then my hand stopped between her legs. Soft. Hard. Soft. Harder. Her breathing was rhythmic and beautiful as she arched her head back.

When she was nearly ready, I knelt on the bed between Tess' legs and pushed them slightly wider with my knees. Then gently, we were connected. Slow, full thrusts to begin with and then increasingly harder. Her eyes were closed tight. I placed my palm carefully on her stomach and my thumb found that place on her body. She pushed against it, silently screaming to be touched.

That was enough. Tess' whole body tensed as she came. I removed my hand and pushed deep as I joined her. The electricity thundered around the room as the crescendo eventually subsided into heavy, hard breathing. I crashed onto the bed beside her, eventually handing her the tissues. I rolled on my side to put my arm across her chest. We lay silently, contentedly. When Tess returned from the bathroom, we fell asleep, naked, which we never did. But I guess that night was full of so many things that we had never done before.

"Morning," welcomed Tess' voice as I opened my eyes to see her looking directly at me, smiling. "Can you close those curtains, it's only seven." I took a moment to wake and returned the smile.

"Anything for you." I slowly rose and shut the heavy cream curtains before going to the toilet and climbing back into bed. "How are you feeling? That was one massive night."

"I'm good. Tired. Massive alright." It looked like she was processing the whole thing, running back the video in her head and calibrating all that had happened. I was doing the same, at speed. "Toilet." I watched her every step across the now darkened room. She climbed back into bed and I wriggled close to her, face to face, so our whole bodies were touching. She felt me, hard.

"Again? Haven't you had enough?" She laughed as she ran her fingers in through my hair. I couldn't help it. I wanted her again.

This was not like us. Like any married couple who had been married for twenty something years, sex was not as frequent as it used to be. Not as frequent as I would have liked. Once it was all the time. Then, over the course of time, it naturally evolved into once a week, or even longer at times. I was okay with that. I was happy if she was happy and I wanted her to 'want to', not just go through the motions to please me.

"Ryan, it's time to go." I heard Tess' voice wake me again. "Checkout at ten. It's nine thirty now." Again, she lay looking at me. I wondered what she was thinking, how she felt.

There were many times in life when I had woken, hung over, full of regret after clearly getting things wrong the night before. But looking into Tess' eyes then, there was none of that. She just smiled and I knew that we shared an unspoken loyalty and a commitment that we had each other's back. We had each other's total trust, which was all we needed, and we had had one truly fucking awesome night.

Chapter 6
1817

"Who's that?" I asked my best mate Tim as I watched the new girl walk up the stairs outside the central coast high school library.

"Some new girl I think, from Sydney. Meg said she's in Year 11. Nice!" Tim seemed as equally impressed as I was. I only saw her briefly but I still remember that moment. It was the first time I ever saw Tess and I still think it unusual that I have that memory, clear in my mind, of someone I didn't even know at that point in time. It was 1996. I was eighteen, in my last year of school. Tess was seventeen, in the year below.

"What time is the game on Saturday?" I asked Tim, one of the forwards in my footy team. I had always loved rugby league and Tim had played alongside me since we had first started in the under sevens.

"Eleven thirty, at home. Port are rubbish, we'll smash 'em." Tim was confident as always and as tough as any guy on our team. He played hard. I was smaller and played in the back line. Speed and skill were my weapons, not brute force.

"Can't wait, they picked up a few players from last year. I'm gonna get there early and watch the sixteens." The bell rang to signal our return to class.

"Not enough players to beat us," Tim mumbled as he strode off to Maths. "See ya." I looked again at the second storey hall way but the new girl had disappeared into the crowd by that stage.

I loved Saturdays, especially when we were playing at home. From my back yard, if I listened carefully, I could hear the crowd. Especially when first grade played at three. That Saturday I slept in as always before digging into my customary bacon and eggs. Mum was my foundation in life; a selfless, beautiful soul who would have done anything for her boys. She never missed a beat and I appreciated her far more than I ever actually told her. Dad was a good man and

I always knew that he loved us, that he was proud of us. He had moved out when I was ten. It was hard.

It had been me, Mum and my younger brother Luke since then. A single parent pension was hardly enough to pay rent, so the rest of life was budgeted down to the cent. That was until we were broke and then we got to the second Thursday, pay day, the best we could. I got a few hours here and there doing crappy jobs, but Mum wanted me to put my time and effort into school. That's what I did, except for Saturdays.

Footy was my reward, my release, my escape. It was my happy place. When Dad left, we lost our house. Mum did the best she could but she inevitably struggled. Everything I knew was turned upside down, except when the whistle blew. Then I was home. I was the best player on the field most days, but I was never cocky. I played for the team, my teammates, and I just loved the clear mind that footy gave me for eighty minutes each week.

That Saturday, I got my chores done as quickly as possible and carefully packed my gear. It was the same check and re-check routine that I did before every match.

"Thanks Mum, I'm going now. The sixteens are on soon, Luke's already down there."

"Be careful Ryan. Be careful," she said those same words before every match. Her boys were her whole world and rugby league was a brutal contact sport.

"Don't worry, they won't even touch me. They never do. Too fast," I reassured her. I wasn't over confident, I had a healthy fear of the game. I just hated to think of her worrying. She knew that there were risks, but she never missed a game, ever.

"Yes, yes, alright. I'll be there at eleven after I finish up here. Make sure you drink enough, okay?"

"Yep, drinking right now. Love you. See ya there." I held my water bottle up in the air as I threw my footy bag over my shoulder and walked out the front door.

I reached our home ground in no time, James Beecon Oval, and the under sixteens match had already started. I saw Tim on the far side of the field. Strange, he was never early and regularly came puffing into the change rooms late to the great annoyance of our coach.

He was talking to two girls. Meg had always had a thing for Tim. She was a year younger and he clearly liked her too.

"There's my boy. Ryan, what's happenin'?" He was full of bravado as ever.

"Mornin'. What's the score?" I asked as I neared the group and immediately realised that Meg was talking to the new girl. I made sure I kept my eyes on the game but I was aware of every move she made.

"Down by four. Four nothing. They just started. Baitsy dropped the kick off and 4 tackles later they scored in the corner. Hopeless." I had reached the group of three and the girls had stopped chatting to listen to Tim's account of the first five minutes of the match. He was a hard marker and he wasn't big on introductions.

"Ryan, this is Tess. She moved up from Sydney a few weeks ago. We thought we might watch your game. Nothing better to do." Meg stepped in. She loved to talk and she was a perfect match for Tim.

"Hi Tess." I wasn't sure whether to shake her hand or what to do. I didn't meet many girls. I was a shy, pimply kid and talking to the opposite sex did not come easy to me. "I saw you at the library the other day. Um. I was talking to Tim." Too much? I hoped that she didn't think I'd been watching her, even though I had. I blushed slightly.

"Hi Ryan," was all that she said in reply. She had a quiet self-assured demeanour and stunning brown eyes. She smiled courteously before returning to her conversation with Meg.

At half time in the under sixteens game, the coach gave the call for us to head into the sheds, as we always did, to get ready for the game. I took my worn-out black boots from my bag and sat them on the concrete floor. They were second hand and old when I got them. New boots were expensive and almost every pair I had ever owned were hand-me-downs, although I polished them up as best I could. But it didn't matter when I got on the field. I made them sing.

Our game finished and we walked off, winning a game that was closer than we expected.

"Where were you today? We should have smashed them," lectured Tim as the whistle blew.

"We won by ten," I replied, conscious of my poor performance during the game.

"We won by forty last year. And their new guys didn't do jack shit."

Meg and Tess were sitting near the sheds. I watched as stealthily as I could, with a messy fringe covering my surveillance of the girls.

"Jerseys in the bag. Make sure they're not inside out or you can wash 'em," the coach barked at us. I stripped my shirt off and threw it in the bag before continuing towards the sheds. I stopped to talk to Luke and looked up to see Tess looking straight at me. Her gazed lingered for just a fraction of a second. I tensed the muscles in my skinny upper body, suddenly aware that I had no shirt on.

The next week at school I was walking along one of the crowded hallways when I heard Meg's voice.

"Have you seen Tim? He should have History now?" She scanned the crowd. Tess was next to her. They were inseparable it seemed.

"Sorry, he'll probably be late like he normally is." I looked at Tess in her short blue school skirt and white collared shirt. "Hi," was all I could muster, along with an abbreviated smile.

"There he is." Meg took off in pursuit of Tim and left Tess and I standing there in awkward silence.

"So, Meg said you came from Sydney," was all I could think of. She was quiet but we just seemed to click. That hadn't happened before. The feeling was magical. We ended up talking for longer than we should of and I was late to class, which I hated. I was on time or early for everything.

The next day, after constant rehearsals in my mind, I asked Tess if she wanted to go to the movies on Saturday night. I anticipated all the reasons that she would give, then say no, and prepared myself for the rejection. But she said yes.

We saw Mortal Kombat. I remember nothing of the move whatsoever. We were completely consumed with each other from the moment it started. We whispered, to the disgust of the family nearest us, and the conversation just flowed. I had never expected it and it was nothing like my limited experience with girls previously.

Then, without any conscious thought, I kissed her. It was pure magic. Soft, sensual perfection. We didn't talk much after that and the family guy was happy. We kissed passionately for what seemed like the whole movie. I had never done anything like that and it was heavenly.

Many years later I read an article about kissing. Somehow our brains process the taste, smell, feel of the person we're kissing and makes chemical judgments on their suitability as a mate to reproduce. It was all very scientific. I didn't need any science to tell me that we were perfect together. I loved her from that night on.

Twenty-three years later, she was every bit as perfect and I loved her completely. So many things had changed in those years but Tess had never changed at all I still looked at her with the same look in my eyes as I did all those years ago.

"What's on Netflix?" I asked Tess as I crashed onto the lounge next to her. The kids were playing in their rooms on a quiet Saturday night as we settled in to watch TV.

"Nicky at work has been watching this. She loves it. It's called You, Me, Her."

"Weird name. I'm easy. Put it on if you want." We liked watching TV, or movies, together. It was a kind of escapism from work, and from life. It was August, 2019. The story followed a happily married couple from the American suburbs who were unsuccessfully trying to have children. The husband eventually paid an escort, a college student trying to make some extra cash, to meet him one night.

After finding out, the wife decided to book the same escort for a night as well to try to understand her husband's infidelity. But the wife fell for the college student, just as the husband had done, and the show followed the throuple's relationship from then on. We loved the show and after a few weekends of binge watching, Tess asked me a question that I never, ever, saw coming.

"Do you think we could do something like that?" She took me by complete surprise.

"What?" Fuck. What did she just ask me? Just say no I thought, it must have been a trap.

"Did you have any college students in mind?" I joked, trying to process the question and quickly dismissing it as a joke.

"No. I'm serious. We were so young when we met, don't you feel like you missed out on certain things that other people our age were doing?" Tess didn't sound at all like she was joking. We had never really discussed the fact that we were so young when we met, that we hadn't really had the chance to explore other people. We had lost our virginity to each other and we had been together ever since.

We were happy. We had two beautiful kids and a beautiful life together. I had never really thought about the fact that at eighteen and seventeen, there were things that we had missed out on. Tess was always everything I ever needed. But I understood where she was coming from.

"I guess I never really thought about it. Is that how you feel?"

"Maybe. Don't you ever think about what it would be like? Other people?"

I was processing a thousand thoughts and my mind was racing. The conversation continued about whether we could try something crazy, not necessarily along the same lines as the Netflix show, but something new. Goose bumps tingled across my whole body as a nervous, tight feeling churned in my stomach: the electricity.

Nothing more was said about it that week but it must have resonated with both of us and each of us jumped online to explore what was out there for a couple like us. I don't know if it was coincidence or fete, but eventually we both found the same website for a club, a swinger's club. I didn't even really know that they existed. It was called Deepest Desires. The website was comprehensive and gave a thorough description of this hidden Sydney venue.

The following weekend, as we lay in bed, the deafening silence on the subject was broken.

"I got online this weekend. There's this place in Sydney. A club where people go to meet." Tess eased into the conversation.

"Yeah, I had a look too. There were two clubs. I checked out a site for a place called Deepest Desires." I couldn't believe the words were coming out of my mouth and it didn't seem quite real at that stage. "It was pretty wild. I didn't even know people did that stuff."

"No way. That's the same place I checked out. In the city. A swinger's club." Tess looked at me and we both burst out laughing. What were we doing? I had no idea where it was leading but I felt the energy even then as we discussed our crazy idea.

"Are you serious about this? It's not really something that people do is it? Not anyone we know that's for sure." I became a little more serious at this point.

"Well, even if they were doing it, they wouldn't be telling us about it would they?"

"True. I wonder if many people do get into it. I mean, it's a pretty out there thing to even think about doing. Are we actually serious about this?" I looked directly at Tess. This was cards on the table time. We had both had a week to think about it and it looked like we had both given it a great deal of thought. She paused.

"Yeah, I think we could at least try. Maybe we could go and check it out one night. We wouldn't have to do anything we didn't want to do. What do you think?" It was a yes. Wow, she was a yes.

"Okay. If you're in, then I'm in. We love the city anyway. We could do dinner and get a nice hotel." I couldn't believe I was a yes as well.

It took some time to sink in, to process. Could we do this? Could we walk this road less travelled? It was frightening, exciting and instantly I felt more alive than I could ever imagine. It was an energy beyond words. This was a totally crazy thing for a quiet, small town couple like us to do so we decided to get some perceived control over the situation. We needed rules.

"The website talked about setting rules before going. Did you read that bit? I thought it was a good idea," I suggested. The rules became an important part of the adventure. Any cracks in a relationship would be blown into canyons if you were not both squarely on the same page in a place like that.

"No, but it sounds like something we should do. I have no idea what they would be though. How do you make up rules for something like that?" Tess asked.

"I've got some. I was thinking about it this week. There are five. Do you want to hear them?" I said.

"Well, you're very organised, aren't you?" Tess laughed and sat up, eagerly awaiting my five swinging rules. I wasn't sure if she was taking me seriously or not.

"Okay, here they are. Number one, be safe. We stay together and obviously it has to be safe sex, safe everything." The gravity of my wife having sex with another man, no matter how safe, started to dawn on me. Saying it aloud was terrifying.

"Makes sense," Tess agreed. I moved on quickly.

"Number two, be honest. If we're going to do this, then we have to be honest about every little thing. Everything."

"I thought it was a given but yeah, it'll do," replied Tess.

"Number three, be forgiving. There are so many unknowns. I think we have to give each other the freedom, within limits, to make mistakes. Really, we have no idea what we're getting into," I continued.

"You really have been thinking about this." Tess seemed both intrigued and agreeable.

"Number four. It's a secret. It has to be. Every little detail. Everything. Can you imagine what people would think if they found out?" Tess was a nurse and her work mates loved to gossip about the smallest things. I hated to think what they would do if they got hold of something like this?

"Imagine what the girls at work would say? Definitely our secret." Tess almost read my mind.

"Number five, hash tag no regrets. If we do this, then we don't get caught up with all the shit that could happen. Who knows what it will be like? I just don't want us to be down on ourselves if it goes pear shaped. I don't know why I put the 'hash tag' in there. Maybe it just sounded cool."

"No regrets. It's a deal," Tess said.

After the first time, I felt nothing but love, admiration and chemistry for Tess. We had been safe in every aspect of the night. We were completely open and honest about everything we did and felt. We were forgiving. There was no road map for this stuff but we were still able to let each other fly. It was definitely a secret. It had to be. No one else could begin to understand unless they had experienced it. And as far as number five was concerned, there were no regrets. I had never felt so close to Tess, so supported and loved.

Chapter 7
The Weird and the Wonderful

"So, Luke has asked if the kids want to sleep over at their place a week from Saturday. It's Charlie's' birthday." My brother adored our kids and their younger cousins always loved having them over. "A night to ourselves. I wonder what we could do." I used my most suggestive voice and Tess knew exactly what I was asking.

"I wonder. What do you think we could do?" Tess was happy to play the game.

"Well, I thought we could drop the kids to Luke's place after Josh's game and then maybe head out to dinner." I paused. "On the harbour?"

"Which harbour?" Tess teased.

"You know that Sydney one," I replied.

"That's a long drive just for dinner."

"And then maybe we just see where the night takes us?" I raised my eyebrows, still asking the same original question.

"And where do you think the 'night' might want to take us."

"Ah, into the city. I hear there's a great club there, you know how much I love to dance," I said.

"Oh, so we're going dancing, are we?" laughed Tess.

"There will be dancing, yes. Amongst other things. I can book the same hotel. Maybe Vietnamese this time."

"Well, I do love Vietnamese. And we do have a night to ourselves which would be a shame to waste. Okay. You book then." Tess held her smile as she returned to her book. The anticipation was instant. I knew what to expect this time.

When I looked back on the first time, it wasn't the sex that I thought of. It was the long afternoon spent in the city hanging out with Tess, talking the night away and sharing memories over dinner. It was the sheer, unparalleled excitement of standing at that terrace door, the feeling of meeting new people, the chemistry. I hungered for the electricity, the indescribable energy that surrounded the whole night. It was life's power chord plugged in, and I wanted more.

It was September and Tess and I had booked a different hotel slightly closer to the club. I thought that less walking through Sydney streets at the end of the night would be safer. Rule number one. Although winter had just finished, the sun shone brightly and the customary Spring winds were behaving.

"We've got harbour views this time. You can see the Opera House, the bridge, the park. This room is way better," Tess said as she opened the curtains. I followed behind with most of the bags.

"Looks awesome," I said as we got settled. "Are you hungry? I'll do the food platter now." I had loved the luxury of our platter the first time and I'd made sure I was equally prepared this time.

"Belle peppers. Have you tried these things? I had some at Meg's birthday. So good." I arranged the cheeses, fruit, chocolates and dipping sauces neatly on the hard wood chopping board that made a perfect platter.

"Not yet. You've done well Ry, very prepared." She went for a chocolate first as always. "So, I thought we'd start at Gallagher's pub. 4 cocktails for thirty dollars. Then to Darlinghurst Road and Vietnamese after that. Sound like a Plan?"

"Sounds like a plan T. Very prepared," I repeated.

We sat on the bed enjoying the view, eating. I kissed Tess, dipping chocolate still on my lips, and took time to relax on the bed. I breathed in the city view and enjoyed the stillness of sharing food with Tess. But inside my heart raced like a revving engine at the starting line and I revelled in the electricity that filled me completely.

In less than an hour, we walked into the small, character filled Irish pub that we had visited the first time and ordered our cocktails. Two illusions and two beachcombers. We didn't drink fast, we were not there to get hammered. We were there to enjoy time together, without the stress and the demands on our time that filled every other day of our busy lives.

"Did you bring your questions?" I knew Tess had hers but I asked anyway.

"Yep, they're in my phone, ready to go. You?"

"In my pocket, paper only though. I didn't even think about putting them in my phone." A few years ago, on a weekend away, we decided to do the New York Times '36 Questions That Lead to Love' questionnaire that I had seen in the paper a few weeks earlier. It was a really cool thing to do and we found out things about each other that we had never known, even after all those years together. Some of those things were pretty heavy and I loved the open, honest dialogue.

One of the questions was about our worst childhood memories. Tess told me about the times her dad would come home drunk after payday and the terrible things that he had put her family through. He was a charismatic, larger than life man when he was sober. But he was a mean drunk and it sounded like he was pissed for much of Tess' childhood.

He was an orphan, and like many indigenous kids of his era, life was tough. It never validated any of his behaviour as a father and a husband, but I could see where those inner demons had been born, and why they still raged within him.

We had decided that we would write our own questions before visiting the club the first time. We could ask anything we wanted. Anything, just be completely honest, rule two. The questions became a key part of the adventure. Every question was answered openly and honestly. It struck me how we really listened to each other, without judgement, and how it helped us to understand each other. Listening was something that couples didn't do nearly enough. The questions were not just about Deepest Desires. They spanned the entire breadth of our relationship, our childhoods and our most private thoughts.

"OK. You go first," Tess said as she sipped her lime green illusion. "This should be interesting."

"Alright. Question number one. Where did you get the idea for this whole thing and what did you think I'd say?" I really wanted to know. Tess smiled and paused to think.

"It's not as if I'd been thinking about it and planning it. It just kind of happened. I never thought that we missed out on anything when first met. We were just kids. It was only when we were watching that show that I thought about it. Leyla and Josh are older now. We hardly had a night away in ten years. I just thought that we could do something for ourselves. Together." She ran her hand along the beautiful, carved table as she spoke, lost in thought. "And I had no idea what you'd say. I just didn't want you to think that I was unhappy with us. Because I'm not. I hoped that you'd say yes."

"It was a pretty brave thing to ask. I'm glad you did. Your turn."

"Right. First one. How many sexual partners have you had in your life?" She looked closely into my eyes. This one wasn't hard to count up.

"Three." I didn't want elaborate at all on that one.

"And they were?"

"Ahh, you know this." This was hard.

"Do I?"

"My nineteen-year-old mistake, Star Wars and you obviously. That's it. No, four, if you count Scully." Soon after we had started dating I had made a terrible, regrettable mistake late one night on a local beach. I had never forgiven myself and Tess had never forgotten it. I couldn't blame her. Soon after it happened, I told Tess everything, I couldn't live with that guilt. That night I learned how hard she could punch, close fisted in the face, to many times to count.

I had gone through the excuses: I was young and pissed, she came onto me and so forth. But there were no excuses for that, none. Star Wars was a girl from uni, a one-night stand after Tess and I had separated for a few months 5 years into our relationship. She had Star Wars wallpaper and that's what Tess called her from then on after I had told her about it.

"And what about you?" I wanted to confirm what I already knew, just like Tess.

"Three, if you count Michael." I was trying to read the room and assess if this was a good idea, or if it was just stirring up trouble. I wasn't sure yet. Tess' number two still hurt, even though we were not together when it happened, but I was leaving that one alone. "Next one."

"Did you watch me with Katy, what were you thinking?" I wasn't even sure I should ask.

"No, not really. We were drunk. No. I didn't want to watch you." She sipped her vodka as a group of women sat down at the table closest to us. "Did you?"

"No. I could hear you. You sounded like you were enjoying yourself. You were safe. I didn't want to watch either." We were on the same page and there was no residual damage. Good, we moved on.

"Number two. Do you ever take care of business yourself?" Tess gave her naughty schoolgirl look and smiled. I loved it.

"Are you asking if I'm a wanker?" I burst out laughing before reigning myself in and hoping that I'd spoken quietly enough that the neighbouring table didn't hear. "I reckon there's only two groups of blokes. The ones who admit to having a pull and the ones who lie about it."

"So that's a yes?" She wanted a definite answer.

"Yes, not that often, but yes. Do you want another drink?" I was surprisingly embarrassed, even though this question was much easier to answer than the first.

"Let's keep walking, pub crawl remember? I loved the New Hampton last time." Tess led the way as we walked back out onto the street and joined the bustling Sydney foot traffic. The fresh air and the walk did us good. We continued our game across the next two pubs and answered openly and honestly. Some questions were simple fun: what's your dream holiday or who are the three most attractive celebrities in your opinion. Others were heavy hitters, probing our insecurities and concerns about this whole adventure.

"Live music, this pub's definitely my favourite," I chorused as we walked into the next pub to see a young duo on the small stage playing 'You can go Your Own Way' by Fleetwood Mac. It seemed rather ironic. I collected the drinks while Tess found a private table with two chairs at the back of the room.

"It's busy tonight. That hen's party is having a good time." I scanned the room as I sat down.

"Yeah, they look like they've had a big arvo already," Tess replied.

"OK, let's keep going. Number ten. Ah. Did you surprise yourself when you and Katy, um, got together that night? Did you always know that you might like girls too? I never had any idea." I was intrigued by this part of our first night at Deepest Desires. Tess paused to sip her vodka and orange.

"Yeah, I kinda knew. She wasn't my first time with another girl." Tess left her succinct answer at that. What the fuck?

"What do you mean?" Intrigued was an understatement. "You haven't been with another girl." I paused. "Have you?"

"I was sixteen I think, we were still living in Sydney. A girl in my street and I used to hang out a bit. She was beautiful. We went to school together." Talk about edge of my seat. I nearly fell off it. "One afternoon she came over while Mum and Dad were still at work and we were watching TV on the lounge. She was right next to me and she just turned and kissed me."

"On the lips? What did you do?"

"Yeah, on the lips. Properly kissed me. I kissed her back. As we were kissing, she put her hand on the inside of my thigh and then down my pants."

"No way. How come you never told me this before?" I never had the slightest hint or suspicion about this part of the girl that I had loved for a lifetime.

"Why would I? It happened before we were together."

"So, what happened next? You can't stop there." I wanted to know every detail. I couldn't help but be impressed and I hung on every word. I couldn't believe that Tess was so calm about it.

"That's about it. We played. We kissed. It was fun. Anyway, it was a long time ago."

"So, did you? You know?" The hen's party reeled in laughter as the live music continued to play.

"Did I what?" Tess was clearly enjoying the game.

"Did you come?" Tess laughed at my hunger for detail and just nodded yes to my pleading question.

"So that counts on your tally. You're on four like me." We both laughed.

"I guess so," Tess conceded.

"Did it happen again? It must have been strange seeing her at school the next day?"

"No. It was just once. We were just experimenting I think. Not long after we moved out of Sydney and I met you. I'd pretty much forgotten about it until now." Shit, how could you forget that? I was still stunned as Tess moved on.

"So, number ten." She looked closely at her phone screen.

"Why did you cheat on me and why did you phone me to tell me what happened, rather than in person? Dog of an act" There it was. I had been waiting for this question. Dreading it. I sipped my beer slowly and took a deep breath.

"I don't have an answer for that. There are no excuses for it. It was the most stupid decision I ever made and I still regret it." Tess was silent, serious, and she wasn't going to let me leave it at that. "I was just a kid and she asked me." Shit, don't blame the girl. It was my decision, not anyone else's fault.

"I just fucked up." I continued. "I would never do anything to hurt you but I know how much I did. I am so sorry." This was hard and the joyous, playful mood had changed. "I don't know why I phoned. Maybe it was easier. I don't know. At least I told you. Most guys wouldn't do that." A desperate tone, begging for forgiveness, soaked into my voice. Tess always had an unreadable poker face when she needed it.

"Well, aren't you just a good bloke then? Wanker." She looked hard into my eyes, giving nothing away. She gave me the smallest smile and then looked at the duo on stage.

"I love you," I said simply, longing for a reply.

"Love you too. Next one." Her gaze softened and I was more than happy to move on.

"Eleven. Okay. Did you feel jealous, seeing me with someone else?" This was awful timing. I wished that I had not asked the question, especially now. I so wished that we were discussing favourite holiday destinations at that point.

"No." Tess thought carefully before answering. "We did it together and we followed the rules. I don't think I was jealous. The whole thing still feels like a dream." Thank goodness for the rules. They were more important than we had realised.

"Were you?" she replied.

"No. It sounds stupid but I kinda felt proud of us. Proud that we could give each other the freedom to do something like that. It's heavy stuff. I could hear you, I knew you were okay. You were close and you were safe. I wanted you to be able to experience some of the things that you missed out on."

"She's enjoying the party." Our hen stood on a chair near us with a pink veil hanging from her head and danced. "It's still only a quarter to seven. Here they go." More of the girls stood and danced where they were. I felt like dancing too.

"You hungry?" Tess asked as we watched the group enjoying the live music.

"Starving. We really should get something to eat before any more of these. Did you want to get going?" I was happy to leave the questions for a while.

"Soon. I've still got this drink left." She sipped her vodka and I hoped that her next question would be easier than the last. I paused to watch the duo playing. "What's your favourite sex position?"

"You're a classic," we laughed at the question together. "I like them all, but doggy has always been up there. Variety is the main thing though. What's yours?"

"On top lately, but it changes." We were interrupted by the cheers of the hen's party.

"How good are they? Love her voice." I said, clapping the ending of the song. "Next one. Do you always tell the truth, or do you have secrets?" I thought I knew the answer but I asked anyway. Again, Tess thought about it.

"Um. I pretty much tell the truth. I don't keep things from you. Only little things like I wish you'd turn your bloody phone off at night." She paused again. "I don't lie to you, not about anything important anyway." She was brutally honest at times and told it like she saw it. I admired this about her, most of the time anyway. "And you?"

"Well, I do have one confession." Her serious stare returned. "I hate spaghetti bol. Just not a fan." It was her favourite dish to cook. "Sorry, but just saying. No, I don't have secrets. You'd see through them in a second anyway. I guess everyone lies sometimes. I try not to. Rule number two."

"What are we up to? Twelve. What do you think about open relationships?" Again, Tess stared hard at me as she asked the question.

"Open relationships? I don't know how that could even work. Na. I could never see us doing that. Ever. The whole reason that I think it worked the first time was that we were together. Definitely wouldn't be into it. Nothing against people who do it and good luck to them but no." I drained the last drops of my beer.

"Good. Me either. Just that night with no ties, no strings. That's about as much as I could do." Tess finished her drink as well.

"Is that why you never thought about calling Katy and Michael?" Until then, I had never asked her about the number swap.

"I guess so, one night was enough. Let's go hey?" We were ready for dinner.

We walked out onto Darlinghurst Road and I was amazed, as always, at the crowded city footpath full of people in a hurry to get somewhere. The energy was something that just didn't exist on the quiet rural streets of home. Besides the many pubs, there were food joints everywhere and the odd 'adult' shop with racy slogans above the door.

"We'll have to check it out some time," I commented as we walked past one with a DD's styled silhouetted logo in the window. It left nothing to the imagination.

"Maybe we will. We won't have time to go down to the harbour. What about the Thai place we walked past before. We could sit outside."

"Done." One of the many homeless people scattered throughout that part of the city sat at the bottom of a dark staircase leading to a second storey. He was holding out a cup. A scribbled cardboard sign said a single word. Please.

Substance abuse and mental health issues must have played a huge part in the lives of the homeless and I felt for each one of them. To the city locals they seemed to be invisible objects but I could not walk past without giving some change at least, and a kind word. I knew that I had my own demons, which had threatened to derail everything I had at times. I felt like I understood just a faction of the hardship that had put them on those lonely streets.

"Table for two?" An attractive young waitress greeted us warmly at the door of the small restaurant, twenty metres off the main road. "You like to sit inside or outside?" I listened closely to her heavily accented question.

"Outside please." I turned to Tess for confirmation.

"Yes. Just here please." The girl pulled out the chair for Tess as we sat at a small table next to a much younger couple, obviously from the city. He had a man bun and both had perfectly matched scarves. Their eyes were constantly on their phones as they chatted and I felt a sense of melancholy for them as they sat glued to the screens.

The footpath dining was perfect for us. It allowed way more privacy than the cramped seating inside and people were less likely to hear our crazy questions, not that anyone would have been listening. But it also allowed us to people watch, which we loved. We could see the river of weird and wonderful humans flowing by and take it all in. I was amazed at how many dogs there were. It seemed like every second pedestrian had a dog, mostly small breeds, and every bike seemed to come with a doggy basket on the front as standard issue.

The waitress called towards the kitchen in a beautiful, strange language and an older woman brought out menus.

"You like any drinks?"

"No. Thank you, we have our own," I said as I gestured to the plastic bag at my feet. I had seen the BYO sign above the front door on our way past earlier in the night and I made sure that we had drinks. It was part of the night and made the questions just a bit easier.

"I put the rest in the fridge," she offered kindly as I fished for a drink each.

"Thirteen. OK. Were you unhappy or bored with our sex life before all of this?" I felt slightly nervous asking and sometimes it felt that Tess didn't want me like she once did. For a moment, I thought why ask the question if I was afraid of what the answer might be. I knew she was going to be honest.

"Of course not. I mean, it's not like it used to be, but we're older now. It couldn't just stay the same forever. We have great sex, but I just wanted to try something different. Does that make sense?"

"Yeah. Yeah it does." I felt a sense of relief.

"Are you happy with us?" Tess bounced the question to me. Again, I forgot the implied rule that if you were going to ask a question then you also had to answer it as well. Fair enough.

"I still love to watch you undress, still want you as much as ever. Sometimes I would like to do it more though. I guess every husband would say the same thing." Tess was silent again. She was good at keeping quiet, implying that she expected me to elaborate. "I'd never get bored with us. You're still smoking hot. Just a bit more would be good." I hadn't planned on this reply and wondered if I was being too honest.

We both looked at the menu as the waitress headed on our direction.

"You like to order now?" she asked, taking a pen and notepad from her back pocket. We seldom deviated from our favourite dishes. Spring rolls, Pad Thai, Thai beef salad and rice.

"Thirteen. When you die, do you want to be cremated or buried and why?" Tess asked. I loved this question. There was no pressure at all, just some simple housekeeping.

"I really don't care either way. Cremation is much cheaper. I kinda like the idea of my ashes being scattered at the footy fields. That would be a nicer place for the kids to visit than a cemetery. Either one is fine." I'd never really thought about it but it seemed like something that a couple should know about each other.

"Same," replied Tess. "It's not going to worry me when the time comes."

As we ate our meals and watched the footpath procession, I thought it was a good time to surprise Tess.

"So, I decided to try something new this week. For some strange reason, I wrote you a poem." Tess burst out laughing.

"Sorry. How sweet," she said as she wiped her mouth.

"Yep, a poem. This whole thing is full of firsts hey?" Ex footy players didn't write poems, but this one did. I took the crumpled piece of paper out of my jacket's inner pocket and began to read.

"It's called 'A Poem For Tess'."
"Very original." She stopped eating and listened intently.

"A poem for Tess that doesn't rhyme
Raw and honest as the beers flow through my blood
Each day with you feels new, I never lost

That excitement from your touch or being in the same room
Tonight, I am in awe of your courage
To take on new things and bravely walk
Where others wish they could
When you think you know everything about someone
It's amazing to be surprised
On this journey with you I feel alive and young
Truly exhilarated and frightened too
It feels like running through a minefield
Hand in hand, heart racing every second
And living our lives to the absolute full where
One crowded hour of glorious life
Is worth an age without a name
I feel safe because it's all been with you by my side
And every step has been taken with honesty
I love the energy of the city
And walking into a bar with no one else but you
Not worrying about anyone else in the world
Where no one matters except you and I
In this wild, amazing adventure
I will love you always and forever Tess."

I folded the page and looked up as she reached out and took my hand. I meant every word.

"I stole the 'one crowded hour of glorious life is worth an age without a name' bit. I love that line. It's by Mordaunt."

"Never heard of him. It was beautiful. Thank you."

"I wrote it when I was waiting for Josh at training. It just sorta came out."

"It's a wild, crazy adventure alright. One crowded hour, yeah, it's almost impossible to put into words. But you did a pretty good job."

I loved those moments, when the world stopped for us. We talked and laughed, just enjoying each other's company and looking directly into each other's eyes. The scarf couple were still gazing at their phones.

"Keep the change," I said as we left the restaurant. It was a modest tip but well received. We joined the river of the weird and wonderful, feeling like both of those things in our own way.

"Are you nervous? It's kinda different knowing what to expect this time." My thoughts immediately focused on Deepest Desires and the night ahead.

"A little. As long as we stick to the rules, it should be fun," Tess replied as we dodged our way along the footpath. She always had an understated calmness. I wondered if she felt the wild anticipation that consumed me. Like the first time, it was beyond words and the electricity was every bit as strong. "You?"

"Nervous?" "Not really. Just excited to feel that energy again. I mean, you know how much I love to dance."

"You're a dancer alright. I wonder what Tim would say of he knew his best mate was a pole dancer in a swinger's club." We both laughed.

"We'll never know, will we?" I shuddered to think what he'd say.

We stopped in briefly at the hotel and I dug into the food platter while Tess was in the bathroom. I wasn't hungry but I kept eating. Maybe I was nervous after all. I joined Tess in front of the mirror to add more after-shave and check my hair. I grabbed the strawberry flavoured breath mints sitting on the basin before heading to the mini bar.

"Should we have a shot before we go?" I had already poured them before Tess had said yes. I hated the name, Cocksucking Cowboy, but I loved the butterscotch schnapps and Baileys combination.

"Why not." We downed the shots and took a last look at the city landscape through the window. We paused for a moment before opening the hotel door, heading back out into the night.

Chapter 8
The Second Time

We were in no hurry as we rounded the street corner and caught sight of the club for the second time. The chatter from the pub spilt out onto the footpath as we walked past it.

"My heart is going a hundred miles an hour," I stuttered. I felt each step slowing until I was hardly walking at all, eyes fixated on the terrace light.

"No one waiting this time," Tess observed. The small, silver number 84 slowly became visible.

"No. Maybe no one will be there tonight. Or they might be in there already. There were a fair few couples inside last time when we got there and it was only twenty minutes after opening time." I had noted that most of the couples were deep in conversation last time when we arrived, and that getting there early allowed those accelerated social connections to happen.

"What time is it?"

"Twenty to nine. It's been open for over half an hour." I had been keeping a close eye on the time all night.

"Nice watch. New is it?"

"It is. This hotty bought it for me on eBay. She likes to shop online. Too much I think."

"Well maybe she won't be shopping online for you anymore. You think?" She was good at making her point, and it was clearly understood.

"The pub looks packed again. I wonder if there's any couples in there looking across the road like we did." I peered through the windows into the crowded bar. Thirty metres more and we were standing at the front door.

"They might be in there checking out whether anyone goes in." Tess turned to scan the pub as well while I pushed the red doorbell. The thirty seconds it took for the door to open seemed like an eternity.

"Hey, how are you tonight. Our friends from the coast, right?" Mav greeted us with a new designer stubble and plain white T-shirt.

"You remembered. Yeah, we thought we might get away for the weekend and just happened to end up here." I pulled the jet-black member's card out of my wallet.

"How's your night been so far?" He was like an old mate welcoming us to a barbeque. He had the same familiar, genuine feel as he did the first time.

"Great. We've just been hanging out in the city. Saw some live music and had a nice dinner." I handed Mav the card.

"Cool. So tonight, it's one twenty plus the fifty dollar locker deposit that you'll get back at the end of the night." Mav returned the card as I paid the one hundred and seventy in cash. A faint smell if incense drifted out the door. "Thanks. Looks like it will be busy tonight." He stepped backwards and motioned us in. Stranger's voices echoed towards the entrance and my skin bristled.

"Thanks Mav." We entered, customarily holding hands. "It's just as nerve wracking as the first time. I love it," I said to Tess.

"What would people say," Tess replied in a terrible English accent.

"What would they say?" I had thought about that exact thing a lot since the first time. "Ok, more people than I thought." We walked past the provocative artwork on our left and in a few short steps we were in the main lounge room. Tess squeezed my hand hard as I swung the plastic bag holding our drinks in the other.

"Love you T," I reassured Tess, and myself, as eyes glanced in our direction. Conversations continued uninterrupted but I could feel the momentary assessments as we entered.

"Hi, I'm Stacey, this is Aiden," said a woman standing near the fan in front of the stairs. She was thirty something, blonde haired and he was tall, well dressed in slim fit pants and a long, black collared shirt.

"Great to meet you both. I'm Ryan, this is Tess." They were standing apart from the other six couples near the lounge and looked relieved to be talking to someone.

"How's your night been?" asked Aiden, smilingly politely.

"Good so far. We had a really nice meal and got to see a bit of the city." Tess was her usual calm, collected self.

"Yeah, it's beautiful. We got a room on the harbour for the night, left the kids with Mum. It's so good to get away," said Stacey.

"Us too. The kids are with my brother in law and their cousins. Hopefully they're in bed soon," Tess replied.

"Nice. How old?" Tess and Stacey compared families as Aiden looked on and I took a brief glance around the room. There were six other couples and a woman on her own, who looked at me and smiled. A younger couple sat on the lounge nearest to Aiden. They must have been early twenties, attractive. I wondered what had brought them here at that stage of their relationship. They were talking to an animated couple on the lounge next to them. The younger woman had a tight fitting red dress and matching stilettos while her partner sat protectively with a hand over her thigh.

On the other side of the lounge sat an awkward looking couple, completely overdressed. She was short, solid, and sat cross-legged in a poorly fitted black cocktail dress. Her short back and sides haircut was almost identical to her partners'. I knew it was judgemental and pretentious but I always preferred longer hair, especially on Tess. I blamed the preference on social conditioning.

He looked out of place in an outdated black suit and brown polished dress shoes that clearly shouldn't have been matched with the suit. It reminded me of my grandfather's old suit. He was in the middle of some fantastic story, with grand hand gestures, and looked to be having a lovely time. Next to them was the single woman, her name was Amy. Regrettably, I'd get to know Amy later. The last couple, sitting nearest the back doorway, were enjoying the conversation with the awkwards and Amy. Our age, they seemed very quiet and looked to be taking everything in just as I was.

"Let's get those in the fridge." Tess interrupted my surveillance and tugged my hand as we started walking towards the bar.

We smiled and exchanged brief hellos as we kept moving towards the door. We walked past the dungeon on our left, which put a grin on my face. I hoped we would be in there at some stage that night. I put our drinks on the bar counter as Mav arranged bottles already in the fridge.

"You cut your hair, it looks great," Sara complimented Tess as she took our drinks. "Locker number?" I was impressed again that Sara had remembered us.

"Nine. Yeah, only a few centimetres. I like it shorter."

"How long since you were last here? It's good to see you two again?" Sara put our drinks in one of two large fridges at the back of the small bar room, keeping a beer and a vodka cruiser for us to begin the night with.

"Five or six weeks maybe. It doesn't feel like that long." I eagerly opened the beer.

"I knew you'd be back. Enjoy your night," beamed Mav with his usual enthusiasm.

We continued down the concrete stairs leading to the back room where another four couples were sitting, drinks in hand. A matching pair of leather jackets, worn by an animated Chinese Australian couple, caught my eye. They were sitting on the lounge to our right as we walked through the room. The doc martins complimented her pink hair perfectly.

The other three couples, ranging from early thirties to mid-forties, stood in a collection of provocative dresses and smart casual attire. We gave the same smile and hello routine as we did in the first lounge and made our way through the door to the next corridor that led to the locker room.

"Hi there, how are you?" We were instantly greeted by a stunning African Australian girl who was standing near the wall mirror to our left. She had the slightest accent that overlaid her Aussie twang.

"Good thanks. I love your outfit." Tess stopped for a moment to take it in. She wore tight, dark pink hot pants with a type of black leather belt stitched into the waist. Her washboard stomach led up to a matching pink bra with tiny bells attached all over it. The black neck collar matched her waist belt and the beautiful afro on top. Her athletic, toned legs and black toe nail polish completed a pretty impressive sight that we had not expected.

Behind her sat a man that looked twice her age, dressed in plain jeans and a black T-shirt. He was staring down at his phone and looked completely out of place. He didn't even look up to say hello.

"Thanks. It's just a bit of fun for the night." She stood on her toes and shook her whole upper body all in the same motion, making the bells ring, as she flashed a wide smile fit for a magazine cover.

"Gotta love the bells. How are you mate?" I tried to include phone guy in the conversation.

"Good buddy, good." He still didn't lift his eyes from the phone.

"I'm ready to dance, let's go," she said as she grabbed his hand and dragged him off his chair.

"Righto." He was definitely a man of few words.

"We'll see you out there." She danced her way out the door as he begrudgingly slipped the phone into his back pocket.

"Odd couple, how is she possibly with him? He must be loaded." Tess opened our locker as I speculated. Later we'd learn that they were not together at all.

We put our phones and Tess' handbag in the locker and she played with her hair at the mirror for a moment. It was almost like the moments in the dressing sheds before a grand finale. I was both nervous and excited. I just wanted to get out there.

Tess looked as gorgeous as ever. Her tight black jeans hugged her curves perfectly and her crimson blouse was modest and under stated, just like her. It was another mental snapshot moment and I stood looking at her in quiet admiration.

"OK, are you ready?" I asked eventually.

"Ready, we'll go to the front lounge hey?"

"Sounds good T. You look amazing. Love you."

"Love you too." We made our way to the front lounge where two more couples had arrived. A nervous looking pair stood near the fan below the stairs, listening to Grandpa's Suit telling another story.

We headed past the pole and stood next to Stacey and Aiden, casually joining the conversation. It was fun to hear people's stories and connect with strangers who were just like us really.

"I can't believe we've been here an hour already, it feels like five minutes. It's nice meeting new people," Tess said. This was unlike her. She didn't always like people.

"They seem really cool."

"Yeah, Stacey is a nurse too. Their kids are pretty much the same ages as Leyla and Josh."

Everyone shared their stories. Who are you? Where are you from? What do you do? There was a real honestly that was there the first time we had visited Deepest Desires. It wasn't sleazy or contrived, these people were just on a crazy adventure like us.

"Who wants to play a game, it's really fun?" Sara appeared from the back of the building.

"Jenga?" Aiden saw the small box in her hand.

"Correct, only this is the DDs version. It's mostly the same with some added rules when each person has their turn."

"No way. Maybe we'll watch first. Jenga, here?" Tess took a small step backwards.

"If you want, there's way more people here now, we'll just see how it works. Although I'm pretty bloody good at Jenga," I replied. The kids and I had played the game often.

"Ready. Now I'm sure you've all played before. Take one brick from anywhere on the column and place it on the top. Easy. The only difference is that each brick has a message written on it. Once you place the brick on top you have to do the task." Sara squared up the wooden stack.

"You'll get the idea. Who's first?"

"I'll have a go." A comical cheer welcomed Grandpa's Suit to the coffee table in the middle of the room, next to my pole.

"This is tricky." It wasn't. He like the attention. "Take off one piece of clothing." The audience cheered again as he placed the small brick on top.

"Jacket." Thank goodness that ugly thing was gone. The guy next to him sized up the Jenga stack.

"Hi." The beautiful bell dancer entered the lounge with a demeanour that was far beyond confidence. Grumpy was nowhere to be seen and she began to move.

"Wow, she can dance. She's beautiful." Tess leaned in and said what everyone else was thinking. The bells were inaudible over the music and everyone froze, taking in every part of her perfectly sculpted body, every movement.

"Dance like no one's watching. That's her. Wow alright." But people were watching, while the odd Jenga brick was placed on the stack. It was some performance. She danced throughout the next song as well before disappearing just as quickly as she had arrived.

"Stacey." The group demanded as our attention returned to the game. She was the first seated guest after Grandpa and his friend.

"I haven't played in ages. This one." She laughed as she read the scribbled writing. "Kiss someone." Everyone took an immediate liking to the game. "Come here." She planted a lingering kiss on Aiden's lips. Safe option.

"Only this place would think of this. Classic. You know everyone has to have a go?" I said to Tess, I was keen to play.

"Ryan," voices yelled above the music when it came to our turn. "Come on." I turned to Tess who nodded. We couldn't say no. I couldn't anyway.

"Alright. Let's see."

"Mr competitive."

"Take off one piece of clothing." Tess cheered with the rest of the room. My jacket was in the locker, I only had my navy-blue dress shirt or pants to choose from.

"Well go on then." Tess was starting to enjoy the game too.

"Shirt." I laughed and unbuttoned my shirt and placed it near the fan. "I should have worn a scarf. Now it's your turn."

"Go Tess." People were good at remembering names in this place. She took a slow drink from her cruiser then shook her head, laughing at her chosen brick.

"What is it?"

"Pole dance." I joined the cheering wholeheartedly. I couldn't have scripted it better.

"I bet she's a great dancer," said Amy who had been sitting next to Tess. She moved closer when Tess stepped up to the pole.

"Sure is." I was fixated like everyone else. Tess swayed her shoulders and hips in opposite directions, perfectly in time with the music. The one hand gripping the pole slid down as she bent her knees, continuing the lateral movements.

"She's good," Dane hadn't said much but he was right.

"She is good," I mumbled to myself under the music. It was only a ten-second performance but it was magical.

"Awesome babe. That was awesome." Stacey rushed to kiss Tess on the cheek as Amy wriggled back to her spot. Applause filled the room. Her quiet confidence shone and people had always gravitated towards her.

"Amy. Your turn."

"Oh no. Lap dance. I wouldn't even know how." She had grabbed her brick before Tess had even sat down. Thin, she looked late thirties. She wore a very short, tightly fitted dress with long arms and a low-cut chest.

"Just make it up. This song is perfect," Stacey encouraged. Amy scanned the room quickly before her eyes settled on me. Not me.

"Well, you're the only one without a shirt so you're the lucky man."

"Me?" I looked nervously at Tess.

"You," Tess replied, giving me nothing at all in her tone or expression.

"Here we go, you ready?" She was already dancing in front of me as Tess slid over to make some room.

"I guess so." I didn't feel lucky. "Be gentle."

She moved forward until her thighs touched my knees. The approving crowd clapped in unison. Slowly, her legs parted to sit on my lap. Her skirt inched up her hips, revealing her black lingerie underneath. My hands flattened onto the lounge either side of me as my body tensed. I wondered what Tess would think as Amy's body moved with the music, ever closer. Her hands pushed my shoulders against the lounge and she placed a lingering kiss on my cheek before finishing the performance.

I was relieved when she retreated, pulling her skirt back down her thighs, and I dared not look at Tess.

"Aiden, your turn," I yelled, trying to mask my discomfort. It would not be the last time I felt uncomfortable with Amy that night.

"Lucky man," Tess said blankly as she resumed her position beside me. "They might be getting lucky as well." We watched intently as two couples from the back lounge walked purposefully up the stairs to our left.

"Nice undies." It seemed almost normal. My eyes fixated on the stairs.

"We loved the pole dance. I'm Dane. This is Loretta," said the quiet couple seated on the lounge next to us.

"Thanks, definitely the first time I've done anything like that. I'm Tess," Dane had sat next to Tess as Aiden left the lounge to kneel at the Jenga stack and Amy disappeared towards the bar. "Ryan. This is Ryan."

"Hi, I'm Dane." He held out his hand.

"Loretta." She just smiled.

"So, have you guys been here before?" I asked.

"No, this is our first time here. First time outside the Northern Territory actually. Sydney is amazing. This is our second night here." Dane was quietly spoken but intently focused on the conversation. Loretta held his arm tight, like Tess had often held my hand. "Have you been before?"

"Just once. It's honestly something that we ever thought we'd be doing, but somehow, we're here," I replied.

"Same. We tried one place at home in Darwin. It was okay, but not like here. This Jenga thing is fun."

"I think I'll just watch; I'd probably knock it down." Loretta gave a shy smile as she joined the conversation. "Are you from Sydney?"

"No. We live up the coast. It's only a small town. A lot different from here." Tess had a way of connecting with people. "We don't get away much. The kids are with the family. It's only one night away but that's enough." I thought of the kids, tucked in bed, for a moment.

"We're here for three nights, it's the longest we've ever been away from our kids. Dad and the family got us this trip for our tenth anniversary." Dane took his own moment to reflect on home.

"Darwin. We'd love to go there. What's it like?" Tess asked. She loved the heat.

Time continued to melt away. As the night unwrapped, couples would retreat to the locker room and return dressed only in their finest undergarments. It seemed so surreal and at the same time it started to take on an air of normality. It was kind of like being at the beach in bikinis and board shorts with strangers. Only this place had a second storey.

"Did you want to get changed?" I asked. Tess and I were among the last to disrobe, although I had been topless for half the night.

"Why not. Everyone else is. I love this song. Let's go." Hand in hand we headed to the locker room. There were now about ten to twelve couples in the two lounge areas and more upstairs. We'd hardly been in the back lounge all night and hadn't been able to keep track of the stair ascensions like we had in the main room.

"Who am I?" I grabbed the corner of the locker and did my best pole dance impersonation, checking myself in the mirror. Tess wasn't impressed.

"Who am I?" She pulled her dress up to reveal her panties and spread her legs slightly as Amy had done. I stopped dancing.

"You look pretty good at that, maybe I could get a lap dance some time."

"You wish pole boy," Tess fired back at me. We undressed and quickly rejoined the party.

"Have you seen the dungeon?" Dane asked us as we sat back on the lounge. He gave Tess a quick glance as I had done in the locker room.

"It'd be hard to miss it. Pretty wild." I replied. I couldn't help but notice that two more couple were missing.

"Maybe we should get changed," Dane suggested to Loretta. They were now the only fully clothed people in the room.

"Um. I guess so." Loretta smiled at Tess, almost looking for reassurance.

Before long, they had returned wearing Ralph Loren briefs and a conservative, but stylish, one-piece lingerie teddy.

"We should try the dungeon. It looks fun," Amy suggested, joining our conversation. Dane and Loretta looked at each other tentatively as I tried to read Tess' expression.

"Why not. There's no one in there. Do you guys want to try it?" Dane said and stood up immediately

"Okay. Can't hurt." It could. "We might just have a look." Loretta said, giving her own naughty schoolgirl look. Go you, I thought.

"Well, I'll give it a go. But be gentle with me," I joked. "You might want to watch out for Tess though."

"Don't listen to him." The five of us grabbed our drinks and ventured into the small room that would have seemed so incredibly out of place anywhere else, but not here.

"Whips. And what are they? Looks painful." Dane gazed at the cabinet of sexual weaponry. "What do you guys think?"

"Last time we were here we used the paddle, that one. It was fun." I pointed it out as Amy took it out and ran the tassels through her fingers. She handed it to Tess.

"Well, you know what that means?" Tess laughed as she looked at me.

"I thought you'd never ask." I climbed carefully onto the frame. Tess landed her blows as hard as the first time and enjoyed every one. The other three watched in silence with a combination of concern and admiration on their faces. "It's so weird how something painful can feel so good, maybe it's the love you put into each swing."

"Don't think so. It'll be harder next time." Tess replied.

"Do you want to try?" Dane asked Loretta. She looked uncomfortable at the idea of being smacked.

"You don't have to," I said.

"Up to you, I'll be really soft," urged Dane.

"Ok, but soft." She climbed awkwardly onto the frame and he gently paddled her bum, even more softly than Katy and Michael had done. She seemed pleased with the applause and relieved that her part of the game was done. There was no judgment or expectation, just that moment in time. Loretta looked more at ease as she swung the paddle softly at Dane.

"My turn," Amy said excitedly. "It must be Ryan's turn with this." Amy handed the paddle to me.

"Ah, OK. Up you get." She put both hands at the top of the frame and spread her legs wide. Another couple stopped and watched intently.

"Ready. You can hit hard if you like." I couldn't hit someone else hard; I didn't like hurting people and the first swing was barely harder than Loretta's.

"Harder," she ordered. Tess raised her eyebrows and nodded. Amy looked back expectantly as the next one landed more forcefully. "Ouch."

We played some more before the paddle was replaced carefully in position. Amy selected a whip next and the pain from the leather on my skin had me wincing with pleasure. When it was eventually returned to the cabinet, I took a long drink as all five of us glanced expectantly at each other.

"Well. That wasn't so bad. It didn't really hurt at all?" Loretta broke the silence. That's because Dane didn't really swing at all, I thought. Quietly spoken, there was an insecurity about her that I found endearing and it was understandable in this place. She was attractive in her own unique way, but looked like she had never known it.

"What now?" Amy hinted as the silence resumed. No one wanted to ask.

"Well, I don't know, maybe we could, if you wanted? Maybe we could go upstairs?" I could hardly get the words out. Dane looked at Loretta and nodded eagerly while Tess took my hand as normal. Amy was already walking.

Chapter 9
Five Is an Odd Number

"I won't ever forget these stairs," I whispered to Tess as we followed Amy up to the second storey. Twelve steps.

"Just watch where you are going." At the top of the stairs, we turned left into the first queen room. Four people lay twisted, pulsing on the bed. A lamp gave ample light to absorb the graphic scene for a moment. A woman glanced at Tess and I as we quickly reversed out of the room. The second queen room up the hall to the right was free.

"This one?" I asked Tess as Amy, Dane and Loretta all walked in.

"Looks like it." Tess followed as I joined them. Five is an odd number I thought.

Amy was the first to unhitch her bra and slide her panties to the floor. She kicked them against the wall and ran her fingers through her shoulder length blonde hair before lying on the neatly sheeted bed.

"Your turn." She looked directly at me. I looked at Tess, searching for confirmation. She stood next to the fruit bowl of coloured condom packets and dams. Tess responded by dropping her black lingerie to the floor. I stared at her beautiful naked body for a moment as Dane took down his Ralph Loren's and lay on the opposite side of the bed to Amy.

"Tess?" Dane asked quietly as Loretta stood at the side, watching.

"Well look at you." Amy's eyes trailed down my body as I lowered my briefs to the floor. Tess lay on the bed and turned towards Dane. "C'mon," coaxed Amy.

Feeling self-conscious, I quickly climbed onto the bed with my back nearly touching Tess. It was comforting to know that she was close. The rules were still working, but something didn't feel right. Amy kissed my chest and trailed her lips up to mine, where her tongue went to work. Her hands covered my body and time slipped into irrelevance.

"Here, why don't you put this on?" Amy reached to the bowl of condoms and handed me the packet.

"Have you ever been with someone with a clit ring before?" Amy whispered in my ear as I felt the movement from the other side of the bed. She put my hand on it. "Be gentle." Her entire body tensed at my touch and her nails dug hard into my thigh.

"Ryan. Yes. Ryan." Amy moaned my name over and over again and I wished that she would stop talking. I caught Tess' eye for a brief moment and her blank expression was impossible to read. By this time, Loretta was naked on the bed. Dane turned and kissed her before positioning her above him.

"Ryan," Amy said again, now clawing my chest. She pulled me on top of her and I instinctively thrust forward, feeling her tight around me. "Ah Ryan," she repeated as she placed her own fingers on the ring. Again, I allowed myself the smallest peek at Tess, lying still in the middle of the bed, staring straight at me.

"This is fucked," was all Tess said. She pulled herself to the end of the bed and stood up, looking for her wireless chemise set on the floor. "This isn't working." She began to dress. I instantly got up and grabbed my briefs, throwing the rubber in the discrete corner bin. Amy propped herself up on her elbows and watched while Dane and Loretta continued.

Tess was already walking out the door by the time my pants were on and I quickly followed. There was no explanation for the three people left on the bed, we were out of there.

"Tess?"

"I'm getting a drink," was all she said as she purposefully marched down the stairs.

"Are you okay? What happened?"

"Nothing. I wasn't just going to lie there in the middle listening to what's her name saying your name. What was that?" I had no answers.

"Number nine for the coasties," Mav turned to the fridges, "yeah, they're opening a second club. Just looking for a venue," he said to Sara. I gently touched Tess' back.

"Don't." She pushed back at my hand and took the drinks from Mav.

"I'm sorry. I didn't. I should have known. I'm sorry."

"Let's just sit down. Hold this, I'm going to the loo." We walked down the steps to the back lounge. Tess turned into the toilet and shut the door hard. I waited for a moment before moving towards the lounge.

"Hello, how are you?" A heavy accent surrounded the woman's friendly greeting. There was no time for a quiet 'sit down' in this place. It was right on midnight.

"Yeah good, good how are you guys?" They were the only couple in the back lounge, and the main room still rang with lubricated conversations. She stood at the rounded bar table with a drink in her hand, dancing, swaying. She was hypnotic in G-string panties and a matching purple bra. He sat at on a stool with thick glasses on, bronzed and toned.

"Great, great. I'm Valentina and this is Matias." Her accent was beautiful. I stared at the toilet door, longing to hold Tess.

"Nice to meet you both. I'm Ryan. My wife, ah, Tess is at the toilet." I stumbled through the sentence. Valentina continued to dance subtly as the door opened. I handed Tess her drink.

"Are you okay?" I pleaded quietly.

"I'm fine." She forced the words through pursed lips.

"I was just talking to Valentina and," I turned to Valentina for help.

"Matias, I'm Valentina," she said directly to Tess with a smile. They didn't force the conversation and Tess and I had time to quietly gather ourselves on the lounge after what had happened.

"I hope you don't mind, I love to dance," Valentina said eventually.

"All good. I love your accent," I said. "Where are you from?"

"Columbia. We've been in Sydney for ten years now. Our English is better but the accent hasn't changed much."

"Are you from Sydney? It's a great city, so different to Barranquilla," Matias said. He was softly spoken and articulate.

"No, the city is nice to visit but we prefer our little town. I could never live away from the beach," I replied. The salt water had always been a refuge, a huge part of me.

"And do you have children back at home?" asked Valentina.

"Yeah, Leyla is ten and Josh is twelve. They're at home with the family. It's nice to get away every now and again but I miss them. How about you?" Tess put her hand on my knee and squeezed. I hoped that it was her way of saying she was alright.

"Just one, Manny. He's home with my girlfriend. A beautiful boy. You like to dance?" Valentina asked Tess.

"Yeah, sometimes. Ryan is a bit of a dancer too, aren't you? Tell them about your pole skills," Tess teased. The laughter returned to the room as Mav leaned over the bar and gave a quick wave.

"No. No skills at all. I wish I did. Tess is far better than me," I said. To my surprise, Tess got up to join Valentina, letting her hair hang across her face.

"Yes, she's fabulous. C'mon boys, dance with us." Tess and Valentina moved closer to the centre of the room, dancing as another couple headed into the locker room.

"Yes Ryan." The girls approved as I stood and joined them. Matias smiled broadly, remaining in his seat and casually tapping his foot.

"Drink Tina?" Matias asked.

"Yes, yes. I might go to the lady's room." Valentina disappeared behind the toilet door as Matias walked up to the corridor bar, looking over our back lounge.

"I'm sorry about upstairs. I didn't mean for that to happen. I'm sorry," I said.

"I know you didn't. I just couldn't do it."

"That's okay. If you want, we can leave now?"

"Maybe, we'll see what happens."

"He looks like a cross between an accountant and a pro beach volley ball player," I said to Tess.

"They seem nice. She's stunning. Reminds me of Shakira, with shorter hair," Tess replied. She was right, Valentina really was stunning.

"How old do you think?" I was thankful that the conversation had moved on from the upstairs, but I was deeply unsettled by it.

"Early thirties maybe."

"Dance with us Maty." Valentina held her arms in the air, drink in one hand, spinning with perfect balance.

"No, no. I'm very happy to just watch. My knee you know." I was happy to watch too. I always loved to watch Tess move. She was both graceful and understated when she danced. Valentina personified Latin rhythm and her beautiful curves were hard to ignore.

"Pfft. Your knee. I'll dance with Tess then. This is so much fun, have you been here before?"

"Just once, it's not really our thing but we had a good time. We were in the city this weekend and just thought why not? You?"

"Our first time. There's nothing like this in Columbia. We came here when we were in our early twenties. Home was a dangerous place. People here don't realise how lucky they are."

"So how did you decide to come here to the club?" Tess asked.

"A friend told us about it. We just thought it would be nice to try something new, you know?" I understood perfectly. We danced for a while, as people floated around the club. I kept waiting for Amy, Dane or Loretta to walk in demanding an explanation. But they didn't.

"Mind if I join you?" Sara said and stopped for a moment to dance with the girls before walking up the stairs to the back bedroom. We had only been there once briefly during our first tour. She returned shortly.

"The spa is free you guys. No one's up there if you wanted to try it."

Valentina looked at Tess and then at Matias.

"The spa Maty, would you like to try it?"

"I would," the alcohol filling my blood whispered inaudibly below the music.

"Tess, what do you think, should we go up to the spa? It sounds like fun." Valentina seemed keen. Tess turned to look at me and I nodded ever so slightly without meaning to.

"Why not, it does sound like fun," Tess replied. Forty minutes before I thought we would be promptly marching out the front door, never to return. I could never have imagined that we would be walking up another staircase with a pair of Columbians for a date in the spa.

The bedroom was larger than any of the front three. The huge king-sized bed didn't crowd the space like the other rooms and the spa sat in one corner, opposite to an open ensuite.

"It's so warm," Matias said as he dipped his hand in the bubbling water. Valentina jumped on the bed, landing on her back, like a kid on a sleepover.

"This bed is so big Maty. So much bigger than ours." She bounced back up just as quickly as she had landed. She unhitched her bra and flung it towards Matias and stretched her arms high in the air, lifting her already firm breasts. She pealed her G-string down her legs and the three of us watched for a moment.

"C'mon people. Let's get in." Valentina's exuberance was infectious.

"This is like a dream, a fast moving one," I whispered to Tess.

"Sure is, ah, looks like we're getting naked again." Tess' spark had returned. I was thankful.

"Looks like it," I replied as we undressed. Matias joined Valentina as Tess and I followed. Matias sat on the opposite side of Valentina and splashed her gently.

"Excuse me," protested Tess as I smacked her bottom while she climbed in as dignified as was possible. Tess sat next to Matias. I was next to Valentina. The spa was only small, room enough for four, and eight legs intermingled in a blurred sea of limbs.

"So, what do you do Matias, when you're not in a spa with strangers?" I joked.

"I'm a civil engineer. We've been working on the WestConnex for a few years. It's close to home so I see more of Tina and Manny. Big job." He smiled at Valentina who was still moving her shoulders to the music. "You?"

"I work with teenagers, most of them have had so much to deal with in their lives. They have some pretty awful stories. I run a community program at a youth hostel. People wouldn't believe what some kids go through at home. Some of them don't even have a home."

"How very sad. That must be heart-breaking?" Sincerity surrounded Valentina's voice.

"Tess is a nurse. Night shifts are brutal. Don't know how she does it. We've got this weekend off anyway." I wasn't keen to dwell on my work.

"Oh, I wanted to be a nurse but I didn't finish high school in Columbia. Not long after we moved here Manny was born."

"At least you get free clothes sometimes at the shop, and no night shift." Matias cushioned her retrospection.

The water bubbled away while we shared stories and lives. We discussed little things, dreams and memories like you would do with old friends. Again, I imagined what our friends from the real world would think if they ever found out. It was the opposite of everything they would have presumed. I lay back in the spa and relaxed, enjoying the strange sense of honesty. The electricity sat above it all, sparking over the fire of sexual energy. My thigh was brushing against Valentina's beautiful, naked body and we were inching ever closer all the time.

"Can you get me a towel?" Tess asked eventually. There were eight, neatly folded, on a table next to the spa.

"I might get out too I think," I said as I carefully manoeuvred past Valentina, dripping on the tiles.

"Yes, yes. That was fantastic." Valentina stood and I handed her a towel as we dried ourselves.

Valentina was the first to lay on the bed, so naturally beautiful like Tess, and so full of energy. Tess walked to the other side and lay down. Matias watched their every move, and finished drying himself.

But standing there, I had eyes only for Tess. I walked around the bed and whispered 'I love you' through her hair, before laying down next to her.

"I know you do," she replied.

"You're beautiful," Matias said to Valentina as he put both palms on the edge of the bed and leant down to kiss her. She instinctively moved over as he lay on the space beside her, placing his glasses on the bedside table.

"Another crazy night hey?" Tess said as I kissed her neck.

"What did you expect? You look beautiful too." I echoed Matias' compliment and we were both right. She moved over slightly, lying her head on the pillow. As I lay down, I reached over her and grabbed her curved bottom tight, pulling her hard up against me.

I kissed her neck gently, trailing up her jaw line to her ears, and bit her ear softly. Then harder. My hand explored every sinew in her thigh, every contour of her back, and the bone of her hip.

"You kiss okay for an old guy," Tess whispered after minutes of kisses, all over her body. Sometimes I forgot what an intimate, magical thing kissing is, and I savoured every second.

"I wonder if you know how much I still love kissing you."

"Well don't stop."

I pushed her flat onto her back and caressed the inside of her leg, my lips on her all the time. I stopped just short of the top and then ran one finger over her stomach, tracing her breasts and nipples. I moved my hand back down to her lower stomach and continued to the soft folds of her body.

"Harder," she breathed. I stopped and began from the start, trailing every part of her. Soft as first, then gradually harder. She stiffened, pushing her breasts upwards, and I my lips left hers to kiss them. I had felt her body stiffen like that countless times before and I knew exactly what it meant.

"Harder." I stopped.

I pushed one thigh apart from the other then positioned myself above her, pushing the other open with my knee. I paused before finding my way inside her gently, carefully making sure it was right. Then I pushed hard, deep. I felt her breath loudly, purposefully.

"Love you T." Her eyes were closed.

"Love you too. I'm close."

"Yes Maty, Yes." Tina and Maty were right beside us but it felt like Tess and I were the only ones in the room.

"Not yet. Let's play for a while." I withdrew and kissed her again. I circled the stubble on my chin around her naval and kept sliding down the bed until my elbows rested between her legs. I gently bit the inside of her thighs before my tongue found that place. Tess groaned and pushed herself against me.

"Don't stop. Don't." Tess said but before she could finish the sentence her body stiffened again, and every muscle screamed.

"Yes Maty. Oh yes." Tess' primal, sensual song was interwoven with Valentina's. Tess writhed in crescendo and all at once she relaxed, only her chest pounding in breathless pleasure.

I knelt up and grabbed her leg, rolling her over onto her stomach. She knew what I liked.

"That was so good." She pushed herself up onto her hands and knees and I was inside her again. She closed her legs slightly as I positioned my knees on the outside of hers.

I delayed the inevitably for as long as I could, I wanted that moment to last.

"I am." Every ounce of energy drained out of me in those blissful seconds. I fell to the side of her on the bed in slow motion, spooning, still connected. "I can't move."

"We're naughty, aren't we?" The question wasn't rhetorical.

"Maybe. I guess everyone is in their own way." I heard voices at the door for a moment before disappearing back into the distant sound of music. We lay silently, still.

"How weird is it to feel so relaxed with two strangers on the bed. I could fall asleep right now," I whispered close to Tess' ear.

"It's nice just lying here. What's the time?"

"Just after one. Getting late."

"You guys are so beautiful together. That was incredible, no?" Valentina's compliment broke the silence. Our backs were facing them.

"Yeah, it was," Tess agreed.

"It was amazing," I puffed. We lay for minutes without speaking.

"Maty, are there any drinks left?" asked Valentina.

"Two. This girl never stops," he replied.

"I can believe that." I said. The stunning Latin dancer lying naked on the bed was a truly beautiful sight. Voices interrupted the silence again.

"We should get up. It's getting late." Tess stood to locate her underwear. I propped my head on a pillow to take in the room. "We've got two drinks left as well."

We made our way down to the bar, collected our drinks, and sat in the main lounge once again. Stacey and Aiden were still there with three other couples.

"Hello again. Haven't seen you two for a while. Enjoying your night?" Stacey seemed both inquisitive and pleased to see us.

"Been a big night, it's been fun, mostly," Tess replied.

"We've been in here most of the night. Ryan, the pole's free if you want it," Stacey teased.

"What about the other piece of the night?" boasted Aiden.

"Well, you know, that was fun too," replied Stacey.

We relaxed again in the company of strangers and again chatted about the mundane, about the little things that filled any normal conversation.

"I'm tired Ry, can we go now?" Tess whispered as we finished our last drink. I was ready to go too. We quietly left the lounge as the banter continued and headed back to the locker room to get changed. That part of the night was the only awkward part, almost like we were putting our real life back on and preparing to leave this strange world.

"We'll see you around Mav," I said as we walked past the bar.

"Back to the coast they go, great to see you two again. Stay safe."

"Bye Ryan, Bye Tess. Thanks for coming tonight." Sara spoke with the same warmness that she greeted us with at the start of the night. Positive energy was all that I could describe it as.

"Still can't believe that room." Tess paused at the empty dungeon to have a last look.

"Who would have thought that we'd be doing this a few months ago hey?"

"Yeah." She just shook her head. I guessed that she was trying to process the whole thing just like I was. We said our simple goodbyes, opened the heavy wooden door and stepped into the cool city air.

I turned to take in the plain terrace building for a moment, as I did the first time. The early hours of the Sydney night were quiet and still. For once, it seemed as though the bustling city was sleeping.

"What do you think people would say if they ever found out?" I asked as Tess tugged on my hand and we began to walk.

"They wouldn't believe it probably, not us. Maybe they'd think it was sleazy or seedy. Don't know."

"But it wasn't, was it?" I waited for an answer of reassurance.

"No, it wasn't."

"Maybe it's the beers talking but it just felt, well it didn't feel normal but I felt okay about it. It's hard to describe. Everyone there was just like us. Nervous, excited, honest. Like, for most of the night we were just talking about families and jobs and stuff." A siren in the distance broke the silence. "It wasn't any of the stereotypes that people would expect."

"I guess not. I don't think any of our friends could have any idea what it's like. We didn't." Tess shivered; she despised the cold.

"I reckon the first thing people would ask is how could you be in the same room together? And how could you just forget all the rules about marriage and family and all that stuff?" I was thinking aloud and I'm sure Tess wasn't interested in the answers at 2am.

"Who knows?" was all she said. The city sparkled at night and the quiet gave it an added beauty that I had rarely seen.

"It's a bit like that saying 'if you love something set it free'. You know, if it returns then it was yours all along and if it doesn't, then it never was in the first place."

"Am I the 'it' in that analogy?"

"My 'it'. We just gave each other freedom to explore, to be free for one night. Being in the same room meant we never have to wonder what happened. It was like the same experience."

"That's a pretty big 'just' when you think about what we did." Tess joined my introspection.

"Yeah. Pretty heavy shit when you think about it. Live and let live." I continued.

"You're full of quotes, aren't you?"

"Everyone must have some sort of fantasies inside them, don't you reckon? We did it together, no lies. That was the most important thing." Maybe I was trying to excuse every cultural value that we had broken that night.

"You got any more proverbs left mate?"

"No, but I remember reading a study."

"Oh, here we go." Tess interrupted.

"It was a study done on thousands of elderly residents in retirement homes across Britain. They asked them lots of things but the article focused on one question. 'What makes a good life?' By far the most common answer was that they didn't regret the things they had done in life. They regretted the things the things they had not done. All the opportunities they hadn't taken." The pace quickened as we neared the hotel.

"Makes sense," Tess agreed.

"Their message I think was to live life to the full. Don't be scared to try shit. That's what we did."

"Well, that was some pretty wild shit that we tried tonight Mr Tanner."

"Yeah, it was."

It was hard to believe that we really did those things. I felt safe and supported in that room with Tess. There were no secrets, no jealousy. She was mine and I was hers. How could we break all of those cultural rules? I don't know. We just did and it was magic. It wasn't sleazy or seedy. It was brave, honest and beyond words awesome. No regrets. Not then anyway.

Chapter 10
Nothing Is Ever Forgotten

"It's nearly nine, Ryan. Get up. Josh plays at ten, he's been up for hours." That was the second last thing that Tess said to me that morning.

"What?" She had walked out the door before I replied. My head hurt. I knew the feeling well.

"Dad, we play soon. Are you taking me?"

"Yeah mate. I'm taking you. We've got time. You got your gear ready?"

"I packed it last night." Josh disappeared as quickly as Tess had done. I got my coffee, loaded with sugar, and stood in the kitchen regretting every word, every beer. The coffee comforted me just long enough for my mind to replay the night before.

"Tess." I mumbled. I knew she would be angry. I walked meekly into the bedroom.

"Yesterday was really hard, with Bill and everything. I wanted to..."

"Don't fucking talk to me." Tess didn't look at me and walked into the ensuite, closing the door. I took my coffee to the back yard to escape, to hide. 'Why do I keep doing this?' I sat for a while. I didn't want to go back inside.

"Dad, hurry up. We have to leave soon." Josh's excited voice broke the silence. "The Rams are good. They'll probably smash us."

"I don't come to your games to watch the score board Josh. You can only do your best. Get stuck in for your team and listen to Brad. He's a great coach." Josh instinctively sat beside me. I thought I always hid my depression flawlessly from him and Leyla. It was only years later that I realised they always knew when I was down. I wasn't nearly as good at hiding it as I thought.

"Did you get scared sometimes Dad when you played? Rams have got some really big forwards. Jet got a broken arm when we played them last year."

"Yeah. Every game. Fear can be a good thing. It makes you sharp. I think everyone probably feels that way. It's normal to feel that way."

"Can we get there a bit early? I want to warm up and practice my kicking."

"Yeah mate. Let's get your stuff and get going." I loved to watch Josh and Leyla play. They looked happy on the field, just like me when I played. I missed playing terribly but footy was a young man's game.

"Are you staying for first grade? 3pm," Tim asked as Josh emerged from the sheds after the game.

"Don't think so. Are you coming?"

"Sure am. I gotta do a few things at home then I'll get here for the kick off. Meg's driving, I'll pick you up if you want."

"I don't think I can. I'll just see what Tess is doing."

"Just see what Tess is doing?" Mimicked Tim. "Grow a pair and just tell her you're coming. Pick you up at two thirty." Tess didn't like to be told anything. At best I'd ask, nicely.

On the ride home, I painfully recounted the way I treated Tess, and our guests, the night before. I couldn't blame Tess for being upset. Josh burst through the door at home, eager to tell her about his win.

"Mum, we won twenty-two to sixteen. I got to play at full back in the second half when Riley got hurt. I didn't score though."

"That's awesome Josh, well done. Is Riley okay?" She still wouldn't look at me.

"Yeah, he's fine, He hurt his knee but they put this giant ice bag on it."

"How did Leyla go?" I asked tentatively, but Tess was already disappearing into the bedroom.

"We lost thirty-nine, twenty-five. No subs. They were so tall." Leyla never minded losing, she just loved playing the game.

"That's okay Ley. I'll be there next week to watch. Can't wait." Josh and Leyla debriefed as always on a Saturday afternoon about their games. Sport was a part of our lives. Being part of a team was something special and all four of us had our own connection to playing.

"So, Tim asked me to go down to watch first grade. I was thinking I might go. What do you think?" Tess was in the ensuite again as I walked into our bedroom.

"You don't have to ask my permission. You do what you want, you always do."

"I was thinking we could all go down maybe? Meg is going."

"I don't want to go anywhere with you. The kids and I are going to visit Mum." She walked out. Her tone spoke louder than the words as it often did.

"See you at two thirty," was all my text said, followed by a thumbs up emoji.

"Beer?" Tim asked simply. "Hamo is running the drinks. Gotta support the club, you know." I never said no to a beer. Neither did Tim. We visited Hamo regularly during the game. Drinking was an escape from the pressures of life, something I had earned after a hard week of work. That's how I rationalised it anyway. In reality, it was me running from that heavy feeling in my chest, running from the dreams that I had about my childhood. It was me running.

"Where's Meg, I thought she was coming?" I asked.

"Nah, she had to take Jet somewhere I think. All good. You keen to stay for a few after the game? Some of the boys are staying back. Just like old times hey? Except that's it's us that are old now." Tim didn't even wait for a reply before replying to Hamo's observations on yet another first grade loss.

"Hi. So sorry about last night, it was outta line. Are you home from Nan's yet? Tim wants to stay for a while." The text was a weak effort at an apology but as expected there was no reply. Her phone was always glued to her hand and I knew she'd have seen the text.

"So? All the boys are here." Tim continued. "Are you staying or is it true that all half backs are just soft?"

"To be honest I'm just as happy to go home. Tess and the kids," I was quickly interrupted by Tim.

"Tess and the kids nothing. You see them all week."

"Well, I'm not walking home. Done that to many times." I replied. I was looking for excuses.

"Meg said she'd pick us up. Sorted." Tim disappeared into the buzz that brought urban sports grounds to life each Saturday afternoon. Sport in small towns meant connection, belonging. For some guys, separated from families all too often, their team was their family. The club was their home. Win, lose or draw their mates backed them. No matter how bad things got, their mates supported them. It was about the closest thing to unconditional love that most of them would find, even though the word love would never be used in that environment, unless we were talking about beers or winning.

I knew just about everyone at the ground. I'd either played with them, coached them or met them at club functions somewhere along the line. But even though I knew everyone, lately I had found it hard to feel close to any of them. In a crowd full of people, I felt increasingly alone. I bounced from one group to the next, making sure that I caught up with every one of them, unknowingly craving attention. There was still something deep inside of me that wanted their approval. Every last one of them.

Tess was the opposite. She would find her seat and that's where she would stay. She was comfortable in one place and she didn't feel the need to validate herself in that space like I did. It always annoyed Tess, my need for approval. The week before she had come to the game with me.

"Are you going to sit with the boys again?" She asked.

"No. I'm just hanging here." I wanted to be with the team but I knew Tess expected me to sit with her. I wanted to be on that sideline yelling encouragement to my team. They respected me unreservedly. They never asked questions or made judgements about every little thing I had got wrong. But I sat in silence next to Tess. She didn't need people. I did.

"I'm just going to see if they need a hand." I couldn't help myself and headed for the bench.

"You can never just sit with your family. I'm not going to settle for second best," she said. "I deserve better than this." What I heard was 'I deserve better than you. You're not good enough.' That's how I always felt and the person that mattered most in the world telling me that only made it all the truer. Sometimes it was like she didn't care how I felt. Or if she did, she wouldn't show it. The only thing is that it wasn't true. She did care. But I couldn't see that.

"You smell," said Tess as I walked into the kitchen that night. I knew better than to touch her when she was angry.

"There was a fire there, it was a bit smoky. We lost again. The Rebels were pretty strong. Too many injuries." My slurred words betrayed me and I knew she wasn't interested in the game.

"I didn't mean the smoke. Helping with the drinks again were you?"

"Nah, Hamo spilt one on me. Hopeless. It wasn't my fault."

"No, it never is Ryan." She turned and walked into the bedroom. I followed her in. "Can you shut the door?" I knew it meant trouble when she asked that.

"How do you think it makes the kids feel when you come home pissed every Saturday? And then it's 'I'll just have a few' on Friday or Sunday, or any other day you want. How do you think it makes me feel?"

"But I'm not pissed. I just had a few. I'm fine."

"Did you just have a few at golf last month when you didn't come home at all? I was worried sick Ryan but you couldn't have given a shit. No text. Nothing."

"My phone was flat."

"Oh, that's alright then. Josh was waiting for you to come home today. You said you were going to watch the game, not hang around for hours after it finished."

"I texted you. I thought you were at your mum's."

"Bullshit. You knew we'd be home. You just wanted to stay and drink with your mates like you always do. What if we wanted to do something as a family today? Your mates come first. They always do."

"They don't. You and Leyla and Josh are the most important people in my life. I'd do anything for you. Anything."

"You know what to say. You always do. But nothing changes. Actions speak louder than words Ryan. We don't come first. Never have."

"That night at golf. I," I started to justify my mistakes again but Tess wasn't going to listen to more excuses.

"I don't want to hear it Ryan. Fuck. I can't do this anymore."

Chapter 11
Your Dad Doesn't Love You

"Your dad doesn't love you. That's what she would say. Every day on the walk home from school. I was only ten."

"And how did that make you feel?" asked Bill.

"At the time, I didn't know what to feel. I was only small. She was older and there was always a group of boys with her. I felt helpless. If I could go back, I'd walk straight up to her and punch her in the face. Then, ah." I was lost in childhood pain momentarily. "Sorry. I know that's a stupid thing to say."

"She hurt you. Sometimes we say irrational things when we're hurt," Bill said calmly.

I looked briefly at my right leg bouncing fractionally on my toes and the clenched fist sitting on that leg. Bill looked as well. They noticed that stuff, psychologists. I hated it that I was so obvious.

"Yeah, I hated her. I tried not to but I did. I try not to now but I still do. My first day at that shitty new primary school and I had to walk home alone. I didn't even know the way but another kid gave me directions. Two kilometres. I went back and measured it when I was about twenty-five. Don't know why. Does that sound stupid?"

"Not at all. That was a formative part of your childhood. Retracing those hard times is not stupid at all. It's a way of coming to terms with what happened."

"Two fucking kilometres. I walked home alone on the first day in that school. And then she started with that shit because she had had heard about me in the playground. Whoever gave her the right to do that? Every day she would say something about my dad. Two kilometres. Back then it felt like twenty."

"She never had the right to do that to you. People don't understand the damage they do with words. Especially not kids. She didn't know you and you should never define yourself by the things that she said."

"Yeah, sorry but I'd still go back and..." What would I do if I could go back and do it all again? "I'd try to help Mum and Dad. But I was only ten, you know?" I started to cry, silently. "I wanted to make everything okay but I couldn't. Them. Me. Tess."

"It's okay to cry Ryan."

"When Dad left, we lost our home and we had to move to an old housing commission house in the poorest part of town. I had to change schools so I lost my friends too. The first day we moved in there was a fight next door. I'd never seen a proper fight before. I peeked out of the corner of our front window. I made sure that the blanket hanging over the window hid my face. We didn't have curtains."

"That must have been frightening as a child?" Bill understood.

"Yeah. It was. One of the guys was bleeding all over his face. He was walking backwards and the other guy kept hitting him until he fell onto the grass. It was our front lawn."

"It's Ok to feel frightened. That's a terrible thing for any child to witness."

"When the bleeding guy went down, the other guy looked up and saw me watching. He saw me. I ducked as quickly as I could but he saw me. I dreamt about him a lot. He was always coming for me and I was running. But I could never get away. I could never get away."

"How do you think those experiences back then affect you now Ryan?"

"No idea. Sometimes I still dream about him. I'm still running. No idea. You tell me."

"I can't tell you that. Those things affect everyone in different ways. What I can tell you is that it's okay to feel the way you do. Somehow, we have to come to terms with these things ourselves."

"So, it's one hundred and sixty dollars an hour for me to figure it out myself?"

"That's not what I meant Ryan."

"I'm sorry Bill that was out of line. I'm sorry. That's not like me. I do a lot of things lately that are not like me. I've kinda lost who I was, you know? I just want to be happy. I want to be a good father and a good husband. That's all."

"Depression can have huge impacts on a person's behaviour. We don't forget the things that happened to us when we were young. But we need to find a way to live with them in a healthy way. Admitting to yourself how much they hurt you might be a good start."

"Maybe."

"The way you feel is not permanent Ryan. You are still the same person even if you don't feel like it at the moment."

"Mum always taught me to be a good person. Dad too. I've always been really close to both of them. But people have seemed so far away lately. Tess more than anyone. I thought that everyone else must have just misunderstood me. I thought that I was a really good bloke. But maybe I was wrong."

"You're not wrong Ryan. Depression isolates people, and it makes us doubt ourselves. People withdraw from the relationships in their life just at the time when they need them most."

"It's just easier you know. Not to have to deal with people sometimes. To pretend to be happy rather than try to explain why I'm not."

"That makes sense. But maybe you're not giving the people in your life enough credit. They'd probably be a much greater support than you could imagine if you'd just open up a bit." Bill's observations were never exactly what I wanted to hear, but they were seldom far from the mark. "Maybe you should do the same with Tess." I was too lost in my thoughts to hear the last piece of considered advice.

"It took a long time to sink in that Tess hates me at times. Maybe not hate me but that's what it feels like. She doesn't say 'I love you' that much. More often she says 'I love you too,' after I say it first. I don't think her dad said those words to her much."

"She doesn't hate you Ryan. You know that."

"Yeah, I know. Maybe that's more like what I feel about myself. I always thought that I was constantly having to deal with her baggage, that I was right. It's hard to admit that my perspective on things isn't always right. It's my baggage that we are both dealing with."

"It's hard for any person to admit that. We'll have to leave it there for now. But why don't you begin with telling Tess some of the things you've told me? Not what you think she feels about you, but how you feel about you. It might be a good starting point."

"Sounds good. See you in three weeks." We exchanged a cordial handshake, some idle chat about the weather and I was quickly on my way home.

Tess had said little about the previous weekend, she didn't have to say anything to make it clear how she felt. I knew she was angry and I kept my distance the best I could, while trying to let her know that I was sorry.

"It's so good to get home. Been a big week. Thank God it's Friday." I made a point of dropping my bag inside the door and intercepting Tess for a cuddle. Although she had been distant all week, she couldn't stay mad forever. At least I hoped she couldn't. I held her tight, for longer than normal.

"A big week for all of us. How's Bill?" Tess asked.

"He's good. I don't think I've ever talked about some of that stuff. It's hard, but it's helping. I don't really feel like cooking. Do you want to get Chinese delivered?"

"Yes please," yelled Leyla as she entered the lounge room and joined the embrace with the same enthusiasm as me.

"Well, that's decided then."

"Can I ring? I know the order, it's written on the menu," asked Leyla.

"Sure can. It's on the side of the fridge. Where's Josh?" I asked.

"Where do you think Dad?"

"It's the weekend Ry, C'mon. Fortnight and headphones," explained Tess.

"I'm glad it's just weekends. He'd be playing that game all day every day if he could." I walked down the hallway to his room.

"Hi mate, how was school?"

"Hi Dad. Good." He moved his ear phones back just enough to uncover half an ear. He never took his eyes off the screen.

"You know I'm really proud of you Josh, don't you? You are such a great kid. I hope I tell you that enough. I love you mate." Bill's advice about telling people how I felt resonated loudly.

"Yeah, Dad I know. Love you too." I'm not sure he heard it all but it felt good saying it. Back in the kitchen I picked up Leyla and held her tight.

"You know I love you, don't you? More than anything in the world Ley." She kissed me on the cheek and squeezed her little arms around the back of my neck like she always loved to do.

"I know. You always tell me Dad." I hadn't realised.

"Alright, you call up for dinner, I'm getting changed."

I walked into our bedroom adjoining the lounge and Tess followed behind me shutting the door. What did I do was my first thought?

"I'm going to run early in the morning, I won't be up late tonight." I nervously filled the silence.

"So, I ordered something a few weeks ago and it got delivered yesterday, not that you deserve it."

"Doesn't something get delivered every day?" I teased.

"Well, this one was for you, not me." She reached under the pile of shoes in her wardrobe and pulled out a glossy black paddle. She sat it against on the floor and began tidying the pile of shoes in the wardrobe.

"No way, where did you get it?"

"There are all sorts of things online if you look."

"You are full of surprises, aren't you? I remember you being pretty good at using one of those things the last time you had one in your hand."

"Forty minutes. But Josh has to set the table since I called," announced Leyla as she opened the bedroom door. Tess tossed the paddle in the wardrobe and shut the door before Leyla had even looked in her direction.

"Thanks T. That was really nice of you." I headed for the shower, quietly impressed with Tess' purchase.

"Josh, dinner is here," called Leyla as she rounded us up and motioned towards the dinner table. We had always made it a priority to eat together, no matter how busy we were. That feeling of connection at the table was a small but familiar comfort each day.

"Tigers tomorrow. We should beat them easy," Josh concluded as he reached the table. "Chinese, awesome."

"Hope so. Just get out there and rip in. Enjoy it. Who do you play Leyla?" I loved the sport banter of a Friday night. Leyla gave us a full run down of the Phoenix players and her game plan. The night was filled with speculation about the games on the following day. Nothing could ever replace walking onto the field and hearing the whistle blow, side by side with teammates, but watching the kids came pretty close.

"He's finally asleep. He'd be glued to that screen all night if we let him. Most of his mates are still on. I'm the mean mum for sending him to bed first." Tess fell backwards onto the bed.

"Leyla was out as soon as she laid down. Couldn't be more different." I stood between Tess' legs and leaned forward until my palms lay flat on the bed, each side of Tess' shoulders. I kissed her cheek softly and edged my lips around to whisper in her ear.

"I love you. Maybe the four of us could do something after the games tomorrow."

"Yeah, that'd be nice," replied Tess. I crashed on the bed beside her and closed my eyes. Work had been hectic and an hour with Bill was truly exhausting.

"I really am sorry about last weekend. I know it was way out of line. I get really down sometimes and I try to hide it. I hate you and the kids seeing me like that. I've got a lot of things to work through and I'm trying. I'm trying."

"I know you are, but we don't need apologies, or you hiding things. We just want you, not some piss happy version of you, until you've had one to many."

"Yeah." I didn't know what to say. Communicating might have been the right thing to do, but it wasn't easy.

"How about you stop talking?" Tess said.

"What?"

"Take off your clothes." I fought the urge to speak and my shirt was off in a second. Sometimes I talked too much. "All of it," she demanded. I dropped my favourite tracksuit pants to the floor leaving only my grey patterned boxer briefs on and then locked the door.

Chapter 12
Flying Paper Planes

"It was Explorer's Night last week." Tess looked at the club website as I hit cruise control on the highway into Sydney. "I think that's more for same sex couples."

"That's cool."

"So, have you ever thought about something like that?" Tess asked just as the city buildings came into view.

"There it is. I just love the energy of the city."

"You say that every time we come here Ry. So, have you?" She was clearly interested.

"Where did that come from? Honestly, never. I have got no problems with it at all, but that's just not me." Tess listened. "I have complete respect for other people's preferences and I don't think that it's any of my business really."

"So, you've never even wondered what it would be like?" Tess was keen to explore the idea.

"I don't think so. If I ever dream about sex, ah," maybe talking my dreams at this point wasn't a good idea. "I haven't ever dreamt about another guy."

"I bet some guys would love your cute little backside."

"Who knows? I guess preference was the wrong word. I don't think people choose their sexuality, it's just who they are and everyone should respect that."

"Yeah, your 'live and let live' idea hey?" Tess had been listening after all on the walk home that night.

"Exactly. I didn't get to some point and decide I'm heterosexual. I just am. People don't choose. Maybe I've got no idea what I'm talking about but that's just how it seems to me anyway."

"I agree. I wonder why people feel threatened." Tess adjusted the air con as a snap shot of her and Katie on the bed danced in my head.

"I've never understood homophobes. Or racists. Hate is such a waste of emotional energy. It just comes from ignorance," I said. It was something close to my heart, and I just couldn't understand the unnecessary hurt that people caused.

"Mum used to tell me about how they were treated when they were growing up. Their whole life was full of dealing with that shit." Tess hardly ever talked about her aboriginality and her cultural heritage. He skin was just fair enough that it wasn't immediately obvious and she had the same brown eyes that I saw in Josh and Leyla every time they looked up at me.

I was always proud of their aboriginality. I loved the fierce independence that came with it, the strength and the humility in their blood. I wished every one could see that beauty and appreciate our first nation's cultures as the wonderful people that they are.

"That must have been so hard. Maybe that's part of the reason that your dad is like he is."

"Maybe." She would never give him any excuses. Never. "Did you bring your questions?"

"Yep, tucked away in my bag. So, the 'other guys' thing must count as one of your questions then, only 19 left. I've still got twenty. Good ones too," I said.

"Don't think so."

"Tonight might be a bit different." My thoughts returned to the afternoon, but mostly the night, ahead. "The Bar Mix. It sounds like a kitchen appliance."

"The bar is only a few blocks from the club. How do you think it works?" Tess scrolled through her twenty questions listed on her phone as I drove.

"The website said it's pretty much just couples meeting up at a bar. Sort of like the club with clothes." I had read the description the night before.

"Like the club without bedrooms you mean?" Tess was more accurate.

"Then I think people can go to the club afterwards if they want. I thought we might go down to the harbour for dinner, like we did after Mama Mia. You got your questions finished?" I was trying to keep my eyes on the road.

"They're finished."

"There it is, finally. I'm over the traffic already," I said as we arrived in the city centre.

"Mr and Mrs Tanner, Welcome to the Hyde Park Hotel," said the smiling receptionist. The roads became more congested the closer we got to the centre of the city. I couldn't believe that people drove around on those stress filled streets every day.

"You wouldn't last in the city," laughed Tess as we headed to the fifth floor in the wooden panelled elevator.

"People are so impatient. They drive so aggressively and then just have to stop at the next intersection anyway." We tapped the green credit card styled key on the door lock and pushed open the heavy door. I always loved the feeling of walking into a hotel room, something I never did as a kid. It was our little oasis, for one night at least.

"Great view." I stared at the people hurriedly pacing along Liverpool Street and into Hyde Park. "That's the Anzac Memorial they built for the First World War diggers." The city skyline framed the park as I took in the living artwork.

"Yeah, we read the plaque a few years ago remember?"

"Not really. That's probably how I knew what it is. Do you want a drink?" I grabbed the oversized cooler bag and began to pack the bar fridge with beers and vodka cruisers.

"No, it's only two o'clock. Big day ahead Ry. What do you think will happen?" Tess asked. I opened one anyway.

"Part of the fun is not knowing what will happen. Just enjoying the night."

"I thought you planned out the pub crawl like last time?"

"Nope, not tonight."

"We'll just let it happen like you said," Tess replied.

"Just as long as there's live music in there somewhere."

"Just let it happen."

We were not in a hurry to get ready; life was one big rush and it was nice to take things slowly. We had not planned to return so quickly but it was my birthday soon and Rachel, Tess' sister, loved having Josh and Leyla stay at their house. The cousins eagerly looked forward to the sleepovers.

Rachel had also inferred that she was happy to give Tess and I some time together. I'm not sure if she intuitively knew that I had been struggling lately or if Tess had said something, but I was appreciative of the gesture.

When the opportunity came, Tess and I only needed to look at each other to know that we were coming again. It was hard not to think about it every other moment, to anticipate the energy of the city, the club. The more I thought about it though, the more it became clear that we were not gravitating towards 'the upstairs'. We were drawn to the entire experience, the feeling of freedom, trust and excitement.

It was the time together where we were the very best versions of ourselves. Brave, confident and most of all, free of the stresses of everyday life. We knew that Josh and Leyla were safe and happy spending time with family and I wouldn't have traded them or our lives back home for anything. But to escape everything for just one night was addictive. Everything else just faded away and it was just us and the city, and for a few crowded hours I felt like I could breathe.

"How about we head down to Darling Harbour? It's too nice to be inside," Tess suggested as we walked out of the hotel.

"Why not? Just let it happen." The park faced us as we hurried across the road, dodging the stampeding traffic.

"You're always in a hurry, slow down." Tess grabbed my hand to slow the pace. She was right again.

"Tai Chai, I'll try that one day." A group of elderly men and women moved gracefully under a large fig tree. "When I'm old."

"You are old," laughed Tess. The central paved pathway was full of people staring at their phones, or taking pictures with them.

"It's like a giant, leafy archway. Moreton Bay Figs, we've got one at work." I looked upwards at the green canopy with the city skyline in the backdrop. The breathing heart of the city soon morphed into concrete and brick as the figs were replaced by the towering architecture. The footpath narrowed and the pedestrian pace immediately resumed to the city speed.

"It's all downhill to the harbour at least," Tess assured herself. St James train Station emptied as people rushed out onto the street. We headed straight down Market Street and eventually descended a large staircase that led to the sprawling Darling Harbour precinct. "It's packed. So many people."

"So many tourists. Five minutes ago, it was all suits in a rush to get somewhere. This is much nicer. Do you want to get a pic?" I already had my phone camera ready and pulled Tess close to me as the harbour behind us framed our touching cheeks.

"You're more beautiful than ever." I honestly meant it.

"I don't think so. I don't feel it."

"Well, you are. Awesome photo, I'll send it to Josh and Leyla. I don't just say that to make you feel good Tess. It's how I feel. You're beautiful, you're the best mum I could ever imagine. I just feel lucky, honestly."

"We're both lucky, I love you too." She kissed my cheek before leading the way through the crowd. "Cocktail time I think."

"Beer o'clock."

"You really are a simple creature, aren't you?"

"I just like what I like. Plus, they're not twenty-two dollars a pop either." We walked casually along the promenade until we reached a spacious beer garden that overlooked the glistening harbour.

"Nice lounges. And we're so close to the promenade. I love watching people just walking past." Tess nodded in agreement as she ordered drinks from the attentive waitress.

"So, question one. I hope you're ready. This might be harder than you think. You first." Tess fished her phone from her bag and began to search for her hidden list of soul investigations.

"Might just wait until Mabel brings out the drinks. Then I'll be ready." I was both amused and impressed by the young waitress' nametag. "She didn't look like a Mabel to me. Why do I have to always have to go first?" I asked.

"Same reason that I always get to choose what side of the bed I want in a hotel," replied Tess. I thought for a moment.

"That didn't answer my question at all. Anyway." I produced my neatly written list from my shirt pocket and took a deep, slightly anxious breath. "Number one. When we're old and retired, what place would you most like to visit in the world?" I was happy to ease into this part of the night with some weightless conversation.

"Well, it's got to be hot. Hawaii maybe, or Thailand. Beaches and good shopping I think. Meg said Thailand was great, and the shopping was so cheap."

"Like Bali."

"Maybe. Josh and Leyla could come too. Where would you choose?" Tess seemed to enjoy this gentle introduction as well.

"I'd love to go to Africa somewhere. Do a safari and see Victoria Falls. Or maybe Scandinavia to see the northern lights. Have you seen those huts with glass ceilings and you can lie in bed and see the northern lights above you? That'd be awesome."

"Sounds freezing. At least Africa would be hot." Tess was nothing if not decisive. "So, we'll go to Hawaii. Okay. What is your biggest fear about tonight?"

"My biggest fear." I had to think about it. "I don't know. Maybe that you met some guy, or girl, that you like more than me and you run off with them, never to be seen again." My humorous tone masked the speculation.

"That would never happen. I love you and the kids. I love our lives. Would never happen." Tess was honest to a fault. I trusted her.

"Well, I'm glad we got that straight, otherwise we might have had to add a 'no running off with strangers' rule." Again, I was aware of the importance of the rules. Honesty above all had been a foundation of those nights, and our twenty questions game had really made a difference. Talking through any insecurities was critical to the whole crazy idea.

"But when you think about it, I guess there are genuine dangers any time we're out in the city at night. Who knows what nut job is walking around the next corner. But we can't live our lives worrying about what might happen. Anyway," I continued.

"Living life to the full hey? That's us." Tess reassured us both. "Okay, I'll go first for number two. What would happen if we met a perfect couple who wanted to swap numbers and have some sort of regular thing?"

"Like Scully did?" I replied. I shrugged my shoulders. "I think no. It's complicated enough without getting involved in something else. The children are our priority and being away from them even for one night is hard. One night is enough so I'd say no. You?"

"One hundred percent agree. It's so much easier like this. No strings and we just walk away at the end of the night." I was relieved that Tess was on the same page. No strings, or chains. "That was easy."

"Next one. Um, do you still find me attractive after twenty something years together?" Sometimes I wondered if Tess had tired of me a little, if that spark had slowly burnt out for her. I honestly didn't know the answer.

"Of course I do. I always have. You work hard to stay fit and you look great. Honestly. I think you're the same bloody weight as when we met just about, it's not fair. I wish I could say the same thing."

"Sometimes you don't show it."

"I will always want you. You're a great dad and I know you'd do anything for your family. What did you think I would say?"

"I don't know, probably what you just said. But sometimes it doesn't feel like, like it used too. Maybe that's more about me than you. You know I think you're as beautiful as ever, because I tell you all the time. But you don't ever say anything, ever. Not that I want you too but I just wonder sometimes." I didn't need her to say it, but sometimes she didn't show it either and that was the hard part.

"Do you really still think I'm still beautiful though, after having two babies? I'm not the same as I was?" Tess asked.

"Easiest question ever. Yes," I said. "Every curve, every wrinkle tells a story of our lives together. I love every one of them. Yes, you are more beautiful than ever. It's not just what's on the outside. You have a beautiful heart, a beautiful soul. You are an awesome mother, you're honest. You don't give an inch on the things you believe in. You make me a better man. All that is beautiful to me too."

"So, what you're saying is that I have wrinkles," laughed Tess.

"I thought that's all you'd hear. I meant the wrinkles in the soul from all of the shit that I put you through. Otherwise, you're just external perfection." I joined the laughter.

"I'm sure I've given you plenty of soul wrinkles as well Ry. I'm nothing like perfect."

"You are to me." It was true. Time slipped by unnoticed as we chatted, laughed and reflected on a lifetime of memories and aspirations for the future. That time spent together, just the two of us, was magic. It was like our first months of dating. There was a newness about those afternoons, getting to know someone all over again, someone that you thought you knew everything about.

"Do you want to go? We'll head up town to O'Reilly's," I suggested.

"What happened to your 'three questions per pub' rule?" teased Tess.

"Out the window. We're really living on the edge now."

"We'll be living on the edge in about six hours." The club was present in both of our thoughts as we began meandering through the city streets again.

"How good is the afternoon? No wind at all." Weather never really concerned me much, except for the wind. I hated it.

"Yeah, it's nice. Last time was freezing." It was as close to a perfect spring afternoon in Sydney as you could get. We walked along William Street until the huge Kings Cross Coca Cola sign came into view.

"That's so sad, have you got change?" Tess asked as we approached and elderly homeless man sitting on the footpath cross-legged. He had a simple sign written on cardboard that said 'Veteran. Help'. I couldn't help but feel a deep empathy for him. Sometimes in life I probably had my own 'Help' sign out without even knowing it. But maybe I was fooling myself if I thought I could ever understand another life full of such overwhelming hardship when I came from a world of relative privilege.

"I wonder what life must be like for him every day. Heart-breaking."

"Thanks mate," he said as I put all the coins I had into the worn bucket hat in front of him. He never looked up from the concrete. A dirty plastic cup sat on a fast-food wrapper in front of him. His thick black beanie sat low on his forehead and meshed into a thick black beard with flecks of grey throughout. His soiled grey jacket and fingerless gloves looked like they had been on him for years.

"I wonder how he got there," I murmured to Tess when we were out of earshot. "So many of the kids I work with are dealing with mental illness or addiction, or both. I'd bet that a big part of it. The homeless story must have a lot to do with those two things."

We walked in silence with the city skyline behind us. I felt a little selfish, dwelling on the many blessings I had in my life compared to that pour soul seated on the street.

"There's O'Reilly's. Cocktail time." Tess warmed to the very rare prospect of afternoon drinks.

"Two Illusions and two Cosmo's please?" Tess stirred the drinks with a mini umbrella as we sat as far as possible from the raucous group of guys at the centre of the small Kings Cross pub.

"I wonder what the kids are doing. I miss them every time I'm away," I said.

"Probably out with Rachel. She wanted to take them shopping. Leyla will love that."

"Josh won't, I dunno how anyone could enjoy shopping," I replied as I watched Tess carefully swirl the ice in her drink. "Next question. If you met your perfect man, would you ever consider leaving me?" We both sucked down the cocktails, peering up at one another. I still preferred a beer.

"I don't think there is such a thing as a perfect man. If there is, I met him a long time ago. He can drive me crazy sometimes but I'll love him forever. He's the father of my children, my best friend. Of course, I'm not going to leave. This whole thing is about us, not anyone else." Again, the little boy from the broken home needed reassuring, especially on nights like that. I knew the answer, but I just wanted to hear her say it.

"Same. Cosmo's are nice, nearly as nice as a beer. Good answer T. Your turn."

"Okay, are you happy with your life?" It was a simple, direct question, but so hard to answer. I paused.

"Am I happy with my life?" I repeated the question, buying time like a spelling bee contestant asking for the definition.

"Are you happy with your life?" Tess asked again.

"I think I'm really lucky. I have two beautiful kids, an amazing wife and a job where I make a difference in the world. We've got a nice home and good friends, everything that anyone could want."

"But you don't seem happy sometimes. I can see it, so can the kids." She knew me better than I knew myself. She was right.

"I want to be happy more than anything, to be a good dad and a good husband. I hate you guys seeing me pissed off or stressed. I know the kids feel it and I don't ever want them to see it." It was so hard to explain something that I didn't understand myself.

"You are an amazing dad and an amazing husband."

"I don't know why I'm angry, or down. That's why I'm seeing Bill. I wish he had some easy answer or a list of things to do to fix everything."

"But what's everything?" Tess asked.

"I don't know. It's not our life. Its things that happened a lifetime ago. Things that I wish would just go away. Feeling abandoned. That feeling of loneliness. That feeling of never being good enough. Always wanting people's approval when most of the time I already have it or it really doesn't matter anyway." I had never said those things before to Tess, or myself.

"Yeah, I see that in you sometimes," Tess replied.

"I am happy with my life. I have everything I ever dreamed of. I've got stuff to work through, like everyone." I downed the rest of the Cosmo. Cocktails were really not my thing.

"I'm getting a beer." I stood promptly. Discussing these things was emotionally draining and this was not what I had in mind when I first suggested the questions.

"It's getting busy," Tess said as I returned.

"Saturday arvo, it's packed. There're accents from all over the world."

"That's Sydney." The bar vibrated with the energy from people eager for a drink after a busy week

"I really didn't think we'd be talking about this stuff when we started the questions thing. I thought it'd be all about crazy sex positions or sex toys maybe. Not all of the hard stuff that's really not fun to talk about," I said.

"But it's good to talk about that stuff. We don't talk about it anywhere else. Maybe it helps." Tess put her hand on mine to stop me scratching at the wooden tabletop.

"I want to be happy; I have no reason not to be. I got hurt when I was young and I don't really think about that stuff. But the scars still affect me sometimes, even though I don't even realise what's wrong. Getting older is hard. I worry more about the kids and their future, about being around for them as they grow up. All sorts of stuff. One of the best things about my twenties was that I had no worries at all. All that stuff was so far down that I couldn't even feel it. Like these weekends in the city. All the stuff just leaves for a while. Maybe that's why I love them so much."

"Maybe."

"I reckon the sex toys questions still sound like they'd be way more fun. Moving on," I tried to lighten the mood, my mood. "How do you see our future together?"

"I think we'll have a great future. We'll pay off the house, travel, retire. We've both got super and we'll look after the grand kids. Maybe you can even coach one of their footy teams. Remember, we've already picked Hawaii."

"You picked Hawaii, but it does sound nice. That's pretty much how I see things too. Hopefully there's a lottery win in there somewhere so we can retire early."

"Might be hard when we don't buy tickets." Tess was a realist.

"I can dream at least. I like thinking about us getting old and retiring. Being able to sleep in if we want, go to the beach when we want. We'll be there for the grand kids and go travelling sometimes. It will be so cool. Maybe we can buy a campervan?"

"Why not? What are we up to? Four." Tess took a measured breath. "Why do you drink?"

"Fuck." I breathed the word, less than a whisper, but Tess could read my lips. I slowly spun the glass of beer on the table with my fingertips. "Same answer as last question. Is that enough?"

"I don't mean to make this hard Ry, I just want to know." Her dad was an alcoholic. I was not. At least I didn't think I was. But maybe she thought my answer would help her to understand him as much as me.

"Why do I drink? Why does anybody drink, or use drugs, or over eat or do whatever they do? I don't know. I work hard. Life is stressful. Having a beer is like one big release valve. For a little while, I can forget all of the shit, it just leaves me. I can just watch the footy, or hang with the kids and be happy."

"Yeah," Tess just listened. One of the great things about the questions was that we actually listened to each other, really listened. It was a powerful thing.

"I don't know if they are all just excuses or reasons. It just makes me happy." Just be honest, I thought.

"It's hard for us sometimes when you've been shitty all week and then as soon as you've got a beer in your hand you're Mr Happy. It kinda doesn't seem right." Tess was just being honest too.

"Fair enough. I don't want to be a bad example for Josh and Leyla. I just try to get through each week the best that I can. It's hard to put it into words. Every morning after, I promise myself that I'll slow down. I don't know why. I don't." I began scratching hard at the table again.

"It's okay." Tess knew I wanted to move on. We left the questions for a while and just talked. Time was a gift and we drew on the energy of the city. The questions were both draining and cleansing. They built a foundation of honesty and trust, both vitally important for navigating what was ahead that night.

"Next pub?" I asked as I finished my drink.

"Let's go," Tess agreed. We took a few shorts steps out onto the footpath, into the river of human traffic and looked up at the massive Coca Cola sign.

"I'm so glad that our kids only drink water. That stuff is just sugar in a can, although I can't really comment on anyone's drinking habits, can I?" Our playful adventure was back on track.

"No, you cannot," Tess laughed. She wrapped her arm around my bicep and pulled me close as we continued. "Have you ever been into a sex shop?" Tess asked as we approached a neon lit sign above a small doorway.

"Nope, have you?" We were kids when we met, we knew the answers.

"Not yet. Do you want to have a look? Might be your big chance for some sex toy questions." We were nearly at the door and she tugged on my arm enough to walk us straight into the shop. A staircase led down to a double-garaged sized room and my naive country boy feeling immediately returned.

"Wow," I said.

"Wow alright. Look at this stuff." Tess sounded as amazed as I was.

"Hiya." We were greeted by a bleach blonde man of about fifty, in a collared denim muscle top with full arm tattoos on both sides. He had countless piercings and his missing teeth suited him.

"How are you mate?" I replied as we absorbed the scene. "He must be getting something for the wife." We both looked at the only other person in the shop in the aisle opposite the entry, a thirty something guy in an expensive looking suit and polished black shoes. He could not have contrasted more with the shop attendant.

"Or maybe it's for someone else," Tess proposed. He stood in a corner, obscuring whatever he was looking at. We slowly made our way down the second aisle, stunned at the range of toys.

"I've never even heard of some of this stuff. Penis sleeve, really? Shit, people must really like anal beads, look how many there are. Look at the size of that. You're kidding." There was so much to take in. I was commentating while laughing as the suit quickly placed something back on the shelf and paced off towards the counter.

"She looks like she's ready to go," Tess joined my confused delight as she nodded towards a life-size blow-up doll hanging from the ceiling in one corner.

"Mm, she needs some clothes the poor girl." Each orifice was accentuated and I couldn't help but feel uncomfortable looking at it.

"I wonder who buys something like that," Tess said.

"Someone who must be very lonely. I don't know. Someone who likes the quiet type."

"The plastic type. Strawberry lube with sparkles, isn't that nice," Tess said as she turned into the next isle containing all sorts of whips, leather lingerie, tubes of lube and a myriad of other sex aids. The suit exited as Bleach Blonde picked up his phone. "We've got to get something don't we?" She grabbed the lube and kept walking.

"That's just wrong." At the end of the isle were three life-sized torsos in plastic packaging. Just the waist down to the thigh, with incredibly realistic anal and vaginal holes.

"The doll's bad enough, but at least she's a bit characterised. They are foul." Tess didn't stop and turned into the last isle.

"Yeah, those things are a worry."

"Here's your specialty," I said as a range of paddles hung next to some type of ball bag chains. "The paddles I mean."

"I don't know, those ball chains with the doggy lead look alright too."

"Don't think so. I might add this to our tennis collection." I picked up a small, dimpled paddle and headed for the counter. I was thankful that both of our purchases were placed into a plain brown paper bag. I didn't want to walk onto the street carrying around our new possessions.

It was dusk as we emerged from the strange little shop in the Cross. I wondered what sort of life the guy behind the counter led, if he was happy. The shop was open until midnight. It must have been hard.

"That was interesting, and weird. There's The Royal." I was happy to move on.

"Yeah, people are definitely into some strange stuff. The music's loud."

"Louder the better. I love it." We walked into the spacious, lavishly furnished bar that choroused with conversations and laughter. The crowd was much younger than at O'Reilly's. Well dressed, they looked made for the city.

"They look like a bunch of rich kids. I wonder if all the beamers are out the back," Tess said.

"Nah, Mum and Dad probably dropped them off, or paid for the Uber." I joined in the judgemental summation of the crowd. It was a beautiful pub, much different from the historic, earthy feel of the others, but it had the same pulsing energy. I couldn't help but love it.

"Do you want a shot with your beer?" Tess asked.

"Absolutely, what are you getting?"

"Not sure, I'll surprise you. You get a table." I sat in the only vacant booth left and ran a hand over the maroon leather upholstery. Pine partitions gave enough privacy for our questions game but the windows on one side allowed us to look out onto the bustling Darlinghurst Road nightlife.

"Do you like slippery nipples?" Tess grinned as she sat the drinks on the table.

"Ah, doesn't everyone? What's a slippery nipple?" I'd never heard of them.

"It's butterscotch schnapps and Baileys Irish cream. How cute are the little shot glasses?" Tess ran her forefinger around the rim of the glass.

"They look like mini vegemite jars. I love schnapps and baileys."

"I know you do. Bottoms up." Tess upended the drink before taking a swig of her vodka and orange.

"That's my girl." I followed her lead. "I love this, you and me. I love you." The rest of the world didn't exist. It was just her and I, sitting on the maroon leather. The rest of the world was just one big gold fish bowl on the other side of the window.

"Love you too. Yeah, this is fun," she replied. That was one of the moments of silence when the gravity of the whole adventure surfaced. My heart beat faster and I leaned across the table to kiss Tess. My lips lingered against hers.

"You're naughty," I said.

"So are you." She raised her eyebrows and the excitement that I was feeling was mirrored across her face. I took her hand and we talked like teenagers about nothing, everything.

"I think we need some more slippery nipples. Back in a minute." I was off to the bar and the paper planes were flying.

"Are you nervous?" I asked Tess as we walked back to the hotel.

"A bit, you know I don't like talking to people."

"You didn't mind last time. Maybe it's easier talking to strangers."

"Maybe."

"It starts at eight. It'll take us about twenty minutes to walk there." I had watched the time closely as it got closer to eight.

"I'd rather be a bit late anyway. I don't want to get there and there's no one even there. I wonder how many people will go." Tess held me close again as the night cooled.

"Don't know, it's all new to me. There's the concrete jungle," I said as we rounded the corner onto William Street and the city sprawled before us. "It just comes to life at night."

"It gets colder at night. But yeah, it's beautiful."

"I wouldn't want to live here but I'm still drawn to the place. It's so different from home. They were nice, the people we met last time, don't you think?"

"They actually were. We spent most of the night just chatting on the lounge or dancing. It's just not what you'd think it would be." Tess paused. "Except for the part that is what you think it would be."

"But even the upstairs is different from what I expected. No one could ever know what it's like."

"Different how?" Tess asked.

"I don't know, I never thought that we'd actually go through with it. It's pretty heavy stuff when you think about it. I thought we'd be in different rooms, or that we might implode with jealousy."

"Were you jealous?" Tess whispered.

"No, I don't know why but no. I don't know why not, I felt more comfortable with it than I thought. It helped that you were close."

"Except when your friend kept moaning your name," Tess reminded me.

"Yeah, except for that. I'd prefer to forget that part." We reminisced about the previous two nights at the club as we walked. "It's like trying to remember parts of a dream. Sometimes it still doesn't seem real." I played moments back in my head and that nervous grand final feeling returned.

After a short stop at the hotel, we headed to the Bar Mix, still not exactly sure what it was or who would be there. The unknown was a part of the energy along with the thought that life wasn't just one big ground hog day. That day was very different.

"I think we just passed it. It must be upstairs." Tess checked the address on her phone. We turned back and eventually saw the small sign above another dimly lit doorway. "The Terrace, there it is."

We walked cautiously up the carpeted stairs to the second storey clandestine bar.

"There must be a crowd in there, it's loud," I said.

"Okay, now I'm nervous." Tess slowed to let me step slightly ahead of her. "Shit, is it too late to turn around."

"Yeah, me too." My heart raced and the electricity cannoned off the walls. I'd never felt more alive. It really was one crowed hour of glorious life. I waited at the last step and reached for Tess' hand. "Are you ready?"

"This is crazy Ry." Her nervous, beautiful smile stretched wide across her face as the web of voices spilled out of the bar.

"Good crazy. This is wild." We stepped into the boutique terrace gallery.

"Welcome to the Bar Mix."

Chapter 13
Light Versus the Darkness

"A footy match is a lot like a night of drinking. During the match you feel great, completely in the zone, and the crowd's with you. Football and drinking are both spent totally absorbed in the moment and that is one of the biggest reasons that I love them both."

"Okay." Bill validated my speculation but otherwise remained silent.

"It's hard to explain. All of the other noise in life melts away for a while. Sometimes I think it's where I'm the happiest. Your team are all that matters in those moments and they have your back, always."

"Which place do you mean?" Bill asked.

"Footy. The footy field. I really miss it."

"And you think that's the same when you are out with mates?"

"Maybe. I know they're not the same. My drinking hurts other people. Like when the final whistle blows and you start to cool down, things change. You start to feel all of the aches and pains that the game caused and you can feel the damage from all those hits."

"The damage that your drinking causes?" Bill listened intently.

"Yeah. It's not as if I go out much, I mostly drink at home. And every morning I wake up thinking the same thing that things are going to change. But they don't."

"That's something you really need to think about. Drinking alone isn't healthy for you and it doesn't sound like it's good for Tess either."

"Tess is okay about it most of the time. She doesn't get on my case most nights. But I know she doesn't like it. If I've done something to upset her, she doesn't carry on, she just shuts down. She won't talk to me for days. I wish she'd yell at me, anything. The silence is the worst."

"It might be her way of coping, to withdraw." Bill spoke but I wasn't listening.

"When I used to play, after the match I often reflected on the heavy tackles that I put on opposition players. Ones that seemed legal at the time. I always played the game back over in my head, the parts I could remember anyway. That's the same for a big night. Each season I would decide 'that's enough', but then I couldn't help but go again when the next season arrived. I didn't want to stop."

"Most people don't just stop drinking. It's a gradual process. Could you try cutting down the amount you have on a normal night or try to reduce the number of days each week that you drink?"

"Yeah, I could. I will. Tess, Josh and Leyla deserve better. I want to do better for them? Tess' dad was an alcoholic, still is. I am not an alcoholic but I drink too much and I don't like the person I become when I drink. Neither does Tess."

"Maybe this is something that you need to do for yourself Ryan, not anyone else. What do you fear most?" I reacted with an abbreviated laugh at Bill's question.

"Tess asked me that question once."

"And what was your answer?" The context of Bill's question was far different from the bar room question that Tess had asked, sitting across the road from Deepest Desires.

"I can't remember." I lied quickly. "What do I fear most?" What does anyone fear? It was an incredibly difficult question.

"I think the thing that scares me most is the thought of my kids growing up without their dad, like I did. Struggling every day, like I did. If Tess ever got sick of the stuff I put her through and she couldn't do it any more, then..." I looked at the ground. I didn't want Bill to see me cry.

"It's okay Ryan. Take your time."

"Then they would be alone, like I was. I mean they'd still have Tess of course and each other. But it would be hard, so hard for them. I don't want them to ever have to feel that loneliness."

"But what do you fear most for yourself Ryan, not for anyone else. It sounds to me that the thing you fear most is being alone, of being abandoned again like when you were younger."

"I hate being alone. I feel lonely a lot."

"The pressure you put on yourself doesn't help Ryan. Psychologists call it unrelenting standards. You set such high standards for yourself as a father, a husband and a mentor at work that you could never be good enough in your own perception of things."

"Yeah, maybe."

"And when you fail to meet the standards you set for yourself, you feel as if you have failed in some way. That pressure you put on yourself affects your happiness."

"I just want to be the best father and husband I can be."

"Well do that, be the best you can be. But that doesn't mean you need to be perfect. Do you remember when we talked about punctuality, how you get upset if you and your family are even a minute late?"

"Yes, that's just how I am."

"Try this for me. Be mindful that it's okay if you are not perfectly on time for everything. If it's a job interview or you're catching a train, then of course you need to be on time. But if you are just going to a friend's place for dinner, take some pressure off yourself and the family. Let yourself be late once in a while."

"I guess I could do that."

"People are not going to judge you if you're a bit late. Not the people that matter anyway. You don't need their approval. Only your own."

"I'll try."

"You can let Tess know that this is something that you're working on. I think it would be good if you also talked to her about your drinking, ask her how it affects her and tell her that you understand how she feels."

"I do understand how she feels, I think."

"Maybe, but you need to listen to her and she needs to know that you're listening. It's been a month since you started the medication, how is that going?"

"It's alright. I still don't really like the idea of it but if it helps me then I'll keep taking it." I hated the little pill that I swallowed every morning, or maybe it was the realisation that I actually needed it.

"And is it helping?" Bill probed.

"Not that I can see, I don't feel any different. I'm still struggling. It's not some magic cure if that's what you mean."

"That's not what it's meant to be Ryan. It's a support mechanism that's just one of many things that helps with depression. You're on a minimum dose that we can adjust if you're not seeing any improvements."

"I'm not upping the dose. I'm just not." Bill could see the agitation in my knee, bouncing on the end of my toes again. I pushed down with my palm to silence the body language.

"How often are you exercising?" He changed course towards another 'mechanism'.

"I'm still lifting weights a bit. I used to run all the time when I was playing footy. But not now. I hurt my knee." My palm began to rub over the worn joint that had finally stopped me playing.

"Every study in the world on depression comes out with the same thing as the single most important coping strategy. It's not medication or psyches, as helpful as they are. It's exercise."

"Yeah, I read about it once when I was reading up on ways to support one of the kids at work. She's this beautiful person but there's such sadness in everything she does. Almost like a permanent grief. Casey. About the closest we've come to exercise is playing table tennis at the youth centre. My knee has been feeling a bit better lately. It was sore for a long time."

"It doesn't need to be running. Anything that gets your heart rate up works. Swimming is great for anyone with injuries or going for a bike ride with your kids would be a great idea."

"Riding with the kids would be good. I can try that." I didn't know it then but exercise, infinitely more than a little white pill, would be a guiding light out of the fog.

"We'll leave it there for today, there's a few things there for you to think about. You can tell me how you're going with them next time."

"I'll be giving the bikes a clean, they haven't been out of the shed for a while." I said my goodbye to Bill and glanced quickly at the blank faces sitting in the waiting room. I walked unusually slowly through the carpark, trying to process what he had said.

"Unrelenting standards. I'm anything but perfect." Bill was right though, he understood me, and this was the very beginnings of understanding myself. On the short drive home, I thought about all the things I could change, how I could be better. It was comforting to think about the idea of what I could be, rather than who I was.

"Hello sexy," I opened our bedroom door as Tess changed out of her work clothes. I still loved to watch her.

"Hello yourself."

"I met Casey's grandmother today at the centre." I kissed Tess on the cheek as I shut the door. "Her name's Carol. She's a north coast koori like your mum." I didn't want to talk about Bill.

"Nice, how is Casey going?"

"Sometimes it feels like she takes two steps forward then two steps back. It's slow going. But when I hear people's story, it helps me to understand them so much more." I had been moved by the old lady's story.

"Casey's or Carol's?"

"Both, they're part of the same story. Carol was one of the stolen generations. They took her from her family when she was five."

"Shit. Like Aunty Jan."

"She said the only thing she was ever told was that someone made a phone call about her parents. Mongrels. How the fuck did they ever think that somehow, they had the right? How? There was no right of reply. No nothing. It makes me so mad. So mad. She was a five-year-old girl who was taken from her family. For what?" My blood boiled at the injustices she had suffered and there were so many more stories like hers'.

"Aunty Jan was three." Tess looked blankly at the floor.

"So, Carol lived in different homes growing up and never had any contact with her family again until she was thirty. When she was finally able to contact her mum, the first thing her mum said was that her dad had passed away a few years before. She barely remembered him." I could have cried as I retold the story.

"That's heart-breaking. Just unforgivable." Tess' family had known that heartbreak and the irreparable damage that it caused.

"But the thing that gets me is how quick people are to judge. They know nothing about all the shit that someone like Carol has been through but they carry on with their racist garbage anyway." First nations Australians were some of my close mates growing up, some of the best people I knew. I played footy with many of them, they were so naturally gifted at sport. But beyond the footy field they were such strong, loyal, beautiful people.

"Racism comes from ignorance. Mum always used to say that only light can drive out the darkness." Tess' mum was right.

"Martin Luther King. Smart man."

"And a forgiving one." Tess had not forgiven.

"I guess the best thing about Carol's awful story was that somehow, she didn't seem angry. She spoke with such integrity and calm. Maybe that just comes with age."

"So how was Bill?" Tess asked.

"He was good. Like a trip to the dentist, painful but you know it's helping."

"I know it's hard for you, but I know that's it's the right thing for you." Tess wasn't the prying type. She valued her privacy greatly and she respected other people's right to silence as well.

"He said that I have unrelenting standards, psyche talk for being a perfectionist and getting down on yourself when you don't measure up." Tess just listened. Again, I was aware of the power of listening, really listening. People are inherently egocentric creatures and I appreciated her attentiveness.

"I'm trying to work on that, you know, don't get shitty if we're late. Don't be so hard on myself at work, stuff like that."

"Sounds good, you don't have to be perfect all the time."

"That's what Bill said. I know I'm nothing like perfect. I know the drinking has been a problem. Just saying that I'm stressed and grabbing a beer isn't okay. I'm trying to work on that as well. Oh, and exercise. That's meant to help a lot. I might try running again, see how my knee is. The weights are good but I really love to run."

"And the medication?" Tess knew I was still struggling and I think she had hoped that the medication would have made more of a difference by now.

"No change. I don't want to increase the dosage." I heard the fridge open in the kitchen and the conversation ended abruptly. "Josh, why don't we give the bikes a bit of a clean?"

Even during the walk through the carpark after visiting Bill, I was thinking about the six brown bottles at the back of the fridge and the other eighteen in the garage. It should have been easy to dismiss the thought of opening one, only minutes ago I had been talking to Bill about strategies, responsibilities and goals. It should have been easy but it was anything but that. My subconscious scrolled through every reason, every excuse to drink. My internal dialogue took on a life of its own, like a little cartoon devil sitting on my shoulder.

'You've worked all day, you deserve it. Just have one or two, no one will even know if stay outside and clean the bikes. It's Thursday night, the footy is on TV, and this is what we do. It's what makes us happy.' The list was unrelenting, endless.

I muffled the sound of the twist top lid opening. The brown bottle took an audible breath in and it was alive. The battle was always against the first beer. After that, the second, third and all subsequent drinks were consumed without resistance. I took the six-pack to the patio outside. Warmish beers were definitely worth it if that meant that Tess didn't know. But she always knew, I was only fooling myself.

"Meg's sick, can you take Josh and Jet to footy training?" Tess opened the sliding door as I quickly placed the last of the bottles behind a pot plant.

"Ah, I'm doing the bikes, can't you take them?"

"I told you this morning, Leyla and I are going over to mum's. She has no idea how to program her new telly."

"Oh yeah." I couldn't take a chance with my licence. Not now. "I can't." Tess took a few more steps before she saw the carefully placed bottles.

"Cleaning bikes? Must be thirsty work?"

"He can just miss it." My normal aversion to conflict was always clouded when I drank. "Work was hard." There was always an excuse and work was the standard fallback line. I believed it, but Tess knew better.

"Shit Ryan, I don't care if you have a beer. It's the lying I hate. I hate it."

"I never lied."

"Do you know how often I find the bottles that you hide, then forget? It's fucked."

"Just don't want the kids to see me drink, I don't want them growing up around it." Another lie, it was Tess I was hiding it from.

"Then don't drink. Simple."

"Don't tell me what to do. If I want to have a fuckin beer, then I will." The brown bottle did the talking from here on, not me.

"I'm not listening to this shit. I'll take Josh and Jet." Tess slammed the sliding door as I collected the bottles and binned them. 'No one's home, the rest of the beers are in the garage. Might as well have another one, we'll feel better then.' The thirst was unrelenting, endless. I opened the next warm beer.

Drinking was never really the problem for me, it was knowing when to stop. I suspect that this is the problem for most drinkers. A beer or a glass of wine in the evening would never hurt anyone but once I started then the stop signals in my brain vanished. I drank to get drunk.

I would eventually learn from Bill that alcohol triggers the release of dopamine in the brain. It's a type of happiness chemical and the brain learns to associate alcohol with pleasure. I was trying to drink myself happy. It didn't work. But as the brain gets de-sensitised to that dopamine release, we need to drink more to get the same feeling of happiness.

Alcohol also affects the executive function of the brain over time, the decision-making part that tells people not to drink. That is one of the reasons why I found it hard to stop, it wasn't just my lack of will power as I had always thought. This was a powerful and dangerous drug. The night dissolved quickly and I remembered little of the argument that started when Tess got home. But as parts of my drunken rant returned the next morning, I knew that I had really messed up this time.

"We're leaving," was all Tess said as she and the kids walked out the front door. It slammed hard behind them. Leaving? My first thought was panic, followed by the rational explanation of work and school. The next thoughts came simultaneously, 'I'm bloody late,' and 'my head hurts.' I searched for the phone. I could hardly get up, never mind work.

Without exception, there was the feeling of regret the next morning. I couldn't even remember Tess getting home, or the kids. It took considerable thought to recall the yelling and the accusations behind the closed door of our bedroom.

The day was spent in states of remorse and regret. Places I knew well. I yearned to apologise, but I knew that Tess didn't want to hear anything I had to say at that moment.

"Tano, what's happening brother?" Tim's Friday afternoon phone calls were like clockwork. He always had something planned for the weekend, especially if the boys had a home game.

"Not much mate. Just got home, been a long day." I didn't really feel like talking.

"You coming tomorrow? It's our second last home game. We ain't gonna make the semis."

"They've been pretty ordinary the whole year. Nothing like when we were playing hey?" I bypassed the question. Saying no to Tim wasn't easy.

"We would've smashed all these teams. You'd still make first grade. Undefeated premiers baby." He loved to reminisce, always wearing his rose coloured glasses. "So, you coming? Josh and Jet can stay for a while after their game, we'll be there anyway."

"Don't think so, I've got stuff to do. I don't want to hang around all afternoon." True to form, Tim persisted but he eventually got the message that I wasn't going.

"Hi Dad," Josh and Leyla said as they stormed through the door. I hugged them both together. For once, I had nothing to say. I just held them. "I love you guys. Where's Mum?"

"She's getting the stuff out of the car." Leyla replied as she walked to the fridge.

"New headphones," Josh yelled as he ran to the PS4 in his room. I tentatively opened the front screen door.

"Do you need some help?" I asked.

"No." Tess struggled with her work gear and three plastic bags full of groceries. She walked inside, never looking at me.

Sometimes I felt like Tess was being totally unfair during those days when she shut me out, that her rage over my harmless indulgences was unjustified. In my mind, I lied to myself. All I had done was fix up a few bikes in the patio, not bothering anyone, whilst have a few well-earned beers. I wasn't hurting anyone and I was just doing my own thing. I was a happy drunk and things only turned ugly when Tess antagonised me. It wasn't my fault.

It was easy to excuse myself from any wrongdoing, but I was gradually learning that I was far from faultless and that my actions hurt others. I hurt the ones that I loved the most. Accepting responsibility was not easy because it meant that, done properly, I had to change. If I excused my own behaviour, then there was no reason to change and I would continue to make the same mistakes over and over again.

"What time does Leyla play in the morning?" Tess didn't answer as she unpacked. "We could all go and then head straight to Josh's game."

"I told Mum I'd pick her up. You can drive yourself." She left the rest of the groceries on the kitchen floor and shut the bedroom door behind her. I put them carefully away and the rest of the night was spent in silence.

"Take the ball on the chest when you catch it," I called to Josh in the backyard the next morning.

"Do we have to go to Leyla's game Dad?"

"She comes to all your games. Yes, we're going to watch her play. Stand more side on when you pass, you get more power." Every Saturday morning Josh would be in the backyard practicing. He began to bomb the ball high in the air, manoeuvring underneath it to make the catch.

"Tess, when are we going?" I called as I walked inside. "Tess."

"They went to Nan's. Can we keep playing?" Josh explained.

We stood side by side like strangers at the netball courts, the silence only interrupted by Nan's intermittent cheering and Josh asking for money to go to the canteen. The same story played out at Josh's game an hour later. I didn't know how to reach Tess and I felt an undercurrent of anger that she was continuing to punish me.

"I'm dropping Mum home, the kids are coming with me," was all Tess said. She didn't wait for a reply.

"Okay, I'll see you at home. You guys did great today."

"Thanks Dad." Their little voices quickly disappeared into the distance.

I was quick to drive home and tidy up the house, a kind of peace offering to Tess. But they were not home and my texts went unanswered. I grabbed the phone as soon as I heard the text notification only to see Tim's name appear. 'Pick you up at two thirty.' I ignored the offer. We had been through it last night.

Another hour went by and Tess was still not home. It was frightening how quickly remorse could morph into anger sometimes and the resulting collapse of any clarity of mind. I was home alone doing housework on a Saturday, being punished for what? All the boys were at the field and I didn't deserve this. Now it was my demons doing the talking. I texted Tim back: 'Yep, see you at two thirty.'

"Three bloody minutes and we're in, go boys." Tim yelled in unison with the rest of our mates on the sideline as we scored early in the game. Meg had dropped us both at the ground.

"She's a gem, dropping you here every home game."

"If only you knew. Does my head in. Here ya go Tanno." Tim handed me a beer from the club fridge. They made decent money every home game and the boys were always willing to help the club by bending the elbow. The battle against the first beer was infinitely harder when it was handed to you by your best mate.

"Thanks." The cold glass felt both comforting and familiar.

"You okay, you're a bit quiet? Work again?" Tim asked. He wasn't the most observant bloke but even he could see that something was wrong.

"Yeah, work. Some of those kids have got so much to deal with, breaks my heart."

"Dunno how you do it mate. Shoulda been a tradie. C'mon Flano, tackle you sook." That was as much support as Tim could offer and I was thankful for the distraction. I didn't want to talk about things anyway. My thoughts turned to Tess and the crushing weight of regret suffocating me. I should have stayed at home.

'Meg gave me and Tim a lift to the game, I didn't know where you were. Are you okay?' I reread the text before I pressed send. It seemed completely inadequate but it was all I could think of. There was no reply as I expected.

"Your shout Tanno, drink up," Tim demanded. The unwritten rule number one of the shout was that everyone involved must drink at the pace of the fastest drinker. This was especially dangerous when he was thirty kilograms heavier than I was.

"First home win in a while. You boys coming back to the pub?" Davey asked. He had played with us for most of our senior grade years. Now divorced, he went back to the pub after every game, home or away.

"Don't think so Davey, I gotta get home." I already regretted coming to the game.

"Don't listen to him. We'll get the courtesy bus with you guys, then Meg will pick us up from there." Tim looked at me with certainty on his face. "Done."

I was already pissed and I didn't have the energy to argue. At home, I would only be ignored anyway. The kids would be in their rooms while Tess kept our bedroom door shut. I'd sit on the lounge alone watching the footy. What was the difference if I was watching it at the pub with good mates? Mates who wanted me there. The brown bottle spoke so convincingly that I thought it was me. But it wasn't. Deep inside I just wanted to be at home, with Tess.

I closed the front door as quietly as I could. Three hours had drifted by at the pub and I had drunk far too much, again, even by my standards. Our bedroom light was on and I could hear Josh chatting away on his new headphones but I rushed to the bathroom and quietly locked the door. I lay on the cold tiles and the room spun violently. I knew what was coming.

"Are you alright Dad?" I heard Leyla's voice through the bathroom door. "I'll get Mum."

"No," I gasped. "I'm okay. Go to bed please." I only just got the words out before the next wave of vomiting began. Leyla's bedroom was on the other side of the bathroom wall. I imagined her in bed listening, frightened. If time accelerated infinitely at Deepest Desires, then these moments were the opposite. Every moment was torturous. Worse than the physical pain was what I knew was to come.

I can't remember anything more after that.

"I can't do this anymore. Not even a fucking call and you come home and do that. How do you think Leyla felt? She spent the night with me." I was on the lounge and peeled open my eyes, adjusting to the morning light.

"I texted."

"I'm not going to let our children grow up watching you do this every week. I've told you again and again this is not what I want but you don't listen." She started to cry. I couldn't speak. "Your mates always come first, they always do. Every fucking time."

"You are the most important person in the world to me, you, Josh and Leyla." I chose my words as carefully as I could in the haze of emotional pain.

"The only person you care about is yourself," Tess said quietly through gritted teeth. It was like talking to a stranger. The rage and hatred in her face was frightening, almost like she was a completely different person. Somewhere deep inside I continued to lie to myself. For a moment, it felt like all the hurt that her father had put her through, all the pain from a lifetime ago, was now my fault. All the pain that ever existed deep inside her now had an outlet to pour over and it was aimed directly at me.

"Tim kept asking. I just wanted to come home. I didn't have dinner. That's why I was sick. I am so sorry." Every word I spoke made it worse. Deep inside I burned at the thought that I was paying for the sins of her father. But slowly I would learn that blaming anyone else for my failures, my weakness, was just plain wrong. Worst of all, those failures could cost me the only things that ever mattered in my life; my beautiful Tess, Josh and Leyla. If the things I feared most were to come true, then it was my fault, not anyone else's.

"You're pathetic. I am taking the kids to mums." Then, they were gone. I scrubbed the mess of vomit from the toilet rim and floor.

Tess' text was short and direct.

'I want you out before we get home.'

My head spun, physically and emotionally. Part of me wanted to take no responsibility for what happened. It was just a night out with the boys, I didn't even really want to be there. But this was not about one night, it was the culmination of a thousand indiscretions and a thousand broken promises to do better. Twenty years ago, those nights were part of our lives. But it had been twelve years since Josh had been born and there had been more than enough time to change. Tess did not want any part of that life anymore.

I turned the car engine off near our favourite caravan park, forty kilometres from home. I only had my clothes, toiletry bag and a blanket. There was also the old towel that lived permanently in the boot of the car. I sat for what seemed like hours, replaying things in my head, wishing that I could go back and change it all. I felt numb, angry, lost. But most of all I felt alone.

Eventually I decided on a long, hot shower but I hadn't paid to stay so I didn't have the entry code for the amenities block. I had parked on the side of the road outside the park, obscured by large banksia trees. Eventually I stood outside the shower block door with my old towel over my shoulder and toiletry bag in hand pretending to have a conversation on my phone. It wasn't long before an elderly man was punching in the entry code and I walked in behind him unnoticed.

The shower was so hot it burned. Nothing more than I deserved I thought. I stood there for an eternity before walking back to the car and folding the back seats down to sleep. I wished that I had thought of a pillow. I used the wet towel instead. I didn't really sleep, the car was stuffy and as soon as I opened the window ever so slightly, the mosquitos came in for dinner.

'What do you fear most?' This.

Chapter 14
The Bar Mix

"Welcome to the Bar Mix," the attractive young woman repeated. "I'm Alyssa." She wore a short black mini skirt and tight singlet top with immaculate make-up. Her hair was pulled back in a perfect pony bun, just like the dancers from an old eighties video clip by Robert Palmer.

"Hi, I'm Ryan, this is Tess. We spoke to you on the phone last week."

"It's great to meet you both. Why don't you grab a drink and make yourself at home, there's plenty of people here already?" The small venue was full. "If you meet someone you like, you can head over to the club later in the night to play."

"Sounds good." I stammered. She got straight to the point.

"Let me know if you need anything. Have fun." Alyssa resumed her conversation near the entrance to The Terrace.

"A play date, doesn't that sound nice," Tess laughed as she kissed my cheek. I scanned the busy room, happy to breathe after the initial panic at the top of the stairs.

"This place is awesome. How would anyone know it's even here? We walked right past it." My chest pounded and I couldn't stop grinning at Tess. "This is wild, this whole thing. I can't believe it's us."

"Wild alright, scary," Tess said. She looked like I felt. A combination of fear and anticipation rippled across her face, like riding some crazy roller coaster upside down. Everything looked different from here. That was the electricity. "I'll get us a drink." We took a few short steps from the top of the stairs to the small bar directly opposite.

To our left were four standing tables and a lounge, all occupied. To the right was a range of boutique lounges, tables and chairs with carefully chosen bohemian décor. Perfectly fitting abstract artworks, woollen tapestries and indoor hanging plants created a quintessential city feel. It was a small space but the atmosphere created by the thirty or forty people there was humming.

"Thanks, there's not one spare seat," Tess commented as I handed her a drink. I scanned the crowd quickly through the slight haze of candle smoke. "We'll just hang at the bar." We walked past the end of the bar and to our left were two bar stools. I sat on the stool closest to the wall facing outwards and Tess stepped between my legs and leaned against the bar.

"Mm. You smell so good. Don't even know what body butter is but I love it. Or maybe it's just you that smells so good," I said. Instantly I felt at ease. I had Tess, that's all that mattered. "You're still the most beautiful girl in the room." We didn't feel the need to force conversations and again it was strange to feel so relaxed in a room full of strangers.

"I think I like this part the most, just you and me talking. Like we used too." I said again as I kissed her shoulder.

"Me too. What did you used to say? Like we're the only two people in the room."

"Something like that." People gave us brief looks, everyone was aware of the other people in the small bar. I guessed that we looked happy, connected. That's what it felt like.

"Do you think this crowd looks a bit older, in their thirties or forties?" Tess asked.

"Maybe. There's definitely more that look our age. But there's all sorts out there." I glanced briefly through the hanging plant to my left. A North American accent caught my ear. A beautiful twenty something Canadian was the centre of attention in a group of six at a table. She had thick, long hair that was dyed bright red. Sierra, we would meet Sierra later.

"Hi there," said a woman in a thick English accent.

"Hi," replied Tess.

"That's yours." A tall, bearded guy with the same distinctive accent handed her a carefully constructed cocktail. "Alright guys, it's rather full in here." Alright meant hello, I think. I loved every part of the English accent and its colloquialisms.

"How are you mate?" My Aussie twang sounded far less cultured.

"Well thanks, not a lot of seats. Mind if we join you?" He replied.

"Sure can."

"I'm Chris, this is Tara?" I reached out to shake his massive hand. He had to be six foot four or five I guessed.

"I'm Ryan, this is Tess. We just got here. It's pretty busy hey?"

"Very. We didn't know what to expect. We've never been to anything like this before. What about you?" Tara asked. She was almost as tall as me, six foot even, with shoulder length blonde hair. She was beautiful with a curved athletic build, just like Tess.

"First time too, we were a bit nervous walking up those stairs." Tess smiled warmly at Tara as she placed her cocktail on the bar. It was our first time at the Bar Mix and I couldn't help but picture the other stairs that we had walked up not so long ago.

"I love your accents. Where are you from?" I asked. I had British ancestry on both sides and there was something familiar, something personal, about the sound.

"Birmingham, the midlands. We've been working in Sydney for two years now."

"Nice. What do you do?" I asked as a guy with tight black leather pants and a large brumby belt buckle leant on the front side of the bar, closest to us. Chris gave him a courteous nod before answering and Brumby shot Tess and Tara another long look before disappearing with two drinks.

"I'm an anaesthesiologist in town. Been doing some long hours lately. Tara's a nurse at the hospital."

"Cool, that's a lot of responsibility. Tess is a nurse too, up the coast." I tried not to sound overly impressed with the doctor and nurse couple. But I definitely was.

"The night shifts don't get any easier, especially with the kids," Tess said.

"Isn't that the truth? They're hideous. How old are your kids then?" Tara brushed Tess' arm as she leaned closer, cocktail in the other hand.

"Ah, Josh is twelve and Leyla's ten, they're with Ryan's family tonight. We just got away for a night in the city. Just the two of us." For someone that didn't like talking to people, Tess looked like she was enjoying herself as much as I was. Just the two of us, our two new friends and a room full of bar mixers.

"So how did you end up in this particular bar?" Chris asked. I guess everyone was wondering the same thing about the other people in the room. What brought people to this place, to this evolution in their relationship?

"How did we end up here? Took a wrong turn I guess. No, a while ago we were talking about something like this, just as a laugh more than anything. But we both found the same website and thought we might check it out." I thought I'd stick to rule two, be honest. "We were at school when we met and we didn't get to, you know, explore."

"Us too, we met at school. We were really young." Tara clearly connected with our story and listened intently.

"So, we ended up here. No expectations. Just thought we'd come for a night out and see what happens. You?"

"Yeah, same here. A friend of mine mentioned the club and I asked Chris what he thought. He was little surprised at first but he came around, didn't you, darl?" She stood on her toes to kiss his bearded cheek.

Tara had asked Chris to come tonight, just as Tess had asked me before we had any idea that this world even existed. I wondered how many other women had those same hidden fantasies. We live in a world where those things are strictly, explicitly forbidden. How many women were unfulfilled, leading lives with secret sexual desires that they dared not acknowledge? I wondered again if Tess was unfulfilled.

How many women wanted to touch another man, or woman? How many wanted to be touched?

So many of my former teammates had amazing, wonderful partners. They were the popular crowd at school. Physically gifted, attractive guys and life came so easy to them in the dog eat dog social order of the schoolyard. The girls loved them and they found meeting girls as easy as a well-directed look or smile. I never felt like I had any of those luxuries. School was tough and I never felt like I really fitted in. Tess was a lighthouse in the fog.

But as time ticked over, the natural, youthful advantages that many of those teammates enjoyed seemed to dissipate. They never had to fight for anything and things like self-discipline or perseverance were never tools that they needed to sharpen. Most had slowly gotten fat, untidy and drank more than I did, although they retained many of their other youthful traits like arrogance and a selfish, entitled attitude to life.

Maybe many of their partners felt unloved, unappreciated or sexually unfulfilled. Those strong women understandably didn't want to sacrifice their family unit, financial security or even their relationships but I suspected that so many of them would have loved the chance to do something wild, something amazing like we had. Especially if it was within the mutually agreed 'rules' and with the support of the person they still loved.

Maybe it could have saved marriages. Or maybe I was completely naïve and it would have eventually destroyed marriages. Maybe Tess and I were an anomaly. But at that moment there seemed to be a room full of happy anomalies.

Broken marriages break children, I knew that from my work and from my childhood. Children come first and that's probably why so many women lived in that unfulfilled space. Someone had to put the children first.

It wasn't necessarily the sexual dissatisfaction that was the biggest part of the equation. It seemed to me that it was the unconditional love, trust and support that so many people lacked. Isn't that what we all want? It was those things that I felt most of all with Tess on those nights, far beyond the primal physical pleasures that could completely cloud every other feeling.

"Yeah, here we are. Same as you, no expectations." Chris seemed to be carefully assessing the whole scene. Even someone as obviously intelligent as him would have found it hard to process everything that accompanied those nights.

"So, Birmingham. Our favourite show at the moment is set in Birmingham," I didn't finish the sentence.

"Not Peaky Blinders," Tara blurted out.

"Yeah, Peaky Blinders, have you seen it?"

"No way. We've seen all the seasons. We love it." You could hear the excitement in her voice. I wasn't sure whether it was the shared appreciation of a television show or the sparks of connection, the electricity.

"How good is Tommy," Tess said. "Those blue eyes."

"Yeah, pure Birmingham. Naughty boys but such a good show. They were a real gang you know, the Peakies." The conversation flowed, all four of us were happy at the end of the bar while the crowd bubbled away only metres behind us.

"This is so much fun, meeting you two and all. I didn't think it'd be like this," Tara said. "It's just like a normal bar really."

"It is a normal bar, just with some slightly abnormal guests," I joked. Chris laughed.

"What's normal hey?" He scanned the guests behind us, "Yeah this is nice."

"We're getting a few looks," Tara said as a well-dressed couple waited for drinks and smiled. I glanced in their direction.

"I think everyone's had a look when they get to the bar," Chris replied. They were a striking couple and it was no surprise to me that people were checking them out. For once, I felt like the cool crowd that I had watched from a distance for so long. Maybe it was just the brown bottle playing with my ego, but it felt good.

"Maybe, they must like what they see," I said before my internal dialogue quickly reprimanded the over confidence.

"So, I wonder what happens after here. If couples meet and hit it off I mean," Tara said and giggled at Tess as the cocktails kicked in. "Do they go to the club?"

"Don't know. They all look like they're hitting it off nicely." Tess nodded at the crowd and she was right, they did look very cosy indeed.

"Later on, people go back to the club if they want, it's only a few blocks away." I was cautious of sounding too knowledgeable about Deepest Desires. "That's what we were told when we got here anyway."

"Are you two going back?" Chris asked. Was he asking us back? Tess looked at me, she must have been thinking the same thing.

"Not sure. Might just see how the night goes." I gave what I thought was an acceptable answer. "You?" He looked carefully at Tara and paused.

"We'll see. No plans at the moment." He looked back at the crowded room.

"I wonder what it'd be like. Bloody exciting. Can you imagine it? Crazy." Tara looked far more excited at the prospect. I could imagine it perfectly.

I noticed the couple that had greeted us when we arrived, still standing at the entry near the bar. He was slightly older than her, and he was clearly not happy. I recognised them from the website, Edward and Alyssa, the owners of the club.

Every one of the people at The Terrace seemed to be having a great time that night, except those two. Throughout the time we'd been there, Alyssa had sat at one of the tall tables near the door with a younger, sleazy looking peroxide blonde guy. He was all muscle and attitude and she was clearly into him.

"He doesn't look happy does he," Tess observed.

"No, they're the owners of the club. She's been talking to Muscles all night." Edward had been doing most of the meet and greet chores as people arrived and he had been mingling with the crowd, often with an eye on Alyssa. "Out of all the people here, they're the only ones that don't look happy."

"Well, they are at work. She obviously likes that guy." Tess had seen the same thing.

"Poor old Eddy doesn't."

"It's after ten already. I wonder where they're off to then." Tara's eyes followed a group of four as they headed down the stair well.

"We've been here for two hours; it feels like ten minutes," Tess replied. I watched the foursome as well.

We were not in a hurry to leave and it seemed that all four of us were happy to enjoy the simple social connection at the bar. Chris and I talked about our footy days while Tess and Tara compared stories about work and family. Again, I was struck by the simple enjoyment of meeting new people.

"This has been really nice, meeting you both. It's not what I expected," Chris seemed to genuinely enjoy our company too.

"There's two more going," Tara giggled into her cocktail. The Canadian accent breezed past us as Tara and Chris excused themselves and walked towards the toilets.

"They're nice," I said to Tess.

"They're lovely. This has been great."

"So?" I smiled. She knew what I was asking. "Are we going back to the club? Looks like people are starting to leave."

"Why not," Tess sipped her drink as she raised her eyebrows at me. She was flying, and I was right beside her.

"We were thinking of heading to the club, it's not far," I said to Tara and Chris when they returned. She turned and gave him a pleading look. I remembered how Tess and I had looked at each other before the first time. Unless both of us were certain, it could have never worked. Tara's eyes were clearly saying yes.

"We might get another drink. Maybe we'll meet you over there." Chris' tone was clearly saying something different to Tara.

Tess and I walked down the stairs, with the embers of the Bar Mix still burning behind us. After warm embraces from our Birmingham friends, we left them to decide for themselves.

"That was so much fun, they were so easy to talk to," Tess said.

"You could see that they enjoyed tonight. I wonder if we'll see them at the club."

"I think Tara would go, but I'm not sure about Chris. An anaesthesiologist, didn't think we'd be talking to a doctor tonight." Tess mirrored what I had thought earlier.

Deepest Desires was only a ten-minute walk, even quicker for paper planes. The Bar Mix had been so relaxed with our new English friends but my thoughts turned to other things as we rounded each street corner.

"Are you nervous?" Tess asked. She shivered for a moment.

"Yes." I answered immediately. "Nervous, excited. I just feel alive. This still feels absolutely crazy, but we're doing it together. It's hard to explain. I feel closer than ever to you. It's like we love each other enough to let the other one do this thing that is just beyond anything I thought we'd ever do. Does that sound dumb? Yeah, I'm nervous."

"It doesn't sound dumb at all, I can't believe we're doing it either. I am nervous, but I feel alive too. Hash tag no regrets?"

"Something like that."

We turned the last corner and the brown terrace building was only fifty metres away. My whole body screamed. The rules bounced around my head. The rules worked here and it seemed, in that moment, that they were relevant across the rest of my life as well. If I could do those things more consistently, then maybe I would be that little bit better. Not just a better husband, father, friend or any of the many other roles I had in life, but a better, more complete person. Forty metres.

"There's a couple at the door."

Be safe, the rational and most important rule was fundamental, here and in life. We had a family and they came first, not our own needs. It would serve me well to remember that when my personal battles resumed.

Be honest, this above all else what was I had learned from our adventures, not just with other people but with myself. If I was to be the person that I knew I could be, then honesty was everything. Developing the ability to admit my faults, recognise my strengths, and allow other people to understand my insecurities would be corner stones to build on.

Be forgiving, this was the rule I loved most when we began this thing. It was the safety net above which we flew and, in my mind, it safeguarded us from any serious falls. Forgiveness wasn't an open invitation to do what we liked, it was an understanding that we would make the best decisions we could at the time, but if we did get things wrong then those mistakes would not be held against us. Tess had been more than forgiving over many years. It was time that I applied it to myself, and my past, and started to chip away at the 'unrelenting standards' that plagued me.

It's a secret: this rule seemed to intuitively work against the whole idea of honesty, but it was an absolute necessity in this case. People would not understand this journey and they had no need to know.

The last rule was 'hash tag no regrets'. I don't know why I put the hash tag in front. It may have been a pointless exercise in trying to sound cool, or maybe it was signalling our intent to the world to live life to the full. Even if it was just at Deepest Desires, that is how we lived. I loved this rule. Make the most of every day, every minute, and squeeze every bit of passion and energy out of life that you could. That attitude was definitely lacking in other parts of my life where sparks barely smouldered under piles of dead wood.

"Hash tag no regrets. That's us," I boasted to Tess. I knew this was the brown bottle speaking, but for once it was not trying to tear me down, it was making sense. That's what it felt like at the time anyway. At that moment, life seemed full of possibilities, as long as I had the strength and courage to chase them. We diverted to the little pub across the road to get drinks and then we were taking those same steps towards the front door.

"Wow, the music is louder, much louder. Look at them." Tess stopped at the entry to the main lounge. The same subtle glances greeted us as we took it in. It was ten thirty.

"This is different, there's way more people. They came to party," I said. The lounges were full and the rest of the room was writhing with people dancing, laughing, and drinking. "Keep walking hey." It was hard not to stare. The energy was far beyond the relaxed, almost formal vibe of the first two nights.

We gave a few courteous hellos and smiles as we weaved through the lounge to the door in the opposite corner.

"Not a lot of clothing in there," Tess said. We both laughed, it was exactly what I was thinking. "See the black one piece? Not much of it." I had definitely seen it. Two more steps down the wide hallway and the dungeon was in full view to our left. We stopped.

"They came to party too." Tess pulled me close as two couples danced, drinks in hand, with one of the women swinging a multi armed whip at a guy on the A frame. He braced himself with one hand while holding a wine glass with the other. Both women were in laced knickers and bra and they squealed with laughter each time the whip landed on flesh.

They looked a little older than us, mid-forties maybe, like many of the crowd in the main lounge. A frame instantly noticed Tess.

"Why don't you get rid of those and join us? There's room." I wasn't sure if he was talking about our bag of drinks or our clothes, but he was talking directly to Tess.

"Ah, thanks." Tess held up the bag of drinks and gently tugged my hand to keep walking.

"That was the guy from the Bar Mix, the one with the black leather pants and brumby belt buckle." I remembered the same look that he gave Tess and Tara at the bar.

"How were his undies? Did you see the little handcuffs at the top when he turned around?" Tess asked. "Gross."

"Yeah, they were a bit out there." The cuffs were only the size of thumbnails but they definitely matched his sleazy demeanour.

"Hello my beach friends, good to see you back in the city." Mav was smiling as always and took the bag of drinks.

"Do you remember everyone who comes in here?"

"Nah, just the ones I like. Locker number ten tonight?" He handed us the key.

"Ten. Looks like a pretty lively crowd in there?" I looked down at the back lounge which was just as busy. The dyed fire engine red hair was instantly recognisable. She stood with a younger Indian guy, chatting with another couple. She looked briefly in our direction then immediately drew her eyes back to the conversation.

"That lot came to party tonight." I nodded towards the main lounge.

"That's the aim isn't it? Did you two go to the Bar Mix? That's always fun too."

"Yeah, down at The Terrace. It was pretty cool." I had loved the whole experience, chatting to Tara and Chris from our spot at the bar.

"You meet anyone?" Mav probed.

"Yes, an English couple. They were really nice. He was some sort of doctor I think." Tess replied. They had made an impression on her too.

"Are they coming back here?"

"Good question, not sure really," I said. Mav gave us a drink each before putting the rest in the fridge. "Might put our stuff in the locker."

We walked through the back lounge, smiling as the couples partied. Most were in lingerie, or underwear of some sort. We put our jackets and phones in the locker and decided to stay dressed for the time being. We headed towards the main lounge where the music was loudest.

"They sound like they're in full swing in there, get it?" Tess was tipsy and laughed at her own joke.

"Yep, you're a funny girl. Very special really." As we walked through the door there was one seat on the end of the lounge to our right. Tess sat and I stood sipping my beer, taking in the whole crazy scene.

"Well, aren't you beautiful," said the man sitting next to Tess. "Must be my lucky night sitting next to you." His seated position accentuated the fat around his stomach and carpet thick hair on his chest. He raised his glass to clink with Tess'.

"Must be." Tess reluctantly met his glass with hers.

"Don't listen to him. I'm Candy, this is Ted." She raised her bottle as well to touch Tess'. "I saw you both at the mix, looked like fun." They looked like mid-forties and Candy wore floral patterned bra and knickers.

"Yeah, it was good. I'm Tess, this is Ryan."

"Hi. Loud in here." I said. I had stopped swaying to the music and watched Ted. He had eyes only for Tess.

"Yes, to loud for me. Is this your first time here?" He asked Tess.

"We've been before, we came down from the coast for a weekend. What about you?" Tess slid slightly closer to me.

"Well, I'm glad you asked. We've been here a few times, we're from out west. We run our own swingers club, of sorts, from our house. We have some bloody good nights out there." Ted looked in his element.

"We don't advertise it or anything, but word of mouth gets around in the country you know. Quite a few of the people here tonight are from out our way," Candy continued, looking equally proud of their country club. Brumby in the dungeon definitely looked like one of theirs.

"That's cool. I bet it's a bit different being in the city," I said.

"No, no. The people might be different, but the rest is the same," Ted preached. If that was the case, then I preferred the city.

"I might go to the loo," Tess interrupted before Ted could continue. "Can you come and hold my cruiser Ry? Back soon."

"We'll see you soon," Ted replied, gulping his red wine.

"Get me out of there," Tess laughed after we left.

"What, don't you want to hear about the outback swinger's scene, I reckon he was going to tell you all about it." Brumby cracked the whip as we walked past the dungeon.

"I think he wanted to show me." She was still laughing. "Not into it at all."

I was conscious that we were one of the few couples left with clothes on. Most must have arrived here from the Mix and immediately disrobed, or possibly arrived hours ago when it opened. I stood outside the toilet and watched, as discreetly as possible, the raw energy rippling in every conversation, every movement. Half-naked strangers danced together and looked at each other with lustful eyes.

My eyes must have been no different, as they scanned every part of the tanned body closest to me. I studied the contours of her legs and the muscles in her calves, accentuated by the platform shoes. My gaze travelled upward to the tight hot pants that moved perfectly with the music. The matching bra contrasted against her straight black hair, swaying as she danced.

"Having fun?" Tess said as she opened the toilet door and I immediately felt ashamed. "I like the white." She kissed me as she grabbed her drink.

"Do you think it's wrong to look at other women, or other men?" I asked without thinking about the question.

"Mm, I guess it depends in what context. In this place, maybe not, but most of the time yes. We don't want guys just perving, like they do. If a girl likes a guy, then she'll let him know. Then he can look all he wants."

"But how does he know, most of the time we have no idea. Biology sucks. Men are programmed to look, to want. But when they act on that they fuck it up most of the time."

"Yes, they do, don't they?" Tess was feeding out the rope.

"Don't get me wrong, I'm not defending any of the shit we put you through. I'm just saying its hard being a guy sometimes, reading the signals and working it all out. No bloke wants to hurt anyone, we're just wired differently."

"There are plenty of assholes out there who care about no one except themselves and their dicks. Wiring has nothing to do with it. Just use your brain and show a bit of respect."

"So how about we get our gear off?" I teased.

"I guess it's hard when you haven't got much of a brain to use." She tilted her head forward as she danced provocatively, ever closer. "Let's go."

Chapter 15
When the Knives Rattle in the Drawer

'Can we talk? I love you.' I sat in my car and reread the text before sending it. I had tried calling her but Tess didn't pick up. I should have been at work that day, but instead I had sat at the beach in front of the caravan park, tearing myself up inside. I imagined the worst possible future, one without my family. It was unbearable.

I had already decided to drive home when Tess' text appeared.

'We need to talk.'

I closed the front door quietly and turned into our bedroom. My knotted stomach growled, I couldn't stomach breakfast. Tess wasn't there.

"Hi Dad, how's Tim?" Josh asked as I walked into the kitchen. "You're so lucky getting Monday off. School sucked."

"So lucky. Um, Tim's good." She hadn't told them. "Where's Mum?"

"She's out the back, I think. Can I learn to ride a dirt bike? Then Jet and me can come next time."

"What?"

"We can come riding with you and Tim. Next time."

"Maybe mate." I was already opening the sliding door to the back yard. Tess was hanging out clothes on the line. I did it most of the time. She hated that job.

"Hi," was all I could muster. I felt like throwing myself at her feet and apologising, but she had heard those apologies a thousand times. I wanted to tell her that I would change, that things would be better. But I didn't know if I could or if they would be. She wouldn't have believed me anyway.

"I love you." It was all I had at that moment but it sounded dismally inadequate.

Tess kept pegging out the clothes. She seemed to be choosing her words carefully.

"You love your mates and your drinking and all the other shit you do. You don't love us. We come second every time." She still hadn't looked at me. "I didn't tell Josh or Leyla. They don't need to know yet."

Didn't need to know what? I wondered whether Tess was talking about the weekend or the future.

"Where were you?" Tess asked as she finally turned and looked at me.

"Grady's Beach, at the caravan park. I slept in the car."

"I thought you'd go to Mummy's house. Or you could have got on it at Tim's place. You'd love that."

"It's been hell Tess. I didn't want to be near anyone else, or talk to anyone. I didn't want to have to explain to anyone. I don't even know…"

"It's pretty simple, Ryan. You really don't know?" Her eyes burned red.

"I'm just trying to do the best I can every day. I never meant to hurt you. I'm just trying to be the best husband and father I can be."

"Well, your best isn't good enough." She walked inside as I sat on the patio chair. Just, just, just. That word was meant to explain my actions, but really, I was only trying to excuse them. She didn't want to hear about me 'just' doing my best. She wanted me to take responsibility for what I did and to change. The worst part was that I didn't know if I could change.

I began to cry. Again, I felt completely alone.

Two agonising weeks went by and I crept into the spare room each night to lie in a sea of regret.

"How do you feel about it Tess?" Bill turned his attention from me.

"I don't mind that he does it sometimes, but it's just happening more and more. The lying is what I hate most." She paused. I could only listen rather than do what I normally did; say anything to fill the silence. Bill was a great role model and again I was learning so much about the value of truly listening to Tess. But over time, I also learned the value in feeling like I had been listened too as well. I'm sure Tess felt the same. If someone really listened to you, then there was at least a chance that they would understand.

"When I was young, Dad chased us out of the house with a knife from the kitchen drawer. We had nowhere else to go so we had to go back and sleep there that night. I didn't sleep. He was passed out on the lounge. It happened more than once."

"That must have been terrifying for a child," Bill sympathised.

"Oh Tess. I didn't know." I wanted to hold her, to make another thousand promises and to make everything better. But I couldn't.

"Every time Ryan drinks and he opens up the cutlery drawer, the knives rattle. I can't help it." Her tears were deathly silent. "The sound of those knives, it's like all that hurt from so along ago is cutting me all over again."

"Have you told Ryan how you feel? About what sort of memories the drinking brings up?" Bill asked.

"Kind of. It's mostly when we argue. I'm not that good at communicating sometimes. Anyway, he should know. I shouldn't have to tell him."

"But maybe it would help if you did tell him, it would help if you told him how you feel. Do you think you could try that?"

"Yeah, I don't know how good I'll do but I can try."

Our session with Bill was one of fi that we did together after that weekend. The problems we had at the time seemed to take a back seat to all the things we had both gone through so many years ago. It was the stereotypical story of sort your childhood shit out before you even start to address all the problems that had ensued as an adult. The sessions were emotionally exhausting.

One of the hardest, but most helpful, parts of sitting in that room with Bill and Tess was that he told me what I needed to hear, not what I wanted to hear. I walked in there believing that the problems we had, the rift between Tess and some of my family and the gut-wrenching arguments were more Tess's fault than mine. I left thinking far more about my own actions, my responsibilities as a father and a husband rather than focusing on blame shifting or feeling sorry for myself.

"You always seem to put your role as a father as your greatest priority Ryan. Do you think that's the right thing to do?" I thought Bill's question was a strange one.

"Yes, doesn't any parent put their children above everything else?"

"Most people might but the most important relationship, the most important person in your life Ryan is Tess. Without that relationship working, everything else suffers." No one had ever said that to me before. I always thought the kids came first and that's how it should be.

"Long before children, it was just the two of you. Think about the time and energy you put into your relationship when you first started going out. That's what you should still be doing. Sure, many things have changed but you get out what you put in and Tess should be your priority."

"It seems like a long time ago."

"A happy, supportive, loving marriage is the best thing you can do for your kids. They understand the tension and the tone of an unhappy household. That impacts on them. Your wife comes first, not anyone else."

"I know they see what's going on, but it's easy to think that they're kids, they don't really understand. Tess is the most important person in the world to me, even if I don't always show it."

"Do you tell her that?" Bill asked. I shook my head. "Josh and Leyla are what, ten and twelve. Before you know it, they'll be telling you that they're moving out. Eventually they'll have families of their own. Then it will be just you and Tess like it was twelve years ago."

Tess took my hand; it was my turn to cry silently. She squeezed tight. It was the first time we had touched in weeks. I missed her so much. I knew that she was listening, really listening to me. Listening to all of the things I had been through and how it had affected me. I hoped that she knew I was listening too. It was such a simple, powerful, yet unappreciated thing to do.

They were some of the hardest hours I had ever done, just talking in that room. But I am not sure that Tess and I would have survived if we hadn't sat there and been totally honest about who we were and how we felt. Those hours made me grow as a husband, a father and a man.

For weeks, I devoted myself to showing that growth, not telling. Tess had said many times that my words were meaningless. The same excuse wrapped apologies were not good enough anymore. I needed to show with actions that I was listening, that I was a better man.

The following weekend I took Bill's advice. We both had sickies on the Friday while the kids went to school and we spent time together. After a morning run, we spent hours on the beach just talking. Listening. Over lunch we reminisced about our early days together and the places we would visit when we got old. It was comforting beyond words to think of happily growing old together.

On the Saturday morning, I made her breakfast in bed. It was a pretty cliché offering and it didn't excuse anything, but it was warmly received and at least Tess knew I was trying. We spent the day at the zoo with Josh and Leyla. They revelled in the calm that we had begun to reclaim, free from the tension and the silence of the last few weeks. They looked happy that we looked happy. Bill's words echoed in my thoughts. The most important relationship was the one with Tess and when it broke down, every other one suffered.

"The kids had fun today. It was nice," Tess said, leaning against the kitchen bench.

"Yeah, who ever thought we'd hold a koala? She was heavy."

"I know you're trying Ryan. I do appreciate it, but I'm not just going to forget everything."

"I don't expect you too. I just want us to be happy. That's all."

"Yeah." I was standing opposite her and she took a few short steps and wrapped her arms around my waste. I locked my arms around her shoulders and held her tight. I don't know how long we stood there but we didn't speak at all. We'd said enough during the arguments and the sessions with Bill.

"Hello there," I said as Leyla walked into the kitchen. I reached out an arm and she instinctively jumped into our embrace. Josh was directly behind her and stretched his arms as widely as he could to bind the four of us together.

"This is all I need," I whispered to Tess.

"Me too," she replied. I slept well that night for the first time in weeks. Even better, I had finally been allowed back into my own bed.

The morning sun found a small gap in the curtains, just enough to lighten the room. She was only half-awake but she had slept topless through the night, something she didn't normally do. I watched her close her eyes as quickly as she had opened them. She had never slept well, same as me. I wondered if good sleepers ever really knew how lucky they were. Every other part of life seemed to be affected when I was tired. I was tired a lot.

I gently pulled the sheet down to see her entire torso. Her eyes remained closed but I knew she was awake. I stared at her naked breasts, perfectly curved. Her stomach was no longer washboard flat like it was for so long. Tess hated her stomach more than any other body part I think, but to me it was perfect. That's where our babies had come from. The small cushion of body fat was a story in itself. Twenty months of creating life, the two most important lives in my world, except for Tess.

"Are you awake?" I whispered. She smiled ever so slightly.

"Maybe."

"How did you sleep?" It was my first question most mornings.

"Okay."

I ran my fingertips softly up and down her arm, between her shoulder and elbow, then down to her stomach.

"I love this bit." I said those words to her often.

"You love all the bits."

"So, you're awake?"

"I'm cold."

"Maybe I could warm you up." I was always so obvious, but at least I phrased the same question differently, just for fun. My hand moved further down to her hip, then around to her bum, which I grabbed forcefully, and pulled her closer to me. She could feel me hard against her.

"Hello." She opened her eyes. "You're naughty." She paused. "I need to go to the loo first." I knew exactly what those words meant. I watched her every step around the bed to the ensuite. I peeled my boxers off and, just for a moment, felt myself under the covers. On the way back, she quietly locked the door.

Tess slowly dropped her panties to the floor and stood naked for a moment. I said nothing. The light caught the edges of her body and outlined every curve. It had been too long since I touched her and I wanted her so badly it almost hurt. Emotionally, and physically, I had missed her so much.

I remembered the first time I ever saw her naked, almost naked, all those years ago. She had insisted on keeping her bra on. She climbed in my single bed beside me and our whole bodies touched. She was so soft and warm, so beautiful. I could have exploded the second she touched me and it was magical to feel that energy again.

Time stood still, again, as we held each other and kissed. Slow, passionate kisses that I had so longed for.

I touched every inch of her thighs and softly mouthed her nipples, running my tongue over them. I traced a single forefinger over her pelvis and down her stomach to the soft perfection between her legs. I touched her ever so gently, placing careful kisses on her breasts, then pressed harder on that exact part of her.

I started slowly, in small pressured circles, in time with my tongue. Her head tilted back slightly as her body pushed against my touch. I pressed harder, faster and her heavy breathing grew into a rhythmic moan. When I felt her whole body stiffen, I raised myself up on both knees, positioned between her legs. I pushed them apart.

I looked down at every part of her before she grabbed my arms and pulled me onto her. Her hand guided me, she was far better at it than I was. I pushed slowly, deeply inside her. I loved to watch the subtle expressions on her face in those moments. Her eyes were closed hard and her mouth opened ever so slightly.

I moved slowly, almost to the point of withdrawing, and then pushed deep again. Each time was slightly harder, faster. I stopped to kiss her neck.

"Don't stop," Tess whispered. I started slowly again, mouthing her nipples. Hungry, I could taste the salt on her skin. She had a divine taste, every part of her.

I resumed the position on my knees, with all of Tess in front of me. I lay down on the bed next to her and lifted her leg, turning her onto her side, facing away from me. Our feet touched first as our whole bodies spooned and I pushed my body against her. I caressed her slowly, running my fingertips over her body, biting her neck, before I reached between her legs and started again. Harder, faster.

She reached behind and grabbed me firmly, stroking up and down. She parted her legs enough to again guide me inside her then brought her hand back to place it on top of mine, almost touching herself as they moved together.

"Harder." Tess said. This time I thrust as hard as I could in unison with our hands. Her hair rubbed against my face and I savoured the sweet smell. Tess pushed back against me and dug her nails into my arm. I had longed for this moment so completely, one I thought might never happen again.

She was close. I stopped again and withdrew. With one finger, I pushed down on her hip to lay her on her back.

"Open your legs," I demanded in a whisper. My lips followed the same path as my hand had done earlier. I kissed her breasts and stomach softly, slowly. I moved down to the inside of her thighs, biting softly, slowly.

My lips barely touched her skin until my tongue found that exact spot. I knew it well and I knew what Tess liked. She took a huge breath in and breathed hard. The rhythm was everything. Then gradually my tongue pressed harder as I moved just the tip onto that spot. Again, her whole body arched, tensed. She grabbed my wrists, which were resting on her hips, and dug her nails in forcefully. She let out a long audible breath and I knew she was in that place.

Eventually I felt her body relax and she pulled me up until we were eye to eye. I gently pushed inside her and felt the wetness around me. This time it was for me and I lingered at the end of each thrust. I kissed her as my soul sang in the place that it loved most in the world.

"I am again," Tess said in a breathless whisper. Of every sensual touch, the kissing was what I loved the most. Tess kissed me passionately, completely and my body let go.

"I am," I mumbled. All rhythm and design were lost in those fifteen seconds as my body took over and I savoured the physical ecstasy that completely filled me. It was a physical, emotional explosion of pleasure that I could only feel with the person I loved most in the world.

I collapsed directly on top of her. There was nothing and no one else in the world at that moment except me and Tess. My full body weight was on her, I could not move. Those were the true moments of electricity, ones that nothing else could come close too.

"I love you. More than anything in the world," I said. I felt like crying, but I did not let myself.

"I love you too," Tess replied. We lay for a while in silence.

"Am I squashing you?" I didn't want to move.

"A little bit."

I fell beside her, physically spent but emotionally jubilant after long weeks feeling so far away from Tess. They were long weeks where I had never felt more alone. Both of us panted as I placed a lingering palm on her hip. I still needed to touch her.

"I feel like I could sleep for days. I haven't slept much lately," I said after minutes of silence.

"Same. I missed you. You make me so mad." Tess rolled onto her side to look at me. I said nothing, I didn't want to ruin the moment.

"It feels like forever since I touched you. I was about to explode." I turned onto my side as well to look her in the eye.

"You should have taken care of it yourself, I thought you were good at that," she teased.

"Nope, I was waiting for you," I replied.

"I did."

"You did what?" She had my attention.

"I took care of it myself."

"Did you now? Was it with your friend in the drawer?"

"Maybe. I wasn't waiting for you." Tess was enjoying this. So was I.

"I thought that thing was just for us to play with."

"You thought wrong," Tess boasted.

"A few nights ago, I had to change my boxers at three."

"Good for you."

"I had the first wet dream that I've had for ages. You and I were doing some wild stuff. I used to have them all the time." I left out most of the details. Tess was there, next to me in the club, but there were other people in the bed. Lots of them.

"I can imagine."

"I guess girls have to take care of it themselves sometimes, you can't have wet dreams."

"Yes we can. I have," Tess said.

"No way." I had no idea. "Nah, that's not a thing. Is it?" I thought she was joking.

"It is. Guys aren't the only ones that have them."

"Really? How could I not know that? I've never heard of it in my life."

"You've heard of it now," Tess said proudly. I was intrigued.

"So, what happens? Do you remember the whole thing?"

"Sort of. Do you remember all of it?" she replied.

"Not really. Some of it I do. And the clean up afterwards. What do you dream about?" I had so many questions. Who did she dream about?

"I don't know, they were a while ago. I hardly remembered when they happened."

"I wish I could remember all of them," I thought aloud.

"That was hard talking to Bill about that stuff you know." Tess said. It was bewildering how the direction, the tone of a conversation could change so quickly with Tess. "I can't forget what happened." She got up, naked, and headed into the ensuite.

"I don't expect you too." I was immediately on guard.

"I don't want you to think that it's all just forgotten and everything is okay."

"No," was all I could say. I wondered why she wanted to discuss this now. Tess dressed quickly and tied her hair back in a tight bun.

"Breakfast time I think." As quickly as the topic appeared, the conversation ended and Tess left the bedroom.

That night we sat eating pizza with the kids, with the ocean sprawling behind the maze of swings they had been playing on. I had made a point of volunteering to drive. The simple commitment was a way to bypass the normal Saturday night urge to have a beer. Until dusk, it was a battle. But it got easier after that.

"It's nice just watching the kids play. They're getting big so fast," Tess said.

"We're going to have a teenager in the house soon. Can't believe it. It seems crazy that we were only five years older than Josh when we met."

"We were just kids really. But it worked out okay." Tess brushed the pizza and garlic breadcrumbs off the blanket.

"Amy's pregnant." I spoke quietly so as not to be heard by the family sitting nearest us, enjoying the silence.

"No? How old is she?"

"Yeah, sixteen. She's hardly going to school. She can't stay at the centre forever. It's a crisis refuge, not a long-term option."

"Is she still cutting?"

"Yeah. It's devastating, the hurt that she's carrying."

"Is there a boyfriend?" Tess asked.

"No, just some guy Amy met at a party. He's long gone. Probably doesn't even know. She's started to talk at least. Hasn't had a home for two years. I told you what her step dad did?"

"Bastard. I don't know how anyone does that to child."

"She's been with friends since then, until a month ago. Remember when I went to the hospital?" Amy was lucky to still be here, although I know she wouldn't consider any part of her life as lucky. "Marg said that she still has to sleep with the light on at the centre. Every night."

"Is she still using?" Tess rubbed my arm.

"We spoke to the police yesterday. Some days it feels like I just can't help her."

"Are you okay?" Tess asked, "Ry?" I picked at the few remaining crumbs on the blanket.

"Nuh."

"You're doing all you can. There's nothing more you can do." Tess knew how these kids and their hurt lived inside me.

"It's not enough."

"What did Bill say, about letting go? You can't fix every one of them."

"I know." Bill and I had spoken at length about my emotional investment in each one of those kids. I couldn't help them all and even if I could, that wouldn't 'fix' me. But it didn't stop me trying.

"Dad, the footy," called Josh, running from the swings. I jumped up with the ball in my hands and bombed it for him to catch. Leyla and Tess joined in. The park lights took over the lasts slivers of sunlight as we played.

"This is all I need." I said. I threw my arm over Tess' shoulder as the four of us headed back to finish the remaining pizza. "Maybe Amy doesn't need me to do anything except listen and support." She didn't need to be 'fixed' and neither did I.

"Sometimes that's all you can do."

"We go back to the hospital on Tuesday."

Chapter 16
Three

We opened the locker and began to undress. I was deliberate and folded my clothes carefully, lining up every crease, while Tess shoved hers in without looking.

"Ahh, just when I think the nerves have gone." She stood looking at herself in the mirror as she had done during the first two visits.

"You look stunning, I love the red." Tess shone in a red lace bralette lingerie set. The see-through side sections in her panties showed the beautiful curves of her hips.

"I should have gotten a one-piece." She continued to look judgementally at the mirror.

"You're so hard on yourself. You look incredible."

"I'm going to get back to the gym."

"Go for it if you want, but go easy on yourself. You look great, you're about the only person who doesn't see that." I hoped that she knew that it was the honest truth.

"You don't look so bad yourself." She turned and pulled me close. She was standing on the platform in front of the mirror and as I wrapped my arms around her, my cheeks rested softly against her breasts.

"This is crazy shit, are you ready?" I asked. I could feel her heart beating madly, just like mine. She lifted my head to kiss me.

"I think so, I love you?" This was still new to us and there were moments where the gravity of what we were doing edged into the dream we were living. Tess stepped down from the platform, took my hand as always, and we were walking.

"Did you ever think we would do anything like this?" Tess asked as we stepped out of the locker room.

"T, three months ago I didn't know this world existed. Smacking each other with a paddle would have sounded wild back then but this, the things we did. Never in my wildest dreams would I have thought that we'd be doing anything like this." We walked through the back lounge as the room bubbled with laughter and small talk.

"Front room? There's no seats here."

"Beer first though," I replied as we walked up the steps to the hallway bar.

"Some things never change," Tess laughed. It was nice to find slivers of normality on this strange planet.

"Hi you guys. I love the lace, it looks beautiful."

"Sure does," I agreed.

"Hi Sara. Thanks. It's busy tonight." Tess flattened the lace on her sides.

"Yeah, it always is on the Bar Mix nights. People get to go out first and make some friends maybe, then come back to the club. What locker are you?" Sara had her hair up in piggy tails and jet-black lipstick.

"Ten, on the middle shelf. This must be an interesting place to work." I asked.

"You could say that. I'm at uni so the weekend shifts work well and I get paid okay." I felt better after the cold bottle touched my hand.

"What course are you doing?"

"Psychology, final year so not long to go. My boyfriend and I will probably move out of the city after that. Too expensive."

"What does he think about you working here?" Tess leaned on the counter.

"He's fine. Besides getting woken up at four when I get home. We'll probably come together some time. Haven't yet though."

"You must see some pretty wild stuff in here?" asked Tess.

"Sometimes, but most people are pretty much the same. They're not that out there. Couples are just looking to meet people and have fun. Most of the time they just drink and talk, like any other bar."

"That's what we did."

"But I think everyone wants the chance to explore, sexually I mean. There're not many places where that happens. But they can do it here." The club must have been a kind of fish tank of human behaviour for a psychology student. We collected our drinks and kept walking.

"The concrete feels weird. The floor is cold," I said.

"Not as weird as walking around like this." Tess looked down. "Or as weird as that." The paddle cracked on flesh in the dungeon. Six people stood in the small room, all enjoying the hidden pleasures that pain could provide.

"Yeah, barefoot isn't really that weird. You ready?"

"Ready," She dipped her head at me. "Are you?" We walked quietly into the main lounge and took the first seats to our right.

"It's loud. Fits the crowd. Handcuffs." I nodded at the guy working the stripper pole.

"He's loving that. What's he doing?" There were twelve or so couples in the room seated at the lounge or dancing, mostly from the Bar Mix. They seemed to be enjoying the rather awkward, albeit confident performance.

"What is he doing?" The dance turned into a strip tease as Handcuffs took down his underwear. Naked, he danced around the pole before jumping and gripping it with two hands and the soles of both feet, his knees pointing outwards. He pulled himself higher up the pole as everything that the missing underwear had covered was on display.

"No, that is so wrong. I can't look," Tess laughed. The group cheered but surely must have found it as uncomfortable as Tess and I did.

"You're a fucken asshole, don't talk to me." I heard the faint admonishment from a woman standing on our left, at the foot of the stairs leading up to the second storey. The guy leaned in to continue talking more discreetly. She wasn't happy and stood defiantly, arms folded, in a black leather bodysuit that barely covered more than the bare essentials.

"I wonder if she's uncomfortable in those stilettos," Tess asked.

"She's not happy." Both of us were trying not to look. The couple next to us shuffled past on their way out to the back rooms leaving two spare seats.

"We haven't seen anyone upset in here yet. It must happen sometimes." Tess ran her hand up the inside of my leg.

"Yeah, cracks into canyons. Ted's enjoying himself. I might have to get a gold chain like that." My attention turned to the bristling crowd in front of us.

"Hi you guys. Mind if we sit?" came the accented request from the door on our left. I turned to see the bright red hair that I had first seen at the Bar Mix. I shuffled over instantly, with Tess following. She sat next to Tess, with her boyfriend perched on the end of the lounge.

"Sure, we were just watching the show." Tess smiled.

"I'm Sierra, this is Darsh," she said as they sat. "Oh, that's some show. You can see, ah," she laughed. "I love your demi." She touched the side of Tess's silk bra.

"I'm Tess. Yeah, he's having fun." Tess courteously shook their hands as they took in the altogether disturbing scene of the naked pole dancer.

"Hi, I'm Ryan. He needs to put it away. I don't know where to look." I was still finding the view rather off putting and turned my attention to Sierra and Darsh. Tess had done the same.

Sierra's dyed red hair cascaded down her shoulders to her low-cut bra line. She wore a red, balconette bra and black knickers. She was the first woman I had seen there with different coloured lingerie. I wondered if she was breaking some unknown rule. Her orange, glittered fingernails and toenails should have clashed with her hair, but they didn't. Darsh was the only one in the room still fully dressed.

"So, have you guys been here before?" Sierra asked.

"Ah, second time." Why did I lie? "First time at the Bar Mix though. That was fun," I replied.

"I saw you there, at the bar. The English couple seemed nice." I wondered how she knew they were English.

"Yeah, really nice, it was something different," Tess said.

"Did they come back?"

"They were thinking about it. I don't think so."

"They still might," I tried not to sound too hopeful. Darsh quietly stood and headed towards the back of the club. "Have you been here before?"

"First time. It's wild."

"Where are you from? I love your accent" Tess asked.

"Canada, Kelowna. I've been here for a few years now. Sydney's the best."

"Sydney's okay. Do you miss home?" Tess continued as she turned slightly to face Sierra.

"I miss family, yeah, but not home. I hate the cold, which is all you get in Kelowna. I love the beach; we go up the coast all the time."

"Me too, the cold and the beach. We're from the central coast, we just came down for the night. I could lie in the sun all day. Do you go up with Darsh?" Tess replied.

"Oh no. He's just a friend."

"It's beautiful up there." Tess teased strands of hair and gently swayed her shoulders to the music as she sipped her drink. "What's Canada like?"

"Well, it's beautiful too," she began.

They were flying. I looked around the room briefly and took a moment to take in the scene. Everyone had dressed down by now. Handcuffs had his pants back on thank goodness and was talking, with his partner, to Ted and Candy near the entrance door. Ted projected a sense of his own superiority with sweeping hand gestures in front of his gut. Another dozen or so people stood chatting as they danced and four couples filled the huge L shaped lounge beside us.

The lights were dimmed but I could see everyone clearly as each couple gauged connections and sent their own messages. Not only were they trying to measure the interest of another couple, they also had to work out whether their own partner was keen. Two people is complex, four is a maze and the room was a sexual labyrinth. Strangely enough, people seemed to be finding each other. There were subtle touches of arms, flicks of hair and burning eyes that were screaming yes.

Tess and I never settled on a safe word or anything that would signal a clear 'no' regarding another couple or situation. We didn't have to. One look could instantly signal a clear, unequivocal no. As soon as Ted opened his mouth, there was no ambiguity whatsoever on Tess's face.

As I looked around the room, I was seeing the same none verbal signals, except they were yes'. Everywhere.

"I'm going to the loo," I told Tess.

"Okay." She continued talking to Sierra. "I asked Ryan first." She didn't miss a beat of the conversation as I left. It was the first time that night that Tess was not by my side. It felt strange being alone. Couples stayed together without exception and I walked directly to the toilets near the back lounge. Darsh was at a standing table with an attractive Asian girl, still looking a little out of place with his clothes on. How strange this place could be.

I walked back into the main lounge with two new drinks.

"For you. You having fun?" I asked Tess.

"Just watching the dancing." Tess nodded at the woman dancing at the pole, "not as good as you but you know."

"One time. I'll never live it down."

"Tess has been telling me how good you were Ryan."

"Don't think so."

"I think we need to see your moves," Sierra said.

"I got no moves. No one wants to see me dance." Conversations continued around the room but eyes were on the thirty something brunette hugging the pole against her breast, pushing her hips from side to side. It was sensual, beautiful. She reached for her drink and sat on the lap of a tanned, solidly built guy on the end of the lounge.

"Ryan's turn," Sierra yelled above the music. The group instantly cheered and called my name. Tess looked at me and laughed. To my great surprise I stood without thinking, which encouraged the room all the more.

"Fuck it. I'll give it a go." I put down my beer.

"Go you," Tess placed her drink on the floor, clapping with Sierra. If I was going on this whole crazy journey, then I was going to enjoy every moment. Why not dance? I had grown up in a culture where guys didn't dance, especially footy players. But I loved to move and it was for me, not for them.

One of the great things about getting older was caring less about what other people thought. It was a truly liberating feeling, escaping the pressure of opinion, and I savoured the sense of adventure that filled the room. But most of all, it was the electricity that I loved. Sierra wriggled closer to Tess. Their shoulders touched.

I grabbed the pole with two hands and threw my head back dramatically. The cheers bellowed around the room. This was a receptive crowd. I strutted around the pole, always gripping it with at least one hand, and I closed my eyes for a moment. The music was in control and I really did dance like no one was watching.

It was nothing more than a short cameo but I think people were appreciative of anyone getting up and having fun. It contributed to the party atmosphere of the night and gave the room a sense of communal enjoyment. This place was all about community, a very special kind.

"That's it, I'm no dancer. Your turn now." I looked expectantly at Sierra. "If you call someone out then you've gotta back it up."

"No, no. I'm happy here." She did look happy next to Tess.

"I think he's right. Your turn," Tess said. Sierra laughed and stood as she sipped her drink. The song finished and a short, rare window of silence surfaced. Sierra grinned at Tess and everyone cheered again as she stepped into the centre of the room. The moody drums of Radioactive filled the silence. Sierra grabbed the pole with one hand low in front of her waist and one as high as she could reach. She pulled her pelvis to the pole and arched back so her long red hair fell away from her shoulders. The fan near the stairs blew waves through her hair and conversations fell away.

"Shit," Tess said. Sierra's legs spread as she lowered herself until her backside almost touched the floor, along with her hair. "Wow." She stood back up as the song kicked in and her whole body began to move. With one hand still high on the pole, she ran her fingertips down her neck and breast then flattened it onto her stomach before sitting it on her hip.

Tess squeezed my knee and grabbed her drink, dancing all the time on her seat. I carefully positioned my arm across my crutch. I had been able to control myself throughout all of the time we had spent downstairs. But not now.

"Now that is how it's done," Handcuffs yelled. The hypnotising, moody tones of the song and the way her body moved consumed every sense, every thought.

"She's amazing. She…" Tess, mumbled. It wasn't only me that felt it. Sierra let go of the pole and spread both hands through her hair and messed it over her face as she continued to sway her hips. She slowly turned around to lean her back against the pole. Sierra grabbed the pole with both hands behind her as she faced Tess and leaned forward, squeezing her shoulders to make a perfect cleavage.

"Yeah Sierra, go girl." Tess clapped as she cheered. Sierra's eyes stayed on Tess, then flickered to me before she stood back up and swung around the pole.

"She's dancing for you." Tess didn't reply. The end of the song prompted Sierra to sit back down, next to Tess. Eyes followed her.

"Wow, that was pretty cool," Tess gave a brief applause.

"Why, thank you. I do like to dance but I can't say I have ever danced at a pole before. I can see why you like it, Ryan."

"I was definitely coerced."

"You loved it." Tess intervened.

"Maybe." All three of us sipped our drinks as the relentless chat of the room continued on. Two couples that I had seen at the Bar Mix entered from the doorway to our left and continued straight up the stairway.

"I wonder what they're doing," asked Sierra with raised eyebrows.

"Play time," laughed Tess. I followed the footsteps of the four playmates until they disappeared into the second storey. Tess' hand touched my knee and I looked down. Sierra and Tess were holding hands.

"Shit," I whispered as I stared for a moment. It was discreet, between their thighs, holding tight. I placed my arm across my lap for the second time. "Go you." Tess didn't hear but turned to see me looking at their hands.

"Are you okay?" She asked, meaning 'is this okay'.

"Yeah, I'm fine. How are you?"

"I'm good."

"You got a friend?"

"I've got two friends."

"Nice. Three altogether?"

"You've always been good with numbers." Tess laughed.

"So maybe it's Tess' turn to dance?" Sierra suggested

"Don't think so. I'm happy just to watch," Tess replied. The three of us quickly became lost in our own corner of conversation, and the other voices in the room faded away. The energy from those two hands touching was truly primal and my mind ran wild with the thoughts of what was to come. None of us were rushing in to ask the question that all three of us were thinking. Like great sex, there was no need to rush and the foreplay was every bit as good.

"This is so much fun. What do you feel like doing now?" Sierra asked. I hoped.

"What do you feel like doing? Is Darsh okay?" Tess replied. Every word dripped with suggestion.

"He's fine. We sort of do our own thing. We could go upstairs if you wanted too." Sierra finally asked and the words exploded in my head.

"Yeah, why not?" Tess said in her understated manner. My mind was doing cartwheels. I fought the urge to sprint up the stairs, three at a time. Three emptyish drinks were placed on the small coffee table near us. Then we were walking up the stairs. Those magical stairs, our own kind of wardrobe portal into a completely different world. A world where wild things happened, amazing things.

I watched the beautiful curves of the two figures in front of me taking each step, a soul mate and a stranger. I had almost played out the whole encounter in my head on the lounge but once my feet hit the stairs everything cleared. Everything except desire.

"That one's full," Sierra stopped at the door of the first bedroom to the left at the top of the stairs.

"What if there's no rooms?" I asked rhetorically. We walked only a few steps up the hallway to see the next bedroom empty.

"It's your lucky night," Tess said.

"Our lucky night. This is wild." I replied. It was a dream inside a dream, our own deepest desires.

The two girls followed me in and Sierra locked the door behind her. It was the only bedroom in the place with a lock. I remembered the first night's tour when Sarah had mentioned that detail. I laid on the bed, propped up by elbows and looked at the girls expectantly.

"Sheet first," ordered Sierra. She walked around the side of the bed and grabbed a fitted sheet from a corner table.

"Good idea." I was surprised by her practicality and how she knew they were there. I had not even noticed them during our previous visits. The three of us neatly tucked in the sheet.

"Now you can get on," Sierra offered. She pushed her hair behind her back with both hands and reached to unclip her bra. Tess did the same.

Sierra pushed her shoulders together again as her bra slipped to the floor. She gently lowered her panties with her thumbs and stood naked beside the bed. I was spellbound. My eyes traced every curve. Her shoulders, hips, breasts screamed at me. She smiled warmly before looking at Tess who now stood naked as well.

"Your turn," prompted Tess. My boxer briefs landed next to the bed, and for a moment I felt a self-conscious tinge at the throbbing from my groin.

"Looks like you're all ready to go," Tess commented. She stepped towards me and squeezed my erection hard as she kissed me.

"He does, doesn't he?" Sierra climbed onto the bed, close to the middle. Tess followed and they lay on their sides facing each other.

"Hi," welcomed Sierra as she put her hand on Tess' hip and kissed her. I lay down beside Tess and reached across her to run my hand down Sierra's leg. I gently kissed the back of Tess' neck, listening to the sweet sounds of their lips exploring each other.

"It's like a dream," I whispered in Tess ear. Touching Sierra was more than electric, it was an explosion of pleasure, and Tess was exploding too. I had no control. My fingertips ran back up Sierra's leg and then between them. They opened slightly. It was new, wet. She pushed herself towards me.

"Mmmm," Sierra obviously approved. Tess reached behind and grabbed me. Pulling, teasing. Then she put me inside her and I felt her surround me. The sound of lips continued uninterrupted, except for the soft moans from Sierra as I touched her. Harder, then soft. Faster, then almost still to start again. The tangle of writhing flesh played in perfect rhythm on the newly sheeted bed.

I stood up and walked around to the opposite side of the bed to the bowl of condoms and dams. I was in no hurry, watching Tess with Sierra was a sight that I never imagined that I would see. They looked beautiful, connected. I carefully rolled the condom on and lay on the bed, next to Sierra this time.

"Having fun?" I said as I moved close.

"Oh yeah, this is amazing." I reached over and touched her breasts, every part. This time I kissed the back of Sierra's neck. The taste, the smell was new. Pheromones blasted into the air as Sierra ran her tongue over Tess' nipples. I rolled back slightly as she propped herself up on her elbow and continued downwards with her tongue, exploring Tess' body. Kisses touched Tess' body and continued down her stomach before finding that place as she winced with pleasure.

Tess' eyes were closed when I leaned across and kissed her. She breathed heavily and kissed me back hard, running her fingers through the hair on the side of my head.

"I love you," I whispered.

"I love you too." Her body arched and flattened in time as we kissed like it was our first time. I looked at beautiful Sierra, knees on the end of the bed, between Tess' half bent legs. The dyed red hair blanketed Tess' stomach. I was drawn to her. I stood and walked to the end of the bed. I stepped back, just for a moment, to see all of her.

I couldn't help but run my hand down the outside of her leg, then up the inside until my fingers reached the soft flesh of her labia. I slowly started to tease in small, tight circles as I watched them both in front of me. The hair on the back of my neck stood as hard as the rest of me.

"Is this okay?" I asked.

"Yeah, it's okay." Sierra replied, lifting her head just slightly. The silence was filled with the sound of Sierra's tongue and the distant music from down stairs. I couldn't wait any longer. I checked that the condom was on properly and gently joined the pulsing flesh on the bed. She pushed back hard against me, inviting me.

Slowly, deeply, every thrust brought me closer. I ran my hands over her perfectly sculpted flesh then gripped her waist as she moved in time with me. My eyes closed and my whole body tensed. Faster, I pushed harder and paused for the smallest fraction of a second as our bodies pressed together. Faster. The sound of our bodies colliding meshed with voices from the hallway.

Every muscle exploded and my body took control. All rhythm stopped, everything stopped as I let go. All I could feel was the ecstasy that had built for weeks surging from deep inside me, through me.

I let out a heavy, low moan and leaned my head back to look at the swirling corniced ceiling. The orchestra fell apart and every instrument bellowed as the last of the orgasm shuttered throughout me. Consciousness returned from my tingling body and I was back in my head. Sierra and Tess continued.

Eventually I stepped back and removed the condom, placing it in the corner bin. Sierra lifted her head and grinned at Tess with hungry eyes. She crawled back up the bed, running her hand up Tess' body as she lay down. Tess looked over at me and I lay beside her.

"That was quick," she laughed as she turned towards Sierra.

"Just getting started," I said.

"Just finishing more like it." Tess turned back to Sierra and their lips met again.

"We can together," Sierra said. I propped my head up with one hand and ran my fingertips over Tess' back. I was a spectator for now.

Sierra's hand reached between Tess' legs and began to move. Tess did the same.

"Yeah, just there." It was so strange seeing Tess with the beautiful Canadian, and yet so natural at the same time. Sierra flicked back her hair from across her face, so as to look clearly at Tess.

"I'm close," Sierra said.

"Me too." Every movement seemed in time, in response to the other. All at once, the symphony of breath turned to primal release, an uncontrollable ecstasy.

"Yes. Yes," Sierra whispered. Tess followed. Eventually she reached behind to run her fingers through my hair again and pull me close to her. Her breathing slowed slightly and her body relaxed. She laughed ever so slightly.

"I was keeping her all to myself Ryan. She's beautiful."

"She is," I affirmed. "That's okay, you both looked like you were enjoying yourselves."

"Oh, we were enjoying ourselves alright. I want to see how a husband and wife do it." It was Sierra's turn to play the spectator. Tess turned to me and I needed no more invitation than that.

"Hello." Our bodies knew each other so well, every contour, and every sound. Sierra watched intently as I again kissed Tess' neck and savoured that familiar smell. It was passionate, intimate connection with a stranger next to us on the bed. Sierra's foot rubbed against my leg and a single finger twirled locks of my hair.

Our tongues collided, duelled, as I moved above Tess and I was inside her again. Time ceased to exist. Everything did except flesh on flesh.

"I am again."

I had forgotten to close the hotel curtains and the dawn sunshine crept slowly up the wall of the room. It was light enough to wake me even though I had only been asleep for four hours. The alcohol still clouded my vision as I squinted to make out an edge of the pearl white Opera House sail through the window. I needed to go to the toilet badly, but I couldn't move and I didn't want to wake Tess.

The night immediately started to replay in my head, ever detail and emotion. The night before had been massive, but there was no regret. I smiled at the Sydney sunlight drawing a bright, narrow line across the room. Fuck, we really did fly.

"What's the time?" asked Tess as I closed the curtain and crept back into bed. "My head."

"Eight." I rolled towards her, face to face, and her eyes forced themselves open just enough to look at me. The edges of her mouth shaped the faintest smile.

"That was some night."

"Some night alright. How are you?"

"Tired." She dragged herself up to the toilet but I was already asleep when she returned.

"Ryan, it's after ten. We have to be out by eleven." Tess touched the stubble on my face.

"I don't even know if I can drive. I brought a portable breath tester, probably blow the thing up."

"She was really nice, Sierra." Tess must have started the replay in her head as well.

"Yeah, she was."

"I can't believe we lay on the bed for that long, talking. I wonder if anyone else wanted the room."

"Too bad if they did. She was twenty-nine." I felt a little guilty picturing Sierra dancing at the pole.

"I remember."

"Well, you still look twenty-nine at least. Good match."

"Liar. Sounded like she loves Australia. Never met a web designer before. I assume that means she builds internet sites."

"I guess so." I would have killed for a coffee.

"Shit, her number is in my phone." Tess' sleepy smile grew wide. I raised my eyes brows in silence, stepping back from that rabbit hole.

"We were down stairs for another hour and a half after that. No wonder we got home so late. Darsh seemed pretty cool." I remembered the number swap as well.

"Some wing man. At least he got his gear off by the time we got back down. Wonder if he made any friends," Tess said as she sat up and checked her phone.

"Who knows? We honestly could have stayed there all night and talked. Lake Okanagan sounds awesome. Maybe we'll make it to Tugboat Bay one day."

"Maybe, sounds like Sierra is more likely to make it to the central coast first. She goes there sometimes with friends."

"Home?" I missed that part. The city is one thing but home? "Are you really going to text her?"

"Are we? No idea. We need to get moving. C'mon," Tess replied. I grabbed Tess' ass and pulled her close as the thought of Sierra sparked beneath the sheets.

"No. You've had enough of that." Tess laughed. "We need to get up Ry."

"Okay. Only 'cause I'll die if I don't get a coffee soon." The shower burned hot on my skin and the memories from the night before echoed like a blurry old film. I watched intently, trying to make out every detail. I wrapped the towel around me and stepped out of the shower as Tess tied her hair back.

"Did you have a good night?" I asked as I rested my head on her shoulder and looked at the both of us in the steamed mirror.

"Yeah, I had a great night." Tess kissed my cheek. "You."

"It was pretty amazing. The best part was seeing you happy."

"There might have been a few best parts."

"You're right. Handcuffs dancing naked on that pole with his ball bag swinging in the wind really was something." I laughed.

"Something alright. What a nutter. Ted's gold chain sitting on his man boobs. He thought he owned the place."

"Sierra's pole dance."

"Yeah, Sierra." Tess grabbed the back of my neck and kissed me again. I pressed hard into Tess' back as I felt the blood rushing instantly towards the front of the tightly wrapped towel. I reached around and slid my hand down the front of Tess' panties as I watched her eyes shut tight in the mirror. She was wet and she couldn't say no a second time.

"That was one wild weekend," I looked back momentarily as we turned onto the Pacific Motorway.

"The girls at work wouldn't believe any of this. They love to talk about anything to do with sex, they'd go crazy." Tess snuck a look at the fading city skyline as well.

"Really, they talk about their sex lives and stuff?"

"Oh yeah, in detail. They love it. Don't you boys talk about it? I thought that's all you ever thought about."

"Yep, think about it all the time. But we never talk about our own sex lives. No way. Do they really do that?" I was intrigued.

"Absolutely, especially the younger girls. We get all the details. You guys must talk about it sometimes?"

"Sometimes, but I don't. Do you?" I was uneasy with the thought of Tess talking about us at work.

"Of course not. I don't even tell them about the boring parts. I just listen most of the time. They'd lose their shit over this."

"What boring parts?" I asked with no reply. "They wouldn't understand. No one could unless they'd been there. It's nothing like I thought it would be." I said.

"Better?"

"Yeah, better."

"Wouldn't you love to tell just one person though? How good it was?" Tess asked.

"Love too, but it would be impossible to explain. Any of it. Rule four remember."

"Rule four." Tess' phone pinged and she fished it out of her bag. "Probably the kids, I called them while you were in the shower."

"Another hour and a half maybe. Tell them I said hello."

"Sierra." Tess said.

"What does it say?" I asked excitedly.

"Hang on." Tess paused. "She says 'Hiya. Had an awesome night with you guys last night. Might see you at the beach some time. Sierra.' Then two love hearts."

"Shit. Didn't take her long to text us. Should we text back?" Tess shrugged her shoulders. "I don't know, what would we text?" We looked at each other nervously.

"No idea. We should at least write back. What do you think we should say?" Tess replied, eyes glued to the phone.

"Ah, how about hi Sierra, no just hi. Had a great time last night too. The beach sounds good." I stumbled to find the right words. "Feels like being at high school again writing a letter to some girl."

"Some girl?" Tess asked sternly. "Sounds like you're inviting her to the beach."

"We...Scrap that." We both thought for a moment. This wasn't what we signed up for and the electricity was moving closer to home. An uneasy silence filled the rest of the trip home before I turned into our street.

"Hello beautiful girl, I missed you so much." I said, hugging Leyla hard as she met us at the door. "How was your weekend?"

"So cool. Aunty Rachel took us to the movies to see Captain Marvel, it was so good. Josh ate a whole large popcorn."

"Where is Aunty Rach?" Leyla returned to the car with me as I grabbed Tess' bag.

"Out the back. Then we got Chinese after. Can I go to Lacey's house later, she invited me?" Leyla continued a full recount of the twenty-four hours that we had been away. I walked into Josh's room where he was glued to the PS4 controller, yelling at his mates through the head set. Conversations were generally short and incoherent when he was gaming. I hugged him as he continued to play. I missed them terribly whenever I was away from them and this weekend had been no different.

Getting back home really was like returning from outer space and it took some time to re-adjust to earth's atmosphere. A sense of clarity kicked in as soon as I saw Leyla and Josh. They were all that mattered, besides Tess. Rational thinking had been shelved for a single day but I was acutely aware that my own desires needed to be reined in. This place was my world, not a brown terrace building in the city. Tess was good at detaching herself from those weekends. But I found it harder.

That energy from Deepest Desires stayed with me, like radiation. Radiation was a by-product of incredible energy and it was dangerous long after that energy had gone.

"Any ideas?" I asked Tess as she sat on the end of our bed staring at her phone.

"I just texted her back. Here." Tess got up and left me to read the text.

'Hi Sierra. We had a great weekend, loved meeting you. The beach sounds nice.'

Chapter 17
Finding the Strength to Be Happy

"You wanna beer, mate?" Tim asked.

"Nope, I'm good. I'll stick with this." Jet and Josh kicked the footy in Tim's spacious back yard while Tess and Meg chatted inside. "I'm going to give it a miss for a while. It's been nice waking up in the morning feeling fresh. Got ten kays in today."

"Nice, you're lookin' fit."

"Fitter than I've been in a long time. It seems like the more people drink, the more they want it and the less they drink, the less they miss it. The first few weeks are the hardest. But it gets easier."

"That's what Flano said, the first few weeks you know. We've been doin' this since we were kids. Old habits hey? Good for you mate." It was nice to hear some encouragement from Tim rather than more questions. He seemed to be getting it finally, that drinking wasn't compulsory and that it had hurt me. It had hurt my family.

Those old habits held on with a vice like grip and every bit of support from the people closest to me made a huge difference. Drinking wasn't always enjoyable, it was just a habit, and it's what I did. It was my dopamine reward after a hard day and over many years my mind had entrenched itself into believing that it's what I deserved.

But over the years, as my brain gradually desensitised to the dopamine release, the 'happy drug' reward faded. But the addiction remained. That's when the glutamate kicked in, a shitty replacement chemical that did nothing more than stop me sleeping every time I drank.

"I'm sleeping so much better lately. I forgot what it was like," I continued.

"Nice. What's that?" Tim asked.

"Cranberry juice and lemonade. Long story. It's bloody tasty and I gotta have something in my hand." That night was the last time I can remember that Tim asked me if I wanted a beer.

"Cool. Good win today by the boys. Couple more and we'll be in the top four," Tim continued. I was glad we had made things clear. I wasn't drinking, on that night anyway, and that was okay. I didn't know what the future held, but the support of mates mattered more than I realised.

"Yeah, I heard. We had a family day. Went shopping and got the kids some nice new clothes."

"Good for you." Tim avoided the normal tirade when I missed watching a game.

"We had lunch at the beach. That girl loves to shop."

"Couldn't think of anything worse." Supporting my sobriety was one thing, but condoning family shopping trips was too much for Tim.

"Maybe."

"Meg shits me every time we're out lately. Nothing I do is right," Tim continued calmly. I missed many markers of where he and Meg were at. That was one of them.

"Shopping's a learned skill. Just learn to shut up. It was good to be together, the four of us. The kids had a swim. I haven't spent many Saturday arvo's with them since they were born."

"You reckon the boys will be piss heads like us?" Tim asked as the ball crashed into the patio chairs.

"I hope not. I can't tell Josh not to drink when he's eighteen, but I'll be doing everything I can to make sure he's nothing like me."

"We were veterans by eighteen Tano. He's already like you, look at him under the high ball. Hasn't missed one."

"It's what I do now that matters. Love him enough, be there for him and hopefully he won't need to do what we did. Tess'd throttle him."

"There you go then, too easy," Tim replied. I admired his blasé attitude on most things but not when it came to the future of my children.

"Remember that movie, Dragon?" I asked.

"Friggen Bruce Lee, legend."

"I read a bit about him just after Leyla was born. You beat your demons or you pass them onto your children. That's what he said."

"What?"

"It's what I do now that matters. If I set the right example, give him the strength to deal with all the shit that the world throws at him, then maybe he won't need to do what I did to survive. Deal with my shit now so he doesn't have to later."

"Beating demons, dealing with shit and worst of all, shopping. You're covering some ground tonight mate." I just laughed at Tim's nonchalance. "I know what you mean though. You're right, it matters a lot."

"It's beautiful out here," Meg said as she and Tess walked out to the patio. It looked like she had been crying.

"Yeah, Ryno was just telling me about his new love for shopping, haven't ya mate?" Tim's support mode was over.

"Yep, just love it." I laughed as I nodded 'no' to Tess. She smiled back with warm eyes. Her support mode never turned off.

"They never stop do they?" Meg nodded at the boys in the yard. "How's work Ry?"

"Same old. We got the grant so that should make a difference to the centre. Some of those kids are really getting there. Some are always going to struggle. We can only support them so much but I'm slowly learning that in the end, they have to find the strength to be happy themselves. No one else can do it for them."

"Easier said than done," Meg said.

"True, but not impossible." I was talking from personal experience as much as my professional insight. "It's beyond hard for some of them. There's a new psych coming in two days a week, Greta. She has been great. The kids have just clicked with her."

"Tough gig." Tim had always hated any type of councillor after family sessions as a kid.

"I think the reason that she is so good is that the kids feel like she gets them."

"Must be nice for them to be able to talk." Meg had always taken an interest in my work.

"She was one of them once, Greta." I sipped the red drink slowly.

"You didn't tell me that," Tess replied.

"Her mum died in a car accident when she was twelve, never knew her dad. She lived with her best friend's family until she was eighteen and worked her way through uni. Did it all on her own, except for her best friend who went to uni too. Inspiring."

"She sounds amazing. Then to end up helping kids like her, that's awesome. Some people get everything handed to them on a platter and all they end up with is a shitty sense of entitlement." Meg spoke quietly as she glared at Tim. "Hardship builds strength. I've been getting stronger lately," continued Meg. Tess' concerned face told the story.

"Ah, yeah. Greta's making a real difference to those kids. I'm learning a lot. She listens but she's not afraid to call them out too. 'Honesty wrapped in love' she calls it," I explained.

"We all need that," Meg replied.

"The kids we work with need love most of all and the trust that comes with it. But that's not enough. They need to hear the truth before they can make any type of change moving forward. It's a starting point at least."

"For sure," Meg was listening intently.

"But a lot of that truth doesn't start with them and the shit they are dealing with now. It starts a long time ago. Those kids dealt with all kinds of abuse, divorce, homelessness, you name it. Greta starts with that and tells them that it's not their fault. It's amazing how much blame people carry."

"I'm getting a beer." Tim headed for the fridge in the garage.

"I sat in on a few sessions, only because the kids asked me too. She had a way of letting them know that forgiving themselves is a start, and that it's okay to feel the way they do after all of the shit that they've been through. She understands why they're lost, angry, addicted, violent. Whatever."

"That must be such a hard job, but so rewarding too," Meg replied.

"Anyway. She's making a difference. Most of all she lets them know that there's hope. The future's not decided by the past, it's decided by the little decisions that we make every day."

"And every night," Meg said as Tim returned. "Tess finally gets to have a cruiser at our place Ryan. Good to see you driving for once."

"My new favourite, cranberry and lemonade." I held the red drink in the air. "You know, the bod's a temple."

"Or a funnel. C'mon Tess, I'll show you the dress."

"Is everything alright mate?" I asked as the sliding door shut.

"Fuck me. Doesn't matter what I do." He scratched painfully at flecks of paint on the wooden outdoor setting. I wondered if that's what I looked like to Bill. "She's never happy."

"Where's this come from? I thought you guys were good."

"It's been coming for a while. She reckons I'm always pissed off. It's bullshit. I bust my ass all day and I come home to this. Over it." Tim stared down at the brown bottle in his hands.

"Why didn't you tell me? You gotta talk about this stuff."

"I don't want to talk about it. You deal with enough drama at work. You don't want to hear about my problems."

"Yes, I do. Of course I do. Nothings gonna change if you don't talk about it. How long has it been like this?"

"Too long. Most of the time we still get on you know. But she's just drifting further and further away. I can feel it."

"I'm so sorry. I wished you had of told me." I felt awful that I hadn't picked it up. I wondered if Tess knew as Tim continued to stare at the bottle. This was clearly hard for him to talk about. Aussie blokes didn't talk about their feelings, or their marriages. Footy or V8's was far easier. They didn't go to the doctor's either because they just somehow thought that everything would be okay.

"It wouldn't have made any difference. Happy wife, happy life," Tim said.

"I never understood that saying?" I protested.

"What?"

"How does that work? Why does the whole family's focus have to be on one person being happy?"

"Because that's just how it is. Everyone knows it," Tim said.

"I'm not arguing that. Everyone does know it, them's the rules. As long as Mum is happy then that's all that matters."

"When mama ain't happy, ain't nobody happy," slurred Tim.

"You do the worst American accent ever. Everyone should be happy? Imagine if we came out with the new family rule, 'as long as Dad is happy, then everyone else will be right'. That's just a stupid, unfair idea that would rightfully get shot down in a second."

"What's up your ass?" Tim wasn't interested in a debate about family dynamics.

"Don't get me wrong, in the end I live by it anyway. As long as Tess is happy then that's all that matters to me. I'd walk on broken glass all day long for her. Just saying, it's funny how the whole world accepts that saying. I never understood it. Unfair."

"Dane got injured again. No fullback for the weekend." Tim was back on his favourite subject.

"Time to retire." I was done protesting. "Tim, you gotta talk about this stuff. Honestly, if you ever need an ear I'm here."

"Thanks. I guess you're right." He spoke slowly. "It's just hard."

"Boys, dinner's ready," called Meg.

I held Tess's hand on the short drive home as I did so often. It was a subconscious warm blanket that wrapped tight around me.

"Did you know?" I asked as Leyla and Josh scattered towards their rooms.

"She's been unhappy for years Ry. She hasn't said much until now. Remember last year at Leah's fortieth? We had to give Meg a lift home."

"Sort of. I didn't think it was anything major."

"You don't listen sometimes. You really don't. I told you Meg was struggling. Tim's a shit sometimes. He doesn't listen either."

"He can be, yeah," I didn't remember much at all about that night and it was one of those markers that I should have seen.

"Thanks for driving tonight. It was nice, for once." It was a small, almost inconsequential effort to drive but I appreciated her acknowledging it. For a few weekends now, I had eased up on the cans or spent nights abstaining. It felt good.

"No worries. I'm going for a run in the morning, you want to come?"

"Sunday morning, I'll be in bed I think. I couldn't keep up anyway."

"Cool. I was happy to drive. I'm trying." Distant yelling came from Josh's room as his gaming resumed.

"I know you are." Tess wrapped her arms around my waist and held me tight.

Words naturally lose their weight as the years go by between two people. Sometimes a person knows a partner better than they know themselves and Tess understood me completely. Actions spoke now and a few weekends of good behaviour was a good start, but she knew how quickly old habits could resume and there was a lifetime ahead.

Tess had heard so many excuses over time and so many broken promises. She had seen me lie to myself so that when I lied to her, I believed every word. Tess had learned over the years to listen with her eyes because the truth was often lost in words. It took me years to understand this and I was grateful for the knowledge because I finally understood that it was my actions that mattered. It wasn't my excuses or justifications, not my best intentions or grandest plans. It was the here and now reality of each decision, one little victory or defeat at a time. Each victory was a way to show, not tell, that I was changing.

I wanted to show Tess, and myself, that change was possible. But even more importantly, those little victories were major battleground wins for my children's future. What I did in the here and now mattered beyond measure to the man and woman that they would become and that thought gave me energy. But this was sustainable, respectable energy that would last over time. At least I hoped it would.

Chapter 18
Careful What You Wish For

"I found her on Facebook." Tess ginned at me and peered beneath her unbrushed morning hair to gauge my reaction.

"Found who?" I asked, tying the laces on the new runners that I had picked up the day before.

"Who do you think?"

"Facebook shits me. Every time I google something I get hammered with adds about it." I looked up and Tess returned her attention to the phone. 'Found her', repeated in my head. I sprang to my feet and crashed onto the lounge next to Tess, staring at her phone. She tilted the screen towards me. Sierra's broad smile was framed with heart shaped birthday balloons in the background. One of the balloons had the number twenty-nine on it.

"No way." I watched intently as Tess scrolled through the feed. "How did you find her? It must have taken ages."

"Not really. There's not as many Sierras in that part of Sydney as you'd think. Public profile, it didn't take long." Neither of us took our eyes off the screen.

"She has brown hair, it suits her. I can't believe you found her," I gushed.

"Look at this one, main beach. That's only ten minutes away from here." Tess stopped at the selfie with our local beach in the background. We'd been there with the kids more times than I could count. I hardly noticed the beach though, I was fixated on Sierra's intoxicating smile and white bikini top. Her tanned skin looked far more Australian than Canadian. My head flooded with memories of touching that skin only weeks ago.

"So, she was serious when she said she comes up here sometimes," I said.

"Obviously. The brown hair does suit her."

"That was pretty wild what we did you know," Tess said as she turned to me, smiling as she shook her head.

"That's for sure, it was out there."

"Does it sometimes feel like just a dream to you, like it never really happened?" She asked.

"Completely. I don't remember all of it and sometimes I have to think hard to even remember parts, just like a dream the next morning. Yeah, it was a crazy thing to do, all of it." We both continued to study the screen.

"Imagine what people would say."

"I still think we did everything the right way, if there is such a thing. We were honest and just gave each other the freedom to do that stuff. But the best thing was we were together the whole time. We did it together." I meant every word.

"There's the red hair. She must have had a boyfriend, he's in lots of last year's posts but none of this year's," Tess said.

"Has she texted back yet?" I asked hopefully. I had fought the urge to ask for weeks. "I love that one." The pictures were very real, far from a dream, and the electricity surged. But this time it was in our home.

"Mum," yelled Leyla, as she walked into the lounge room. "Can we go now?" Tess immediately killed the feed.

"Yeah bub, in a minute. We're picking up Mum and going into town. Josh is coming," Tess explained.

"Cool, I'm going for a run."

"Nice runners."

"I got them on yesterday, the old ones were pretty ratty." I waved the family off and headed directly for the ocean, about two kilometres from home, where the path snaked along the foreshore. The salted air was a comforting reminder of my little victories the night before and provided an atmosphere for clarity of mind. But that morning my hazy thoughts were filled with radiation: images and 'what ifs'. Sierra.

"Morning," chirped an elderly woman that I saw regularly on my runs. There were a cast of locals that I passed more often than not, each one keen to offer their morning greeting. I enjoyed the familiarity of seeing those strangers' faces day after day. It was my time to think and make sense of the world, to reflect on choices and directions. But this direction was altogether different.

"Sierra," I whispered, not knowing why I had said the name aloud. Memories of her and Tess bounced around inside my head. A year ago, the thought of anyone even touching Tess would have torn me to pieces, but not now. The

Facebook pictures rained into the narrative as I ran faster. Most of the time I jogged casually but at that moment I was moving at speed. What if we did this, I asked myself.

"How was the run?" Tess walked into the garage as I scraped the dried mud off my shoes.

"Good. I was just thinking that you never got to answer my question."

"What question?"

"Did she text?"

"Who," replied Tess, amusing herself.

"Did she?" I was still sweating from the run and wanted an answer. "Not keeping secrets, are you?"

"No, she didn't." The tone changed immediately as Tess answered the back handed question.

"Oh. That's easy then." My head dropped to concentrate on the runners. "Should we text?"

"Did you want too?"

"Doesn't worry me. Do you?" I was treading carefully.

"I asked you first, you seem pretty keen."

"We could, maybe just see what happens. Could be fun." I still wasn't looking at Tess, but I could feel her studying me.

"What would happen? I don't know how that would work. Just take her down to the local maybe?" Suddenly the 'seeing what happens' idea didn't seem like such a good one. "You honestly think it would be a good idea?"

"I guess not." I looked up from the floor.

"No, I'm not going to see what happens. Not into it." Tess was right, rule number one.

I spent the rest of the week lapsing into the "what if?" It was new territory again and it scared the life out of me. But part of me wanted it, because in a way it scared the life into me. Most days, most weeks, were long and slow, surrounded in the mundane that was such a total contrast to the memories of flying with Tess.

"That was a shitty week. I only just made it to Friday. Corey got two years." I sat my workbag in the dining room as I always did. The emotional energy I spent on every one of those deserving kids left me feeling empty, thirsty. I wanted to 'fix' all of them and make everything work. But I couldn't.

"What for?"

"He stole another car. Crashed it into someone else. I waste so much of my time on meaningless paper work, jumping through hoops for tools who have never spent a day working with these kids. If they'd just trust us to do our jobs, it'd be so much easier."

"Maybe."

"How was your day?"

"I slept most of it. It was the longest night shift ever."

"Busy?" I often got so caught up in my own mess that I forgot how hard those twelve-hour night shifts were for Tess.

"Nope, dead quiet. I'm exhausted."

"You look tired."

"I've got a headache. I think I might go back to bed. Are you okay with dinner?"

"For sure. Those night shifts are too much. Maybe it's time to think about something else. Kat got a job with Community Health, didn't she? She's working regular hours."

"The pay is not even close to the hospital. We need the money." Tess headed for bed and I lay down beside her, running my fingers through her hair. I pulled through the small knots at the ends of the strands as she winced ever so slightly.

"Don't stop." It wasn't long until she was asleep. I loved to watch her sleep.

Soon, the meat was ready to start making the enchiladas and I opened the fridge to fish for the cheese. Meg's bottle of Sav Blanc had been sitting in the bottom for weeks. Cooking and drinking had gone hand in hand for years, especially on a Friday night. But wine was never an option, that awful tasting stuff couldn't be a problem. Or so I thought.

"Just one glass, Meg won't mind," I coaxed myself, proud of the start I'd made to dinner. I took a deep breath in after the first mouthful. It didn't taste as bad as I remembered and the first battle was lost. It didn't matter if it was a glass, a bottle or a can.

A drinker just wants alcohol, just like a coffee addict craves the caffeine. We all have our preferences when it comes to taste but it's the drug we want. People are addicted to many things. Some crave sugar highs or the little dopamine hits from social media that fill the need to feel connected. Others try to fill the empty voids with food, whatever shape they took. At that moment, I just wanted alcohol.

"Awesome, burritos," said Josh. "I love them."

"Enchiladas little man."

"You must love this song Dad, you always play it."

"It's okay." I danced as I divided up dinner onto plates and edged the volume up again. The empty sav blanc bottle sat behind the speaker, next to two beers.

"Ley, dinner," Josh yelled. The distant flush of the ensuite toilet caught my attention and I immediately grabbed the bottle and stuffed it into the bottom of my lunch bag.

"Did you not hear me say I had a headache? A twelve-hour bloody night shift and all I get is ACDC." Tess' tone said more than the words. I slammed the button on the speaker.

"I made enchiladas," was all I had.

"Really? Good for you." Tess didn't wait for a reply. Leyla and Josh grabbed their plates and sat up at the breakfast bar.

"Are you two okay here? Mum's got a headache."

"Yeah. Are there carrots in this?" Josh asked.

"I'm just taking this to her." I ignored most vegetable related questions and tentatively opened the bedroom door. "I got you this."

"I'm not hungry."

"I didn't realise it was that loud."

"It was."

"I'm sorry."

"It's always louder when you drink," Tess replied to my surprise. I had hidden the bottle.

"It's been a hard week. I didn't mean to wake you. I'll leave this here." I left the room in silence.

"Nice Dad, except the orange bits." I bypassed the kids on the way to the garage where the half-empty box of beers lay next to my golf clubs. They had sat there for weeks and served as a beacon of my improvements every time I went into the garage. They were warm, but that was inconsequential, I was thirsty.

"Love you beautiful girl." An hour later I was tucking Leyla into bed.

"Love you Dad. Where's Mum?"

"She's asleep. Night shift remember."

"I'm never going to be a nurse."

"Don't blame you. Night." I left Leyla's door ajar.

"Just until the end of the game," Josh yelled over the noise of his headphones before I said a word.

"Yeah mate." The energy to argue was gone. I slumped on the lounge as the next bottle took breath and grabbed my phone. I hit the Facebook icon and the search didn't take long. "There she is."

The next beer disappeared as quickly as the last and I willingly lost count after that, although I had the presence of mind to hide every bottle behind my golf clubs in the garage.

"Save." I had examined every photo, every post. But this one I liked the most, in her bikini top at the beach. Her kind, inviting eyes and beautiful smile contained no hint of the hardships of the real world, only memories of a single, perfect night. I scrolled through the year's posts, there were only fourteen. I expected more. The past year's posts were just as satisfying and I savoured every little insight into her life.

"Huh?" I woke with my phone still in my hand and a half-empty beer balancing on the lounge.

"I said, I'm turning this off," Tess demanded angrily, aiming the television remote. I raised my head enough to see the time display on the microwave, 12:52am. At some stage the bottles stopped being shipped to the garage and four more lay on the floor in front of the lounge. Tess looked down.

"Yeah." I squinted through heavy eyes which shut down almost immediately as Tess returned to bed.

"Dad. Dad." Leyla's voice swirled with the pain in my head that had woken me hours earlier. "Did you sleep on the lounge?"

"No bub, I was getting ready for a run," I said through closed eyes.

"On the lounge?"

I pulled myself up and rested my head in my hands.

"What a fuckin idiot. Why?" I whispered as Leyla began breakfast. "Why?" I immediately got rid of the bottles as the normal highlights reel played over in my head. Hiding the bottles was all I could manage before crashing back onto the lounge.

"Leave the Wheat Bix out Leyla," ordered Josh. "What's Dad doing?"

"Going for a run."

"Morning Josh."

"Morning Dad. Are we still going to Aunty Rachel's house this today?" Josh asked. I winced at the thought of a day out, one that I had been looking forward to all week before my big night.

"Shit, I forgot."

"Mum, Dad said shit." Tess plugged in the vacuum cleaner.

"We have to leave in an hour. Rach expects you to be there."

"I know, I'll be okay." I sank into the lounge, fighting the urge to be sick. A coffee and a searing hot shower was all that I could focus on. It was a long shower.

"How's your headache?" The vacuum rang out as Tess turned her back.

"It's fine."

We arrived at Rachel's house and I shrank into the corner chair of the back patio, cuddling the Gatorade keeping me alive. As usual, Rach had asked me to bring a speaker and I could only hand my phone to Tess as she pulled it out of her bag. The music began, louder than Tess, or Rachel, would normally tolerate.

Tess stared at my phone.

"Are you for real? Fuck Ryan."

"Pardon?" The music was hurting, everything was hurting.

"What were you doing last night?" Tess stared at my phone in her hand.

"I'm sorry. Meg's Sav Blanc was in the fridge for weeks and I had a few beers."

"I'm not talking about a few beers. What were you doing last night?"

"What?" I took a long drink of the Gatorade.

"You tell me what."

"Sleeping on the lounge." My tone searched for mercy. Tess shook her head and stood to walk away. "Sit down, please." She sat. I rubbed my temple and took a long sip. "I'm sorry. I was looking at Facebook. Sierra. I just missed that feeling and wanted to feel it again. I didn't mean any harm."

"So why did you save her pictures to your phone?" Tess still wouldn't look at me and continued to examine my phone.

"Why? To remember. There was only one. I'll delete it now."

"There's three." Tess never checked my phone; we had complete trust in each other and I had never given her any reason to doubt me. Not since I was eighteen at least, which was a lifetime ago. I groaned under the weight of guilt and self-loathing.

"I thought there was one. I'm sorry." The smell of the barbeque only increased the nauseous storm inside. "How did you even know?"

"You went to sleep with the phone in your hand. Didn't you feel me take it when I woke you?"

"No."

"I was just looking for a few minutes, I promise. It didn't mean anything. You found her first, not me." Tess' glare burned, raged. She was unrecognisable in those moments and it terrified me.

"I was honest and we both had one look together. Together. That's completely different to pining for her on the lounge pulling your dick over her pictures. Fuck you." She stood and walked away.

"I wasn't pulling my dick," I whispered. I slumped back into the patio chair and all I could do was breathe.

"You're getting greener as the day goes on." Rach laughed as she sat beside me. "You haven't moved since you got here. Big night?"

"I'm suffering. I've been so good lately. Last night was just dumb." I shook my head. "Dumb."

"Is Tess okay?"

"Yeah, she's good." I knew she wasn't. For the rest of the day, Tess didn't even look at me, never mind speak to me. I was spent by the time I lay down in bed. Tess lay quietly with her back to me.

"I know it was a stupid thing to do. I didn't mean to disrespect you." The silence continued.

"It was only for a few minutes. You looked her up first." Tess sat up immediately. The regret was instant.

"You're kidding me. I showed you straight away. It was something we did together like the rest of it."

"I guess."

"That's completely different to you pissed on the lounge getting off on her fucking pictures."

"I wasn't getting off. I was just looking and wishing we were back there together. I miss that feeling." There was no rely and I was thankful for the merciful comfort that sleep offered. It had been a torturous day, one that I was more than happy to leave.

Over the following days Tess remained distant. These were dangerous and very deep waters that we were swimming in and I had been somewhat naïve about what could wrong. Cracks could become canyons and Tess seemed so far away.

I came to realise that trust and jealousy were a part of the same package and if the trust broke down, then everything else could be torn apart. I had let Tess down and I was truly sorry for that. I hated to think of her, thinking about me on that lounge looking at another woman. That was a betrayal in its own right. Betrayal wasn't always a physical act, it was about trust and the truths in our heart.

I could never stand the silence and the distance that the arguments put between us. Later that week she was standing in the ensuite facing the mirror. I stood behind her and put both arms around her waist, holding her tight.

"You were right about everything you said. I know it was wrong and I understand how hurtful it must have been. I am sorry." I looked at her mirrored eyes as she studied me. Tess nodded.

"You just make me so mad. That wasn't okay. For a smart bloke, you are such a dumb ass sometimes." A hint of a smile began to surface.

Weeks later I sat in the sterile, white walled reception area outside the familiar consultation rooms. I tried to follow the subtitles on the five o'clock news which were at least five seconds behind the footage. A mother and what looked like a ten-year-old boy nodded agreeably to the receptionist and took a seat at the opposite side of the room. I wondered why he was waiting to see a psychologist, what 'slings and arrows' life had aimed at him. Maybe if I had been talking to someone at ten then I would have coped better.

"Ryan, how are you?" greeted Bill, motioning me into the small, lightly furnished room.

"Good thanks Bill. How are you?"

"Busy as always but well thank you." Bill was neatly dressed in black dress pants and a deep purple business shirt. I guessed that he was about fifty, with strands of grey hair running over his ears. His calm, supportive demeanour suited his occupation perfectly. "Please, take a seat. How have you been?"

"Good, mostly. I have been managing work better and I'm learning to leave it where it should be, rather than bring it home." Work was always discussed at those sessions and we spoke in detail about managing the stress.

"Great, it's not easy. How's the family?"

"They're all fine. The kids are going well at school and we've been making more time to do things as a family. That's been a huge thing for me, that time together. They're enjoying it too." Bill perused the notes he had taken from the last session and looked above the rims of his reading glasses.

"We spoke about that last time. It's good to hear Ryan."

"I feel like things are changing. I'm happier and Tess is too. I mean, I think that she can see that I'm trying at least. It's not just words, she can see that I'm actually doing things differently, most of the time anyway." I honestly felt like I was heading in the right direction, except for my Facebook mistake.

"Well, it's part of the bigger picture, if you're happier, then that carries over to your relationships."

"It's just small steps and I know I have a long way to go. It feels like I'm growing up. It had to happen eventually."

"Well you've been working hard at this and you should be proud of the progress you've made."

"I am" Yet again, my knee started to bounce and I pushed down hard with an open palm to stop it. "We've spent heaps of time together, the family. It's been, ah, it's been really good." I was disappointed that there was not more conviction in my voice because every word was true.

I wanted to explain the whole Facebook mistake but all of that was off limits. My unrelenting standards meant that the last months of happiness were smeared by those minutes of failure. I was rightfully proud how far I had come and I was more determined than ever to keep going.

"My dad used to say that things are never as bad as they seem and never as good as they seem either. Sounded strange at the time but I think I understand it now," I said finally. I never dealt well with pauses of any length in a conversation.

"Smart man. People tend to accentuate strong feelings, we all do it."

"Maybe I'm not doing as well as I think but I'm trying and that feels good. I'm drinking far less and that feels good. I don't know if that's something I should be proud of, something that lots of other blokes do anyway."

"Of course, you should be proud of yourself Ryan. You're clearly happier and I'm sure your family appreciates what you are doing. Change takes effort and time and it's okay to celebrate small successes," Bill replied. I had done my celebrating on the previous weekend.

"Some days I still struggle, it's hard." I found it difficult to look at Bill sometimes. I would focus on the wall behind him or the plastic plant in the corner. Maybe it was easier to explain those things to him without the intimacy of eye contact.

"We all struggle. It's part of being human, but acknowledging it and talking about it takes the edge off things sometimes."

"I pull myself out of bed and there's still this sadness, like an ache somewhere. Maybe it will always be there. That part of our humanity sucks." Bill smiled subtly, knowingly.

"Yeah, it does. But there are other parts that balance the struggle out."

"Like footy?" I half joked. "I turn on the TV and it's so full on. I worry about what Leyla and Josh's future will be like. Will there be any jobs left, will they be able to afford a home, will the climate completely shit itself and condemn them to I don't know what."

"Slow down. There are enough things to worry about in this world without worrying about things that haven't even happened yet. Sometimes when things are going well our brain looks for something else concern itself with. Maybe keep things a bit simpler for the time being."

"I guess. But sometimes it's hard to be strong each day. I'm trying. There's been times lately when I've gone weeks without a drink, but it's still in the back of my head. I'm loving running and waking up without a headache, but it's still there. Last weekend I messed up. I thought I'd just have a few quiet ones, but that didn't happen."

"So why do you think you kept going?" asked Bill. It was an impossibly hard question, and I found myself answering the same questions all over again.

"Tess asked me that once. Why does anyone drink too much? All my mates do." I was stalling for time to think.

"Not your mates, you."

"Tess says that a lot, 'not your mates, you'. I don't really think about it. Sometimes when I get home from work I am so wound up. I'm short with the kids and all I can think about is the shit in my head. I want to relax, switch off, but I just can't."

"Your job isn't easy, but there are other ways you can manage that stress," offered Bill. I wasn't listening.

"After the first drink, I can breathe. My brain sees the glass in my hand and just lets go of things. Then after the next few I can feel myself relax. Everything seems to get easier, better. I forget the shit for a while."

"Okay," Bill crossed his legs, but remained silent.

"Then after that it's the energy that I love. I start to come alive, that part of me that used to be happy. It's so good to know it's still there. I like to cook and listen to music."

"That part of you is always there. You might need to find other ways to get there besides a beer. That's a dangerous association when your happiness depends on a drug. That's all alcohol is."

"Yeah, part of me knows that. Part of me doesn't want to know. Dangerous, yeah. On a big night, the drinks after that definitely take me into dangerous territory. That's when nothing matters. Every single thing fades away, even the most important things. It scares me, looking back at those nights. But when I'm there. I love it."

"We've spoken about moderation Ryan. It seems like the most damage to your marriage happens when you're in that place. You're not a kid anymore."

"No, I'm not. I lose control. I don't even remember some of it. It's weird, sometimes that loss of control is the only time I feel in control."

"How so?"

"I choose how wasted, how far from reality I get. Sometimes it's like the further away the better. And the further I walk, sometimes I wonder if I really want to turn around and take the long walk back. Getting hammered is so easy, it's all downhill. Sobriety, or even moderation, is an uphill slog. It's so hard."

"No one said it was easy Ryan. But what's the alternative? You fight that uphill battle or you risk losing everything and the choice to take that long walk home won't be there anymore."

"I know."

"Your marriage, your family, your home. They're what's at stake here Ryan."

"I know." Hearing it articulated so clearly was frightening.

Christmas and New Year's came and went, I had two weeks off, as did Tess and it was magic. We spent time at the beach with the kids and we were really able to unwind. Tess had begun to join me on my morning runs, although more time was spent walking and talking, which was fine by me.

"Don't you feel like a hypocrite," Tess asked. It was not the normal response when someone shared their New Year's resolution.

"What?" I didn't understand her reservation.

"Doesn't that resolution make you feel like a hypocrite when we did what we did?" I took time to process the question as we walked. It was early in the new year and we compared resolutions as always. Tess' was pretty much the same every year, some variation on healthy eating and exercise. Mine was about a prayer that Mum had often prayed with me when I was little.

"God give me the humility to accept the things I can't change, the strength to change the things I should change and the wisdom to know the difference between the two." I remembered her words well. I would always end it with a heartfelt 'Amen'.

I was a Christian. Most of my friends and family did not really know and none of them were spiritual in any way. It was not something I spoke about. I didn't go to church. But when I first heard about God as a child, no one said that my faith was dependent on my church attendance, it was about my relationship with him. It was personal and it was what I believed.

"Do I feel like a hypocrite? That's a bit rough. I don't know. Why do you ask that?" I was still processing.

"I don't know. Wouldn't religion tell us that what we did was wrong?"

"Was it wrong? Pretty good question. Maybe." I didn't expect the conversation to curve in this direction and it was difficult to answer.

"It didn't feel wrong. That's still a good resolution," Tess reassured me. She could sense my voice tighten. It was an infinitely rare thing to hear Tess back tracking, if that's what it was.

"No, it didn't." We continued walking in silence. It churned in my mind. Was it wrong? Every accepted societal norm would scream yes. But I thought that there were only three tests that Deepest Desires had to pass. Firstly, was it okay with Tess? I trusted her judgement completely and I knew that I had her support.

Secondly, was it okay with me? As we walked, I asked myself that question and I knew that I was at peace with what we did. Maybe it was my carnal desires clouding everything that was wrong about it but I was truly okay with it. It was never about other people, it was about Tess and I flying.

The last test was the hardest, was it okay with my God. No matter how I spun it in my head the answer was no. That was clear. This was way beyond the limits of how he wanted people to live. In God's eyes, yes it was wrong. But so were the multitudes of broken marriages between people who stood in churches and committed to each other for life. So was the act of working on Sundays when we were supposed to rest. So was the idea of judging other people for their sins.

People's lives were full of 'wrongs', one after the other. But all those 'wrongs' still did not make what we did right.

"You know what my favourite part of the bible is?" I asked Tess.

"Not a clue."

"Judge not and you shall not be judged. I believe in a forgiving God and I know he would forgive us. Anyway, I wasn't expecting to be called a hypocrite because of a simple New Year's resolution."

"I didn't call you a hypocrite, I just asked if you felt like one." Tess deflected the accusation.

"Not much difference. No, I don't." I growled. But somewhere deep inside I did feel exactly like a hypocrite. I knew it was beyond the limits but I had done it anyway. More than that, I had loved every lustful second.

Chapter 19
The Last Time

"Number eight." Tess finished her drink faster than normal. She re-read the question on her phone. "If I ever had a one-night stand, could you forgive me?"

"Okay, you really wanna know?" I shook my head, taking time to really think about the question. "I never know what you're gonna ask next. Could I forgive you? Rule two. I hate to say it but yes. It would destroy me, eat me up inside but there's nothing you could do that would stop me from loving you. I just couldn't imagine not being with you."

"How sweet."

"A much better answer would have been no fucking way. But that wouldn't be the truth then, would it?"

"I guess not."

"So, I hope there's nothing you want to tell me at this point?"

"Nothing," she said casually, oblivious to the packed bar room surrounding us.

"That's good. So, could you?" I tentatively asked, forgetting for a moment what a stupid, loaded question it was.

"I already did." Tess dipped her head and eyeballed me hard before a slow smile spread across her face. Long ago I had stopped trying to explain that I was a stupid, drunk eighteen-year-old kid. There were zero excuses for something like that.

"Okay then, moving on. Do you want another drink?"

"That's an easy one, yes." She held up her empty glass as I downed mine. The Royal Crown was one of the newer pubs in Kings Cross, with the ornate wooden furnishings of all the more traditional venues. It buzzed with a younger city crowd and I loved the energy that filled every corner of the place.

"There's a signed Ramones poster behind the bar, how cool is that?" I said, placing Tess' vodka and orange in front of her.

"What's a Ramone?"

"Who," I laughed, flattening the A4 sheet of paper from my pocket. "Okay, my question. What is it like to live in a world where you can have sex whenever you want it?"

"Whenever I want it?" Tess clarified.

"With me I mean. You only have to look sideways at me and it's on but I have to," there didn't seem to be a suitable word, "wait."

"Well poor you, it sounds terrible in your world, waiting around all the time."

"It really is." Our eyes were fixed on each other. We both enjoyed the banter and playful stand offs. Laughing together was sweet music.

"What's it like?" Tess thought. "It's great to know you're there when I need you. Maybe I should get a little bell to put beside the bed."

"Great idea. A sex bell. Can I have one too?" I asked.

"If you want. You can ring it all day, won't change anything. Honestly, it's great to know you're still attracted to me and I still love having sex with you. I just don't feel like it all the time. I can't just switch on the second you feel like it. It just doesn't work like that."

"I know. It's just hard sometimes, having to wait. It's different to when we were younger."

"Well, we're not younger anymore. I'm going to the loo."

"Cool." Tess disappeared around the end of the bar as I returned to the watching the weird and the wonderful on the main street of King's Cross. It was late January and it was oppressively hot. The pub was full of people laughing, talking loudly above the barely audible music. There was a happiness, an optimism that I could almost touch. It seemed a world away from the comfortable monotony of my real life.

"They're a band." Tess stated on her return.

"Who?"

"The Ramones. Don't they sing that dead pet song?"

"Pet Cemetery."

"Yeah, I never liked it. Dead animals are a weird thing to sing about."

"Depends on what you think is weird I guess. Your turn." Tess was already scrolling.

"Yeah, number nine. Has there ever been a guy you've met that you thought was good looking?" She assumed her standard poker face.

"Have I? Um, I guess the short answer is no, at least I don't think so. There's a younger guy that we work with a bit, he's at the centre two days a week. He's obviously a good-looking bloke and he's so good with the kids. Everything about him is cool and calm, they love him. He is so genuine with them. I don't think there's any sexual attraction, which is what you're asking, just a kind of plutonic admiration if that makes sense."

"It does. I was just curious. I thought that's what you'd say but sometimes, you know?" I didn't 'know' and I thought it best to leave it at that. I had no return question for Tess on this topic. I was happy for it to sit mysteriously in the bigger picture of our adventure. It didn't need to be explained or justified. I was happy that Tess got to explore that part of herself and that I was able to be a part of it. Very happy.

"Time to break the seal. Where were the toilets?" I asked.

"Do you ever look?" Tess asked on my return.

"Look where?"

"At the guy beside you, just to see how big it is, when you're standing there next to each other."

"You're a funny girl. No, I don't."

"You must sneak a look every now and then. I would," Tess asked.

"Never." I replied

"Don't believe it. You must have looked at least once."

"Not once. Ever. It's the unwritten rule of men's toilets. You look straight ahead the whole time. No peeking."

"There must be some guys that look, surely?" Tess wasn't convinced.

"I wouldn't know, I'm always looking straight ahead. Can't go breaking the rules."

"I still don't believe it," Tess protested.

"It's not hard to believe. Even if you're talking, everyone is looking dead ahead."

"How do you know they don't look? If you're never looking." Tess seemed pleased with her entrapment.

"I just know. It would be pretty obvious if someone was having a peek." It did make me wonder though, I had never really thought about it. "Was that one of your questions?"

"No, just interested."

"Nine. If we started playing dress ups at home, what outfit would you choose for me?" I asked. It was as much a suggestion as a question.

"Dress ups? Definitely a space man's full body outfit, with the helmet." She laughed, remembering my failed space analogy. "But you might not be able to breathe. I don't know. Probably something like a policeman, with a big batten maybe."

"I've already got a big batten."

"Have you? I haven't seen it."

"I think you have. I'll keep an eye out for a police outfit."

"And what outfit would you choose?" Tess asked

"Well, you already do the lingerie model just perfectly."

"Funny. The last one you bought was nice, not sure about some of the others."

"I like buying them for you. You look stunning in them."

"They're not for me, they're for you." Tess stared at the group of couples walking on the footpath only metres in front of us.

"For us. I'd choose a French maid's outfit with one of those miniskirts and black stockings. Low cut neck and piggy tails, definitely piggy tails."

"Well, that's very specific, you've obviously given it a lot of thought."

"No, it just came to me. French maid or dominatrix, either one. As long as there's piggy tails?" Both options sounded appealing. "Do you want a shot? Might be fun."

"I thought you'd never ask," Tess replied as she raised her empty glass. She looked free and picture perfect beautiful. We had left the runway. Just like the first time, the partly open window allowed a breath of wind to ripple her dark hair. That's what happiness looked like.

After three more pubs, and dinner, we had finished all of the questions and headed back out onto the footpath. It was nearly eight and time to think about other things.

"I love this part, just walking, taking it all in." I said as we headed back to the hotel.

"I need to walk off some dinner. It's still so hot."

A slight easterly breeze found us as we rounded the building opposite our hotel.

"Oh, that's good," Tess said falling backwards onto the king-sized bed. I headed straight for the beers I had put in the fridge earlier. Flying required fuel. I lay on the bed next to her, propped up on elbows.

"Are you nervous," I asked.

"Always."

"I am, like being in the sheds before a grand finale. Good nervous."

"Everything comes back to footy with you. It's exciting, but scary. Just like the first time." Tess stared out at the beating city. The window was floor to ceiling and the curtains were fully open. "It's like we can see the whole world from here."

"I've been thinking about Tim and Meg today. I wonder how they are going," I said. Tess shook her head.

"Meg texted last night. Doesn't sound good."

"I feel like I should be doing more. I know Tim would be hard to live with but it's not too late. Meg still loves him, I know she does."

"Sometimes that might not be enough. This is not something you can fix Ry. It's between them and they have to work it out if they can. Maybe it's you who needs to listen, just be there for him."

"Maybe." Tess was right as usual. "I still don't really understand what happened. Maybe I wasn't listening. I wish I could help."

"You can. Just be there."

"That view is breath-taking," I replied and sat up to get a better look at the city.

"Sure is."

"What do you think makes a marriage work?" I asked.

"I thought we finished the questions."

"Could be that the 'work' part is what makes a difference. Marriage is something that people have to continually work at, because you prioritise what matters, not just take it for granted."

"I don't think it's just 'work' that matters. Makes it sound like a job," replied Tess.

"I meant putting in the effort, trying. What do you think it is?"

"Its happy wife, happy life. I…"

"Here we go." I cut in. "Don't you think that theory is an insult to femininity? The concept that women need to be put on this pedestal above men to be happy.

I thought the whole idea was about respect and equality not, um, that thing." I completely lost my train of thought as Tess ran a finger down her cleavage.

"What thing?" Tess teased.

"You know, the thing." I slurred ever so slightly.

"What were we talking about again?" She was laughing at me, not with me.

"You know," I had to think, "about happy marriages. What makes some people last. Did you know one out of three ends in divorce, it's improved since the eighties. You didn't answer the question."

"I did answer and maybe you got the whole happy wife thing wrong anyway. It just means stop being a bunch of wankers and don't piss us off."

"Is that what it means? Hard to argue with that." Now she was laughing with me, or I with her. Tess had a simple, black and white view of the world much of the time and it was impossible not to love.

"What makes a marriage work," Tess pondered. "I think communication is a big part of it, being able to communicate but also to listen."

"Bill said that. I've been trying to work on that," I replied in sudden introspection.

"It takes time to learn but it gets more important as time goes on. But trust most of all, trust and loyalty. They go together."

"Yeah, they do. I know I haven't always got them exactly right." For the most part I was a trust worthy, loyal, loving husband but I was far from perfect.

"One out of three mate, you've got some work to do. Oh, and forgiveness. If two people are going to last, then there's got to be some of that too," added Tess.

Forgiveness seemed to be reoccurring theme over the past few years. But instead of drowning in blame or admissions of guilt, forgiveness seemed to be a liberating cornerstone of healing. That's as long as it started in an honest place.

"How do I look?" asked Tess.

"You look like the most beautiful girl in the room."

"I'm the only girl in the room."

"You always have been." Tess looked stunning and tonight she had dressed in her own style, rather than in the semi-formal manner of the first few times that the website had advised. She wore tight black jeans that sat perfectly over her curved frame and a pair of ass kicking Doc Martin boots that I just loved. They were Tess to a tee. Her t-shirt was dark blue with a low V-neck that showed just the right amount of cleavage. She was understated and quietly confident. "You look stunning in every way."

"Thanks. Sometimes I don't feel it."

"You do. It's after eight. We've still got a fifteen-minute walk," I said as Tess continued to study the city landscape.

"Welcome to Deepest Desires." I was happy to see Mav's beaming grin behind the rustic, black door. He knew how to make you feel immediately welcome. "The coasties, hi guys." I could hear Juice WRLD playing in the background and the bass heavy tones suited the club well.

"Hi Mav, how's it going?" I beamed back.

"Always good. Love the boots." Mav tipped his head at Tess' Docs and I handed him the entry fee. With our customary plastic bag of drinks in one hand, we stepped into the rabbit hole once more.

"Scares me every time. Stay close," Tess whispered behind me.

"Always." A couple chatted quietly in the first smaller lounge and didn't look up as we entered. I squeezed Tess' hand tight. "Scares me too."

"Just drop your drinks off, you know where. I'll see you in there. Enjoy your night." Mav breezed past us to resume his post as barman and we followed behind. The main lounge had about five couples, each with a drink in hand, enjoying the early sparks of connection. Nearest the front room was an immaculately dressed couple around our age. She wore a black cocktail dress with high heels. He matched in tightly fitting dress pants and a dark blue-collared shirt.

"Hi, how you going?" I greeted politely as we continued, following Mav through the main lounge.

"Well thanks," he replied. Both of them smiled warmly at Tess and I. There was a younger couple beside them. They were similarly smart in a short red dress and an altogether too small-collared shirt with the top buttons undone. They were deep in conversation with the couple beside them who had already dressed down into matching black teddy and briefs.

"It just seems so strange all over again to see people in their undies," I said as we left the main lounge and stalled in front of the dungeon to our left.

"But they were nice undies."

"Very nice. Yeah, I think I can get used to it again." I looked into the gothic, perfectly arranged dungeon. It was a world that I had known nothing about not so long ago and it still seemed so foreign, yet so alluring.

"Can't wait to get back in there tonight," I said involuntarily. I stepped back. I didn't want Tess to know how much I had enjoyed this place before.

"We might give it try," Tess replied. The pleasure and pain relationship was one that many people would never get to experience in a sexual context and I had never really thought about it until Deepest Desires. I was drawn to it. "We might even try it at home."

"Yes please, this night just keeps getting better." I replied excitedly. Tess raised her eyebrows as I took another few steps and sat the drinks on the bar. The back room down the stairs had two couples in quiet conversation who seemed oblivious to anyone else around them.

I closed the locker and grabbed a breath mint from the bench before stopping and taking a few long deep breaths.

"I'm going to the bar," a deep voice said as the short red dress flashed through the locker room door.

"Prick," she said in the happiest of voices. She wobbled slightly on her heels and grabbed the wall. "Well, hi you two," she greeted as she took her heels off and sat on the step leading up to the mirror. I couldn't help but stare for a moment at her beautiful, long brown hair and perfect complexion. She was drunk.

"Hi," said Tess. "Don't worry, this one's a prick too."

"I'm not really. A tool maybe but not a prick," I said half defensively.

"That's good. I could use a tool tonight," she replied.

"I'm Tess, the tool's Ryan." Tess sat in the single seat and swivelled around to face her as she took off her stilettos.

"I'm Charlie, that was Liam, he's at the bar, I think. He cheated on me you know. Four years and he just fucked everything. Maybe I'll fuck everything." She stood and pushed her hair back behind her shoulders.

"I'm sorry to hear that." Tess shot a judgmental glance at me. "They can be mongrels."

"He can be." Charlie replied. "Anyway, I'm going to enjoy myself tonight." She fumbled with her locker key and Tess nodded quickly to make an exit.

"That's good. You do that," encouraged Tess.

"I need a drink, ah, we'll see you in there Charlie," I said, leaving the locker room with Tess close behind me. As we turned the corner Liam marched towards us with a scowl and a drink in each hand.

"Hi mate." I said. He just nodded without word. That full wall mirror in the locker room always felt like a magnifying glass reflecting exactly where a couple was at. If you were not on exactly on the same page, then I always had a sense that this place could rip you apart. Deepest Desires was not a place for grudges and emotions were amplified in the extreme. I hated to think what it would do to any negative energy between couples.

"That's not going to end well," Tess said quietly. She smacked me hard on the backside as we headed to the bar.

"I do need a drink. Well Liam seemed nice," I scoffed. He had an arrogant look of entitlement that appeared to lack any remorse or understanding of the hurt he had caused. I knew Tess would have taken an instant, and permanent, dislike to him. Maybe I was being overly judgmental about someone I didn't know at all. Maybe he was just some bloke who made a mistake, like me.

We grabbed a drink each from the bar. Another couple joined us at the counter as Tess subtly nudged me with her elbow, prompting me to say hello.

"Hi, how you going?" I asked as Tess collected our drinks. It was the well-dressed couple from the front room and I couldn't help but admire the shapely cocktail dress.

"Good, good. Still a bit nervous but enjoying the night so far." He replied.

"I know what you mean. It's like being at a school dance except you don't know anyone there," I said. Tess handed me a beer.

"Exactly, well I'm Rob, this is Marie. Great to meet you."

"You too. I'm Ryan. This is Tess."

"Nice to meet you. At least we know someone at the dance now," he said politely.

"I love your boots." Marie commented to Tess. "I wasn't sure what to wear." She sipped her wine anxiously.

"Thanks, I'm not very good in heals. And they'll come in handy if this one gets out of line." Tess nudged me again with her elbow to the amusement of Rob and Marie.

"Did you see that room?" Marie motioned towards the dungeon behind her. "I wonder if anyone goes in there. They have whips."

"I think they might. It's only early." I didn't want to sound too knowledgeable about a room like that and I certainly didn't want to give any hints about how much I wanted to get in there again. "We might grab a table?" Another couple walked towards the bar from the front lounge as Tess and I headed for one of the tall tables near the locker room door. Rob and Marie followed.

"This place is like nothing I've ever seen, have you been here before?" Rob asked immediately.

"Just once. It was really cool just to meet people and," it was hard to explain, "feel like that again."

"It was a nice night," Tess said, "not what I expected at all."

"And you?" I asked.

"No, no. First timers. This is all kind of scary, but exciting," Marie replied. She stood with perfect posture, almost touching Rob they were so close. A part of her did seem scared and I understood it well.

"So, what brought you to a club like this?" Rob asked.

"Good question." I had a million answers but it was so hard to articulate. Rule two. "Well, we were very young when we met and we've been happy ever since, we've got two beautiful kids. But I guess we were just curious and we wanted to give each other the chance to," the chance to do what I thought, "to do this." They listened intently.

"How old are your kids?" Marie asked.

"Leyla's ten and Josh is twelve," Tess replied as I guzzled my beer. Marie looked at Rob and smiled.

"Wow, we have a ten and twelve-year-old too. Kye and Wil," said Marie. "We were pretty young too, when we met."

"And why this place?" I had to ask. They looked at each other again, minus the smile.

"I guess over the past few years, ah, things changed and, and I don't know, we were curious too," Rob replied. I don't think his answer even scratched the surface of why they were there. No one owed any explanations in this place. It was just a crazy meeting of worlds on that one night.

They were quietly spoken and there was a kind of vulnerability about them that made them even more endearing. There was a softness in the way they spoke and both Tess and I enjoyed the simple act of hanging out with them. But it was hard to ignore the curves of the cocktail dress and Marie's curled brown hair hanging over her shoulders. She was beautiful.

"Should we head up to the main room?" Tess asked.

"For sure, I love this song," I replied.

"A seat would be good." Marie looked downwards towards her heels.

"Sounds good. Did you see the pole in there?" Rob asked.

"Oh, we saw it. Might even see some dancing later hey Ryan?" Tess teased. We walked into the main lounge which was now humming with seven or so couples. Another two of them had dressed down. We stood next to the stairs, with the fan next to us, taking it all in.

"No seats, let's go into the front room," Tess suggested.

"Okay, after you." Tess led the way with Rob and Marie following.

"I'm glad you kept walking Tess, I was a bit nervous in there," Marie said as we sat on the empty bench seating in the front room. "That photo really is, ah, graphic." We all looked at the naked couple on the wall.

"It is. Looks like the club's user manual," I replied.

"Hi there," greeted a full-figured woman in a strapless white dress as she walked into the front room. Her partner followed in single file, led by the hand. He was thick set with a powerful build and reminded me of one of the footy players I had grown up with.

"Howdy. Kieran, this is Michelle," he said simply.

"How you going, it's a bit quieter in here." I was appreciative of the extra company and his relaxed tone. "This is Tess, I'm Ryan."

"Nice to meet you. This is my wife Marie, I'm Rob." Rob stood and gave Kieran a formal handshake. It was hard not to like his gentlemanly demeanour.

"But the music is still loud enough," Michelle said as Kieran took a seat. She stood at his side and her whole body moved with the music. I felt like moving too. "Nice photo. I thought there'd be a few more in the bed."

"This place is like something out of a movie. We saw it online but I never thought we'd be here." Kieran said thoughtfully. He gazed up at the photo along with Michelle.

"So, this is your first time?" asked Rob.

"First time, yeah. We came into town from Manly for the night."

"First time too. It's been fun so far, a lot more relaxed than I expected," said Rob.

"How about you guys?" asked Michelle.

"Ah, second time," replied Tess. People were obviously interested in the swinging credentials of potential partners.

"Well, you might have to tell us all about it later on," said Michelle.

The conversation flowed so easily. It still amazed me that I could feel so comfortable with strangers. Maybe it was the fact that we were all blank canvases to the other couples. There was no history, no preconceived ideas, just the here and now. But surrounding the canvas was the electricity. Everyone must have felt it. It dripped off every word, every movement.

"This is so much fun, just chatting. Somehow, I thought it would be different," said Michelle. She had not sat down once. They were younger than us, mid-thirties maybe, and she was instantly likeable. She had longish blonde hair and smiled constantly. As the night went on, it was Michelle's kindness and honesty that I admired most. These were the traits that I loved in Tess as well.

Michelle made sure everyone was included in the conversation and the room had a sense of inclusiveness rather than the seedy self-interest that people might have expected. She had a quiet confidence and she made me want to dance too. Kieran was easy to talk to, like one of the boys, and was ruggedly handsome. It was impossible not to like them.

"Well, this is nice, evening everyone." A tall, sandy haired man with a thick American accent walked in from the main lounge. He was followed by a much shorter blonde-haired woman. He was dressed only in Ralph Loren briefs, while she had on a lace edged red teddy. They looked at home with a Jim Beam can and wine glass in hand.

"Hi everyone," she waved with a sweeping hand gesture. The accent reminded me of Sierra and disjointed memories of the three of us in that room flooded my head.

"Hello, come join us," Michelle said enthusiastically.

"Great, I need a seat. Still a bit jet lagged. We only flew in from Florida yesterday," Ralph Loren said.

"Wow, long flight. You must be exhausted," I replied

"Yeah, but ready to party you know. I'm Jamie, this is Rose." They took a seat between us and Kieran. The other two couples did their introductions.

Everyone spoke openly, honestly about their lives, relationships and a gambit of topics that I never would have imagined sharing with strangers.

"I might just go to the ladies. Rob?" Marie gestured for him to follow and he obliged immediately. They were gone for what seemed like an age before returning, dressed down, with drinks in hand.

"Well don't you two look fantastic," complimented Jamie. He was right, they did.

"Thanks, we thought if we'd come this far, we might as well, you know," said Rob.

"He's right, you look great," Michelle continued. "I love your chemise Marie. Two kids, you look amazing." Marie shrank into Rob's shoulder at the compliment. She looked slightly uncomfortable with the attention.

"Thanks, I really didn't know what to wear. It was Rob's pick."

"He did well, didn't you Rob?" complimented Rose.

"Well maybe it's time for us to show off our new purchases for the week, c'mon big fella," ordered Michelle with a grin.

"I guess so then." Kieran laughed as he downed his beer. He was definitely a footy player. Before long they had returned, and Michelle gave a quick spin and a curtsy before jumping back onto the seat in fits of laughter.

"Where's your spin Kieran," laughed Tess as he walked across the room. His frame carried a few extra kilos like everyone after the kids had come along, but he looked relaxed and seemed to be enjoying the night.

"Don't think so, bad knee you know."

Again, I was drawn to Michelle in her white teddy. It was perfect for her full figure and she seemed so comfortable in her own skin.

"Dance with me," Rose asked Jamie as she danced in front of him. He stood and held Rose's hand, drink in the other, subtly swaying with the beat. He looked down at her and kissed her cheek.

"Any time." They had a kind of freedom about them, another 'dance like no one's watching' vibe. They were around our age and looked like they were loving the Sydney nightlife. He must have been six two or three, lean and laid back.

"That's me," yelled Michelle as she got up again to dance, almost on Kieran's lap. "C'mon Bear, dance with me." He shook his head and looked happy watching Michelle.

"So, have you been to a place like this before?" Michelle asked Rose.

"Oh yeah, plenty of times. The swinger's scene is pretty big in the states. The clubs are much bigger than this but I love this place already. Have you all been before?"

"No, no. First time for us." Replied Michelle. Rose looked in our direction.

"You guys look so hot." Instantly I mistook the comment for a compliment. "Might be time to visit the locker room." We were now the only clothed couple in the room. It seemed completely counter intuitive to feel self-conscious because we were the only clothed couple in a room of strangers. But that was Deepest Desires. Nothing was normal.

"Ah, I need a beer anyway. Anyone want a drink?" I felt an uncharacteristic shyness at the attention.

"Let's get it off," called Tess, raising an empty glass and standing to the cheers of our new friends. She still surprised me at times, even after all those years.

"Locker room it is then, after the bar though." We walked back through the main lounge, full by this time, and past the dungeon. A younger skin and bone couple were perusing the whip cabinet.

"Let's get it off." I laughed. "Look at you go Mrs Tanner."

"You only live once."

"How much have you had to drink?" I asked.

"Just enough." We collected drinks from the bar and again stood at the mirror in the locker room. It was like a time out space from the explosion of senses in the club and a chance to return to earth for a few moments.

"You having fun?" I asked.

"Yeah, they seem really nice." After finally getting her Docs off, Tess stripped off quickly. I was standing in my normal tight black briefs and again looked at us in the mirror. I felt a real pride in my physique, lean and muscled at an age when most of my mates were putting on the pounds. The weights I did each morning got me through the day, they were a kind of mental armoury against the stresses of life. I worked out to survive, not to look good, but it was a bonus. I worked hard at it and at that moment I felt good, really good.

Tess, on the other hand, was just a natural beauty. She enjoyed getting to the gym with friends, but she didn't have to same drive that got me out of bed early every morning of the week. To look at her, people might not have immediately picked her indigenous heritage, but to me it shone as bright and beautiful as ever. She ruffled her hair and looked down at her laced black one-piece teddy.

"You look amazing, really. I don't know what I ever did to get so lucky."

"One crowded hour of glorious life hey," Tess quoted.

"Yeah, one crowded hour alright."

"Eight. That's a lot of people," she mumbled as we headed out of the locker room.

"I hadn't really thought about that. Breath mint just in case."

"Just in case what?" Tess questioned, before laughing. "Let's go Tano."

"Alright. Lead the way." By this time, almost every couple in the place had dressed down. It seemed like a kind of 'when in Rome' sort of unwritten rule. There were roughly fifteen to twenty couples throughout the club as we walked through to the front room, each living their own crowded hours. Two couples walked up the staircase in the main room just as we entered and I stopped momentarily to stare, knowing what came next.

"Hey, here they are," welcomed Michelle as she continued to dance in front of Kieran. Rose and Jamie both locked their gaze on Tess and we took a seat.

"We're missing two," I said. "Where's Rob and Marie?"

"I thought you would have seen them, they just went back to the locker room."

"Missed them."

"Maybe they stopped in at the dungeon," said Kieran.

"They really didn't seem like dungeon sort of people to me," Tess replied.

"And what do dungeon people look like?" I asked.

"Like you, a bit strange looking you know."

"We're all a bit strange." The funny thing was, I was a dungeon person, whatever that was, although I had never known it. I loved being in there with Tess and I was sure that most other people would love it too as long as they were there with the right person.

We never saw Rob and Marie again, even though we had walked back through the club to the bar a few more times. They seemed like kind, gentle people and I had loved their company from the moment they sat down. In the haze of alcohol, music and banter, it was now just the six of us in the front room and the night steam rolled on.

"Dance with me Rose," asked Michelle who had been dancing all night.

"Love to," replied Rose as they took each other's hand in the middle of the room. I watched every movement in the symphony of flesh and lace, every curve and every spark. Tess watched just as closely; she could hear the symphony too.

"C'mon Tess, do you want to dance?" said Rose.

"Ryan is our dancer, he'd love to get up there, wouldn't you Ry?"

"I'm good, you girls are doing an awesome job." Really, I was fighting the urge to get up and move. I desperately wanted to dance but remained at Tess' side. I found myself thinking about that question, wondering who would ask, if they'd ask.

"C'mon you two."

"You twisted my arm," I said as I got up, keeping hold of Tess' hand and clutching my beer in the other. I stayed close to Tess with my back to the girls. I turned, letting Tess go as Michelle and Rose moved closer and the three of us danced in the middle of the room.

"Yeah Ryan," Rose yelled in her thick accent as Jamie stood and took a long sip of his Jim beam.

"C'mon you, dance with me." I pulled Tess to her feet and for once she didn't take any convincing. Avicii pumped through the speakers and Tess' lips touched mine for a moment as I pulled her to the middle of the room. Jamie joined the girls as Michelle grabbed Kieran's hand and pulled him into the circle.

"Dance like no one's watching," I said to Tess.

"That's how you always dance. I love it," she replied. But people were watching. Eyes ran up and down bodies, glances met for fractions of seconds and I could see electricity everywhere, lighting up the room. Our room.

Before we'd started this crazy journey, I thought that it would just be two people in a room. Never in my wildest dreams did I think that there would be six. But like the first time it didn't seem strange or wrong, there were no moral judgements. It was just living in a single moment. At that point in time, there was no yesterday or tomorrow, there was no world outside the front door only metres away. There was just that moment and we were flying above it all.

The song finished and there was a brief silence as everyone instinctively reached for their drink.

"That was awesome. I love that song," Rose said.

"I could dance all night," replied Michelle.

"Or maybe, if you guys wanted to, maybe we could check out upstairs," Jamie said. My heart pounded, partly from the dancing, mostly from that single word. Upstairs. There was a momentary pause before Michelle replied.

"Why not?" Eyes met again, but it was partners looking at each other. It was a single look that asked 'are we doing this.' Six mostly empty drinks were placed on the table or the floor. Then we were walking. Single file, we headed silently into the main lounge, Rose leading the way. It was just after midnight.

Eight couples were left in the main lounge and they hardly noticed the six of us walking up the stairs. They knew exactly where we were going and exactly what we were going to do, but they barely looked up from their conversations.

"Are you good," I asked Tess at the back of the line, yet again reaching for her hand. It was my lifeline to reality, my security blanket, and it was all I needed.

"I'm good, watch where you're going." I savoured each step and the electricity that charged through me. I watched Michelle's beautiful, full figure take each step a metre in front of me, the curve of her legs and the cascade of blonde hair into lace. Rose turned left at the top of the stairs into the empty bedroom, simply furnished with a queen-sized bed, bedside table and chaise lounge.

As I entered, I stepped to my right, in front of the lounge, and Michelle sat on the end of the bed.

"This is crazy, I can't believe we're here." She looked at me, then began to unhitch her teddy. No one replied and I took a long, deep breath. Jamie stepped past Kieran and reached an arm around Tess, cupping her bum in his hand. He leant down to kiss her on the lips. Like many of my dreams, I remember the feeling more than the details. It was a feeling of trust, and love, for Tess. Anything other than that armoury of emotions would have torn me to pieces.

I turned to look at Michelle and at the same time, Rose stepped towards me and kissed me. It was slow and deep as she ran her hands down my torso onto my hips. She pushed gently and guided me onto the lounge directly behind so I was lying flat with my head on the leather cushion at the end. She positioned a knee either side of me on the lounge and leant down to kiss me again. At the same time, she slid her hand into my briefs and began to squeeze, to massage. I pushed my hips towards her hand as she pulled, tighter, harder.

"Do you like that?" she whispered in my ear before biting it softly. Before I had even thought about replying, she kissed me again. I pulled her lingerie down enough to bare her breasts and rubbed my palms gently against her nipples. Our tongues explored. It was a completely new kiss, a new taste. She kissed harder, gripping me all the time. My thumb slid under her panties and my fingers ran down the soft flesh on the inside of her thighs.

"You taste good," Rose said. Her lips trailed down my neck as her soft hair brushed my face. The new smell filled my senses. Rose stood up, watching me all the time, and pulled her lingerie down to her waist, then slid it over her hips onto the floor. I paused for a moment and took in every part of her, this unbridled American that had only arrived in the country the day before.

As she stepped forward again, I jumped up to my feet and walked around the side of the bed to the condom filled fruit bowl on the bedside table. Tess and Jamie were on their side, kissing, as he caressed her exposed breast. Her eyes were closed and she seemed completely unaware that I stopped and watched her for an instant.

Kieran and Michelle were already making love next to them. She glanced at me from her missionary position on the bed as Kieran buried his head in her shoulder and kept a powerful rhythm. I quickly turned and took the five steps back to Rose.

I ripped the condom packet open with my teeth as Rose stepped forward and clawed her nails down my chest until they touched my briefs. She pulled them to the floor, ending up on her knees in front of me. She started to work her hand up and down the length of me again and kissed my thigh. I closed my eyes and felt my whole body rippling as I inhaled deep, long breaths.

Rose stood and her lips went straight to mine as I positioned the condom and rolled it down onto me. I grabbed her bottom with both hands and ran them around to her hips, then up to her breasts where my thumbs pushed back and forth over her hard nipples. I wanted to touch every part of her.

"I think I love Australia already," she whispered between kisses.

"Glad you like it." I didn't want to talk. Again, Rose gently guided me onto the lounge and I lay down on my back as she assumed her position on top. Except this time, when she took me in her hand, she guided me inside her. I instantly thrust upwards as she pushed down and dug her nails into my chest again. Slowly, forcefully, she moved back and forth on me. She pushed her chest out and closed her eyes hard as I gripped her hips and matched every movement.

The smell of her perfume, mixed with sweat, surrounded the lounge. Each small groan she made was like a new language. Foreign, yet somehow familiar, I knew exactly what she was saying. I looked up at the Victorian styled cornices on the roof of the room and, for a second, wondered about all of the stories this old Sydney building could tell. There would have been few more engaging ones than those that were happening at that moment.

"Yes. Yes," Michelle said as the sound of flesh colliding on the bed became louder. I knew there would be no commentary from Tess, she was the silent type. Rose sat tall, with one hand on the raised side of the lounge nearest the wall. She drove harder, pulling me deep into her, running one hand though her hair.

I pushed my torso up so that I sat upright and wrapped my arms around her, kissing passionately all the time. I grabbed her ass hard and pulled her into me as I thrust while she ran both hands through my hair. I swivelled so that Rose's back faced the bed and stood. She wrapped both legs around me before I lifted her off me and stood her on the floor in front of me. It was my turn to guide her.

With one hand on her hip, I gently turned her body and pushed her back onto the lounge.

"Hands and knees," I ordered. I put my hand between her legs and massaged the soft, wet flesh. Her body shuddered at my touch. I stopped for a moment, making her wait, and her entire body tensed. I teased, harder and harder and then stopped again, barely touching her at all.

I sat one knee on the lounge, with one foot remaining on the floor, and put myself inside her. This time I was in control and I thrust purposefully and slowly, but hard, and crashed my body into hers.

"Yes," Rose whispered. I pushed my head back and closed my eyes. She reached behind and clawed at my stomach. My hands flattened as I ran my palms over every part of her outer thighs, her hips and her behind. They pushed forward to the arch of her back and around to her ribs and breasts. Back to her hips, I gripped her hard, so that I could pull her into me with every pounding thrust.

From my standing position, I had full view of the room and of the bed with the four naked bodies on it. Kieran and Michelle were still in missionary positions. He was propped up by both arms and moved at a seemingly unsustainable speed. Michelle's knees and shapely calves stood either side of him as her hands ran up and down his back. Blokes really do have hairy asses. What a strange thought to have at that moment.

I turned to Tess and Jamie, who were in exactly the same position. My beautiful Tess. Any negative sentiments or jealously seemed to be washed away by the ideas of Tess being happy, being free, and at the same time being more mine than ever.

The lounge was directly opposite the end of the bed and Jamie was elevated just slightly on his knees. Because his torso was slightly elevated, I could see every single part of them both. Everything. There was a raw, primal beauty watching that connection of flesh, but I only allowed myself the briefest glance before my attention turned back to Rose.

She grabbed the end of the chase lounge and pushed herself backwards in time with each movement of my hips and closed her legs slightly to tighten each entry and withdrawal. My palms continued their exploration of her body as the sweat started to glint in the subtle light. One hand moved forward around her thigh to her inner thigh and my hand ran over the creases of flesh to that spot.

"Mmm. Yeah." The words were more like breaths. She stopped pushing herself back onto me and started to softly thrust her hips forward onto my single fingertip. Each push forward of my body matched the movement of my fingertip.

I pushed then withdrew, harder and harder, until I knew she was almost there. Again, I slowed everything, almost stopping, but not quite.

"Again," asked Rose. I pushed hard and deep inside her again and began another slow rhythm that my fingertip followed. The pressure on that spot was key, hard enough to fly but not too hard.

"Yeah, yes. Harder." Rose's echoing breaths were audible only in our little corner of the room. Every muscle tensed as I pushed harder, pressed harder and I felt the sweat surfacing across my body. This time, when her body screamed that she was close, I didn't stop. The harmony of flesh kept time and Rose's body sang for those moments, every muscle tensing as her head flew back wildly. Then her head dropped almost to the lounge, and everything stopped as each muscle relaxed.

Again, I started to thrust harder, faster. Except this time, it wasn't for Rose. She responded immediately, pushing back against me in time. My hands resumed their mapping of her body and again she closed her legs slightly, tightening her body around me. I was close. The alcohol coursing through my body was a cushion against reality but it was also a physical barrier to reaching climax.

I reached forward, grabbing her breasts and pulling her into me, pulling myself deeper into her. Then I felt that fuse ignite deep inside where my body took control and I could do nothing but enjoy the ocean of pleasure that flooded my head. Self-control left my body as the metronomic rhythm faded. I could see nothing, hear nothing. I could only feel the explosion that left my body in those few moments when the rest of the world ceased to exist.

I opened my eyes, not realising that I was standing completely still. My head drooped forward and I immediately, instinctively, took my hands off Rose. Ensuring the condom was secure, I gently withdrew as she stood and turned to face me. She put one hand on my cheek and kissed me as I carefully peeled the rubber from my body.

"That was incredible," Rose said in between kisses. I wanted to turn and look at Tess again. I dropped the parcel in the bin next to the lounge and turned to the bed. Tess was now on top of Jamie, her tanned back and black hair facing me. Kieran lay beside Michelle, kissing her breasts. She looked straight at me and swiped the hair from her face.

Without really thinking, I walked to Kieran's side of the bed and took another condom from the basket. Rose followed and sat on the corner of the bed. Kieran looked up at her as I returned to the base of the bed and gently crawled up to Michelle.

"Is this okay?" I asked Kieran who simply nodded and stood, taking two steps to kiss Rose. I moved up to Michelle, between her legs, kissing her thighs and then her stomach. My elbow touched Tess' but I didn't dare look this time. I kissed Michelle's nipples then mouthed them softly, and I ran my hand up the inside of her thigh.

"Hi," Michelle said as she guided my lips to hers. It was a new taste again, and a searching tongue.

"Hi," I whispered. She put both hands on my hips and ran them over my back, pulling me onto her. She clenched my hair between her fingers and I felt the wetness as I guided myself slowly into her before a sudden, hard drive forwards. I propped myself up onto my straightened arms and began slowly, gently. I could hear Tess' heavy breathing beside me. Michelle looked like she was a million miles away. She was flying too.

Michelle's hand slid down her stomach and her fingers found the part of her body that wanted to be touched most. I could feel her soft knuckles pushing against my stomach, gradually quickening all the time, until a loud gasp as her whole body pushed upwards. She opened her eyes just for a moment to look at me and her mouth gaped, sucking in enormous breaths that moved her entire body. She fought to stay silent, lost in those moments of ecstasy, before everything stopped and she sank deep into the bed.

She smiled up at me and shot a subtle glance at Kieran and Rose.

"You were the first, besides Kieran, in such a long time," whispered Michelle. I could only kiss her and smile as warmly as I could. I knew exactly where she was coming from but I had no idea as to what to say to something as intimate as that. Tess and Jamie were silent, except for the faint grind of flesh and I continued to avoid looking at them as best I could. I edged off the end of the bed to put the empty condom in the bin and Kieran quietly returned to the bed next to Michelle.

"Hey you. Having fun?" He asked. She kissed him without reply.

"Those two are enjoying themselves." Rose motioned towards Tess behind me.

"I hope so. She's something special that one."

"Yeah. Seems like it. They don't look finished yet." Rose took my hand and pulled me towards her. Again, she kissed me, scratching my chest softly. I kissed back. Her hands continued down to my thighs and she dropped to her knees.

I stood with my eyes closed while her blonde hair moved rhythmically at my waist. I could hear the noise of her lips on me. I looked back down at her through alcohol soaked eyes and then around the room, at the four people on the bed. Just at that moment Tess stood up. She looked straight at us.

Of all the moments, all the mental snapshots from our wild adventures in the upstairs, that one is the one that I remember most. What was she thinking at that moment? My dick was in another woman's mouth and she was looking straight at us. For a second amongst all of the ecstasy, I felt disgusted in myself. What had I done? It was madness. Then I remembered that we had done it together.

At that moment, Tess smiled. It was warm and forgiving. There was such strength and understanding in her face. Everything was okay. This was the moment I remember most from all the hours, all the nights that we spent living that crazy dream. It was proof that we had each other's back, proof that we meant what we said. Let each other fly.

Tess mouthed the word 'toilet' and walked out of the room towards the king bedroom ensuite. Being alone upstairs was not a good idea, especially for a woman, no matter how respectful the other guests were. I ran my fingers through Rose's hair, gently pushing my pelvis back and forth. Kieran and Michelle resumed their position at the side of the bed and I watched every intricate detail of their union from where I was standing. Jamie lay beside them watching.

"That was interesting," Tess said, barely audible above the music as she walked back into the room. Rose looked up briefly. "Someone just kissed me while I was sitting on the toilet. He asked me to come to bed."

"Shit, what did you say?"

"Nothing, just got out of there." Tess returned to the bed with Jamie and I closed my eyes as Rose continued. Minutes felt like seconds and my tensed body readied itself again.

"Love you babe," Kieran said to Michelle, prompting my eyes to open. He traced his hand over her breasts as they lay side by side. Tess fell to the middle of the bed next to Michelle. Rose stood and kissed my chest before sitting on the end of the bed. There was an awkward moment of silence.

"Now that was amazing," Rose said to everyone as Jamie stood and discreetly dropped the rubber in the bin. I scanned the floor for my underwear and we dressed in silence. Michelle sang quietly to the song floating from the main lounge.

The six of us made our way down the stairs and, as always, I found the security of Tess' hand.

"Drinks?" I asked but Tess was already headed directly to the bar. "Are you good?"

"Yeah, I'm good." Tess and I stood at the bar with Jamie and Rose. Michelle and Kieran arrived moments afterwards.

"The front room is empty. We might have a drink in there if you're keen?" offered Kieran.

"Sounds great," Jamie said. The six of us took our drinks and sat tentatively on the bench seating of the front room. We were a group of strangers, wearing only their underwear, who had just done amazing things, wild things, together. The peculiar thing was that it wasn't awkward, or weird, sitting there afterwards. We talked like old friends who had a thousand shared memories. But in reality, we had only one.

For two hours we chatted, laughed and shared our lives openly and honestly. Other couples came and went as we enjoyed the simple pleasure of social connection. Normally this came long before the physical, but nothing was quite normal at Deepest Desires.

Tess and I listened intently to what life was like growing up in Florida and stories from childhoods spent on the northern beaches of Sydney. We shared our own small-town experiences and crazy adventures into the city. We discussed each other's families, dreams and most private desires that people would not have shared with their best mates. The time melt consumed those beautiful two hours in a moment.

"That was really cool, just talking. Really cool," Tess said as we walked slowly, deliberately, back to the hotel. It was almost like we wanted that night to last for just a little longer and to hold onto the energy that powered every second.

"I wonder what happened to Rob and Marie," I said as a siren rang out in the distance. "Do you think they went upstairs?"

"Don't know, I don't think so. They were talking to us most of the time, they didn't seem the type to just meet another couple and go straight up."

"No, that's what I thought. Marie was shy, but she really seemed to enjoy hanging out."

"Maybe that was enough for them, just being there, talking to new people in their undies. That's a pretty big leap for some people," Tess replied.

"Yeah, it is. Twelve stairs is a whole other level."

"Puns again? You're funny."

"What?"

"I wonder how many marriages that place could help." Tess sighed. "Probably not as many as it would destroy."

"This whole thing has made me feel more alive than I could explain. It's the electricity. Not just the sexual energy, it's the life energy, every part of me. I'm better at work, I bounce out of bed in the morning, it's made me treasure you and the kids even more if that's possible."

"Wow, who would have known," Tess scoffed.

"I know right." I was attempting to be serious. "I mean it. I just feel alive and thankful. For you, the kids, our crazy weekends away. Everything."

"Yeah, it's been pretty good." She was understating what I could hear in her voice.

"It's not the sex, like people would think. It's not. It's having the complete trust and support of the person you love most to do those things. Its feeling connected to you, other people, the city, myself, life. Do you know what I mean?"

"So, you love connecting with yourself is what you're saying."

"Good on ya."

"I know what you mean," admitted Tess.

It was euphoric, addictive like a drug, and I wanted more of that feeling. I wasn't to know that using up that kind of energy wasn't sustainable and that it wouldn't last. Not that kind of energy anyway. Those highs had balanced out against the deepest of lows. But for that moment I was still flying and I loved every second.

The summer air had cooled in the early hours of the morning and the city was as silent as it got. It was three twenty am on a Sunday morning and we could see the city lights contrasted against the dark void of Hyde Park from the elevated views of King's Cross. We didn't talk any more about the night. We revelled in the day together, family, future and we slowly came back down to earth.

We would never discuss the details of that night again, neither of us felt the need. We both had the memories of something wild locked away and that's exactly where they would stay.

Chapter 20
Forgiveness Frees the Soul

"That was the longest drive home ever. How's your head?" I asked as we turned into our quiet, suburban street.

"Sore. Never drinking again sore. There's Josh." Josh stood in the middle of the road and booted the footy high in the air for Jet to catch. They scampered off the road as they heard the car coming and disappeared inside.

"I wonder what Jet's doing here."

"Have you spoken to Tim lately?" Tess asked as we unpacked the car.

"Nah, not since last week."

"Meg wasn't answering at all last week. It's not like her. She didn't sound good last time we spoke."

"Might give him a call this arvo." I hadn't spoken to Tim in a few weeks, which never happened and again, he didn't pick up. But he did reply to my text. 'They're gone. Everything is fucked.'

That afternoon, Tim opened the front door slowly. He had clearly been crying and walked back into the house without even saying hello.

"She's gone Tano. I dunno what I'm going to do. She took the kids and left."

"No. Tim." What do you say at a moment like that? No words could make the smallest possible difference. I felt like holding him, but he definitely wasn't a hugger. "I'm so sorry mate. I shoulda been here." We sat for what seemed like minutes without speaking. I put my hand on his shoulder as he fought the sound that each quiet sob made.

"What happened?"

"Who knows? One fight too many. She's never fuckin happy. Or maybe I stuffed this all up." Tim was a big bloke; rugby props were some of the toughest athletes on the planet. But at that moment he looked small, broken. Most of all he looked alone.

"I don't know who I am anymore." He didn't look at me, he just stared out the window from his seat at the dinner table.

"I don't think anyone really knows. We just make it up as we go and do the best we can."

"Last Thursday I helped run the bottles at training. Some of the young blokes were going to the pub. I miss those days. I really miss them, being part of a team. The boys never ask questions, they're never on ya case. They just get it. I went out and came home late. Pissed. I didn't text Meg. That's all it was, it just went from there. The beginning of the end. Or maybe that began a long time ago."

"Maybe the boys get us, maybe they don't. They don't have kids or a wife to go home to after training. I don't think they get what that means. They're young, it's their time to live without responsibility."

"I know. It wasn't just one night. She's been, she just hasn't been happy for a long time and I don't know whether she pushed me away or I just walked. I'm tired Tano and fucken miss 'em so much."

"Any bloke would." My heart broke for him.

"I don't blame her. They're my world, Meg and the kids."

"Yeah, I know that feeling. You're not alone Tim."

"Well, I feel completely fucken alone." He looked at me with shattered, red eyes. "I'm sorry. Thanks for coming over."

"You don't need to say sorry to me. I'm not going anywhere. You want a coffee?"

"Yep." We sat in silence for a while. The mundane chat about footy, work or whatever just didn't seem to matter when the only things that really mattered to Tim were gone.

"Finding out who you are is a long, tough journey. I've been going through the same things, asking myself the same questions," I said eventually.

"But your Mrs didn't take your kids and leave, did she?" He turned his head away. He didn't want me to see him cry.

I could only sit in silence with Tim, I had no answers for him. It was not time to tell him things would be okay, not time to talk about staying positive. His world had crumbled and all he could do was breathe.

My heart ached for Tim as I drove home. I had been where he was, trying to make sense of who he was and what his future held. I suspect that most of us will never fully understand ourselves because we are looking through a biased lens. But eventually most of us will come to some level of understanding of who we are and the million little events, and some major ones, that contributed to us arriving in that place.

That long journey is one thing, but I found that being able to accept my true self and all the things that happened to me was the true challenge, the true liberation. But we are ever evolving creatures, not static entities. From there, it was up to me to use that acceptance as a platform for growth and change. Change is both hard and frightening but it's also inevitable. Understanding myself that little bit better was a major pre-requisite in making sure that the changes I made took me in the right direction.

I was no different to Tim and there but for the grace of God went I.

It was early March, 2020 when I started to feel the pull of the club again. We had a few friends over for a barbeque and after they had left, Tess and I were dancing in the lounge. It was slow, intimate dancing, just the two of us.

"Do you think about what we did at all?" I asked.

"What did we do?"

"Do you think about the club?" Tess smiled wickedly as I swung her around.

"Yeah, sometimes. Some of it is hard to even remember," she replied.

"Some of it?"

"Do you," Tess asked, "think about it?"

"Sometimes. Yeah, I think about it." Tess listened. "I've got all these questions I want to ask, about twenty of them."

"Good for you."

"I was thinking." I searched for the right words. "I was thinking it would be good to ask them."

"Ask them whenever you want."

"Maybe, sometime soon, only if you wanted to. Maybe we could go again." I tried to gauge Tess' reaction. "To the club." We danced silently for a moment.

"No. Not now." Tess let go of my waist and paused the music playing from her phone. "I'm getting tired. I might go to bed." She kissed my cheek then headed to bed without waiting for a reply.

I climbed quietly into bed soon afterwards. I reached out and Tess reeled away from my touch. She turned, facing her back to me. I had well more than twenty questions at that moment, none of which I would ever ask. The next day, Tess was far, far away. She didn't talk much, or look at me. This journey had always had an element of playing with fire and fire was unpredictable.

That night, Tess and I lay on our bed. She spoke about a few unrelated comments I had made at the barbeque that had annoyed her. Maybe I was over reading her reaction.

"4 times. We never used to leave the kids at all. I think we should leave it for a while. I need to get back to the gym anyway. It's alright for you, you never put on any weight. No."

I couldn't believe that Tess had put on an ounce, she looked as good as ever. But that wasn't really the point. She didn't want to go and that was that. I ran my fingertips along the length of her arm like I always did. It was going to be harder that I thought to leave something like that. Tess dozed as we lay silently on the bed.

"We're so lucky. We've got two beautiful kids. They are the best of both of us," I said.

"Yeah, we are, there's still those teenage years to deal with but they're beautiful."

"Remember the first time we ever went to the club? We were sitting in the pub before it. You asked me what I feared most. I've thought a lot about that question. I never really answered it properly. I thought you were talking about the club."

"I was," Tess said.

"I've been thinking about what I fear most in life but I never asked you. Not that night. What do you fear most?" It had taken me an age to figure it out but Tess' response was instant.

"Being alone."

"That is the exact same answer as mine, to the word. We're so alike in so many ways," I said.

"And so different at the same time."

We never returned to the club and I never asked again. The last time we visited Deepest Desires was in January, 2020. Tess and I were blissfully ignorant of the way the planet would change forever in the coming months and years. Smoke had filled the air for weeks already but the worst bush fires in Australian history were only around the corner. There were times when the smoke lay so thick over us that the days turned into apocalyptic nights.

We stood endlessly with our most valuable belongings and photo albums in suitcases at the door just watching the direction of the wind on our weather apps.

That summer we lost an estimated three billion animals, 3000 homes, five million acres of bushland and thirty-three priceless lives.

After years of devastating drought and months of catastrophic fire across the Australian east coast, it started to rain. It kept raining. Then came the floods. The ground had been scourged of the vegetation that held it together and the floods washed it away, along with houses, livelihoods and many people's sense of hope that our climate might somehow right itself on its own.

But the warning shots from mother earth did not stop there. That December, 2019, in a wet food market somewhere in Wuhan Province, China, a microscopic virus found a way to travel from its host species to humans. COVID 19. The social distancing that came to define that pandemic was a heavy blow to the swinger's scene. A scene that operated on social connection, very close connection, not distance. But that incidental outcome was nothing compared to the tsunami of change and hardship that would hit the world.

With the virus, the racist beliefs that lay dormant in so many hearts found a voice as our planet and country seemed more divided that ever. The parochial sentiment between states echoed loudly as borders closed and the political rhetoric that fuelled the divide machined into gear. Behind every speech about protecting 'our own', about the responsibly of following the health advice, rang loud the greedy self-interests of politicians clawing for the next vote.

2020 was a landmark point in time for humanity and I think that it was the first time that many people across the world really understood the gravity of our planet's direction. The virus, the changing climate, the political and social unrest around the world were an ominous message that life had changed forever.

I wondered if humanity was really listening and whether the clear message that mother earth was sending us was being heard at all. I still wonder if we are listening, and more importantly, if we have the wisdom or the will to change. I thought often about the future that my children would live in, along with future generations. The long months confined at home waiting out the fires and the virus gave everyone a lot of time to think.

Deepest Desires seemed far from important during those times, but it stayed with me. I spent considerable time thinking about the path that we had taken. Was it okay? I had been over that question already. We had broken so many social, cultural and religious rules. Rules set in stone, important rules. For the most part, I was still at peace with it, despite the ongoing dialogue with my God.

Tess and I had stuck to the rules which was key to the whole journey. We had supported each other, respected each other and I was strangely proud of us.

I often thought that some other couples we knew could have benefited so much from what we had done. Others could not have got within a mile of the place without self-destructing. I honestly would have loved for them to feel that kind of energy. But we could never tell anyone, and both of us stuck steadfast to that rule. We had too.

Those nights stayed with me. Something as heavy as that becomes a part of you. I remember Michael Hutchence saying that performing in front of a stadium of screaming fans was so incredible that the rest of life seemed a little mundane. I was no rock star and the club was a world apart from what he was talking about but I understood what he meant. The weeks after each visit were kind of flat as I came back to earth from those incredible highs.

They were big nights, really big nights, always following the same crazy plan: pub-crawl, questions, dinner and then the club. If memory is like a camera, then I had an album of snap shots and photos, with very little video footage. But the feeling was as clear and close as ever, that feeling of being alive with this electricity charging through me. Sitting above that I remember the love and respect I felt for Tess.

"Are you awake?" I asked Tess as my mind raced.

"No. I'm tired."

"You get some sleep beautiful girl." I leaned over and kissed her on the cheek while her eyes remained shut tight.

Tess fell asleep quickly but my mind couldn't rest, as usual. I often thought about my years on the footy field. I got into a fair few fights when I was playing. Tess hated it. I never understood how I was such a mellow, respectful guy most of the time but when the whistle went, I changed. One bad refereeing call and I saw red. If a guy put a shot on me, then I reacted every time, with force. After the game, I was always so down on myself for fighting, reacting, letting my team down and I never knew why I did it.

The second last game I ever played I mouthed off to the ref, big time. I got ten minutes in the sin bin at a crucial part of the second half. They scored and we lost. In the sheds after the game, I found myself apologising to a young guy for letting the team down. I had shed blood for that team, won premierships and given so much over the years. I didn't really owe anyone an apology.

"I don't know why I lose it sometimes. I don't mean too," I said to him. His name was Jake. He seemed to understand.

"It's because your body is in the fight or flight mode. You don't back down. All the boys respect it. Don't worry about the ten minutes, we probably would have gone down anyway," he explained.

"Yeah, maybe." It struck me how on the mark his words were and that I had never realised it. When that whistle went, my team and I went into battle. We hit hard and got hit just as hard. Rugby league is the toughest game on earth, there is constant physical collision throughout the entire eighty minutes. I loved it.

Fight or flight. As I sat in that dressing shed, I remember thinking how it became clear that all my life I had chosen flight. I ran away from the contact, from the conflict that I had endured as a kid. But when I walked onto the field and that whistle blew, I spent eighty minutes of every week in a place where I would not run, I would not back down for a second. I would fight. And I fought hard, with every ounce of strength I had inside me. For those minutes on a Saturday afternoon, I would stand my ground and if I ever felt like someone had wronged me then it was on. It was the only time I chose to fight, even though I never knew it.

"Only three more weeks till my birthday," Josh said happily the next morning, strolling into the shed. "October 27."

"Yeah, I remember the date." I paused and thought of those moments when I first held him in my arms. Women deserve unwavering, unqualified respect, and watching the person you love endure childbirth and bring a new life into the world was something beyond understanding. The birth of my two children were the two greatest moments of my life and Tess was the one that gave them to me. "A teenager in the house, wow."

"I'll have a car soon."

"Ease up. I remember the second you were born. I cut the cord connecting you and your mum. I had these really sharp doctor's scissors but it was still so tough to cut."

"I might ask for an electric scooter like Jet's. You shoulda let the doctor do it."

"No way. It was the proudest moment of my life, that and when Leyla was born. Your mum was amazing. She was so, so strong."

"What are you doing?"

"Drilling holes for the hinges on the bench doors. Wanna help?"

"Yep, can I drill?"

"How about you get the screws we need."

"What's all that?" Josh asked, pointing to the seven hand written A4 pages pinned on the wall above the bench.

"It's my plan. My plan for getting old."

"You're already old."

"Maybe. They're seven things that I try to follow every day. A guy called Bergland wrote them. Dunno who he is." The pages had been there for about a year but I found myself being drawn to them more and more. Looking at it, it occurred to me that fighting, really fighting, never had anything to do punch ups on a footy field. It had everything to do with fighting my own challenges and finding peace with who I was and how I felt. Fighting meant living with integrity and doing what I knew was right.

Fighting meant honesty, forgiveness and finding the strength to be the best person I could be for the ones I loved most. But it also meant being the best person I could be for me.

"That first one is a hard one. Stop holding grudges against yourself and others."

"Well, I hate the Rams. They broke Jet's arm."

"That was an accident. That kid didn't mean it. Did you see him watching the ambulance drive off?"

"No."

The more I thought about it the more it boiled down to one word, forgiveness. I wondered if this Bergland dude was a religious soul. The power of forgiveness was immeasurable and it resonated completely with me.

"The second one says embrace who you are, warts and all. It's about liking yourself, even the parts that aren't perfect." It was hard because I honestly liked who I was for the most part. I was proud of the family and the life that I had built through years of hard work and perseverance. But the self-doubt, the dark parts of me were places that I mostly ignored, until they spilled out and into a brown bottle. Learning to love myself seemed almost impossible at times, but I was taking little steps and I was heading in the right direction.

"What does vocalise mean?" Josh asked.

"Vocalise means talking about things. Vocalise your imperfections shamelessly. It means own up to your mistakes. Pretty much it's about taking responsibility for things." It was an Australian cultural norm to take the piss out of yourself. But the point of this idea was not to do it in the flippant, larrikin way that was normal, but in an authentic and constructive way. Admit when you're wrong, take responsibility for your shit and mean what you say when you talk about addressing it.

"Don't get it," Josh said.

"Number four says to practice emotional regulation. Kinda like just staying calm, like on the footy field when you're under the pump."

"Like Jet, he's always calm."

"Yeah, like Jet." It took a while to work out that this was another form of my dad's advice when I was a kid: things are never as bad as they seem or as good as they seem. I whole-heartedly embraced the idea and slowly I was improving the emotional self-control that I thought Bergland was talking about.

That idea dove tailed straight in number five: stay on an even keel via equanimity. I had to look up the meaning of equanimity. It meant calmness and composure, especially in difficult situations. I loved the concept and I consciously tried to keep on an emotional 'even keel' the best that I could.

"What's that one say?" asked Josh, struggling to read the scribbled handwriting.

"It says apologise whole-heartedly for any wrongdoing. Like when you dumped Leyla on the tramp the other day. You shoulda said sorry." This one was something I thought I was already doing but it was the ability to recognise mistakes and really take responsibility for my wrong doing that needed work.

"She just ran off to Mum. I couldn't."

The last was truly the most profound for me, it wrapped all of the others into a succinct mantra and I held it close as I got older.

"I like the last one. It says move on, let go of negative emotions and regrets."

"Like in a game, when the other team scores."

"Yep, just like that." I had dwelt on the profoundness of that idea many times since I had started seeing Bill. I loved that it was the negative shit I could let go of, if I chose, and I could keep all of the good stuff close to my heart. That idea was at the centre of my growth as a father, a husband and a person.

Next to Bergland's seven rules was a small magazine headline that I had cut out. It was a Chinese proverb written in calligraphy over a sunset background: 'Forgiveness frees the soul.' I loved how clearly it articulated that forgiving others reaped the greatest benefits for ourselves, not them. Forgiving others was profound but forgiving ourselves was an even greater freedom.

"There, all the holes are drilled. You want to help me screw the hinges on later?"

"Not really."

"Dinner," yelled Tess.

At dawn the next morning, I ran along the path bordering the beach. The beauty of that place never got old and each sun painted canvas was as unique as it was stunning. There was an energy in this place too, but it was a healthy, sustainable energy.

I was a broken person, but we're all broken in one way or another. Some of us are just better at covering over the cracks with lies, a bottle, possessions or whatever. But somehow my broken pieces fitted back together to make a complete picture. There would always be cracks and fault lines but that was just part of being human. I was okay with that. Tess had been my glue for many years but she deserved better than that and I didn't need to be held together anymore.

That morning was a clear masterpiece and I was out the door before dawn. The first rays of crimson sunlight seemed infinitely welcoming as my feet hit the concrete with the waves caressing the shore. That new light powered me each morning. I thought of Dad who loved an old Spike Milligan quote, 'Blessed are the cracked, for they let in the light.' Maybe coming to terms with those cracks, embracing them, could help others. It most definitely helped me and the light blessed me as much as anyone else. Maybe that was the whole point. My healing helped the ones I loved because our lives were one story.

Some days I thought that I had finally found a sense of peace, something as close to contentment as I would ever find. I had a fulfilling, yet demanding, job where I made a difference in people's lives. I had a fulfilling loving marriage with the only person I had ever wanted to be with. My kids were happy and growing into beautiful people. Each morning I saw the sun rise while I exercised in some way and I took the energy that it gave me into the rest of the day.

But other days just felt dark, like I had no control of the sadness that was always there no matter how much I tried to run from it. On those days, I reached out my hands as far as I could, clutching at something that would help. Those demons would always be there and alcohol remained a crutch in the corner, waiting to be picked back up. But on those days, I kept fighting and I just had to get through them the best that I could, hoping that tomorrow would be better.

I often wanted to ask Tess if she saw a new sense of peace in me, or if she still saw the sadness that she knew only too well. I never asked though. I knew that she would be brutally honest, which is all she knew, and I wasn't sure that I wanted to hear her answer. But at least I knew for sure that every single day I gave everything I had for my family and that was all I could do.

I'd always have a sadness inside me. I think everyone does. Life is full of 'slings and arrows' and we all have our demons. But I was learning to live with mine and disarm them by accepting them.

The footy field was always my happy place. One pissed night I asked Tess to scatter my ashes over our local ground. I meant it. But footy was a young man's game and it was just a memory of a place where I felt completely at home. A place where life couldn't touch me each Saturday afternoon.

If footy was my happy place, then running was my drug. My endorphin chasing time out from life. The more I ran, the fitter I got and the fitter I got, the more I ran. I got up early to run. The pre-dawn stillness was a world without noise, without fear.

Forgiveness frees the soul. That thought had always stayed with me. It was a hard thing to do, to forgive. But holding on so tight to the hurt and pain helped no one. It was like if I let it go then I was letting every person that hurt me off the hook. They walked away, without any of the justice they deserved. But in reality, the only thing that forgiveness did was to free me.

No one else really knew of the things I held onto and they had made their peace with those things a long time ago. To move forward I had to look backwards first. I had to find peace in what happened a lifetime ago. My dad didn't leave me. He was just trying to do the best he could, be the best father he could be while battling all of the same demons that attacked me. He loved me and Luke more than anything. He endured a lot as a child, things that I could never imagine. He never abandoned us. He was there by my side every minute of every day.

When I was young, the only things I ever wanted was a loving, supportive wife and children that I could love. Tess gave me all of that and at that moment I felt lucky, rich. But as time went on I couldn't help but feel that something was missing. In my heart, I had always longed for a best friend. Eventually I came to understand that it was Tess. She was my best friend. She was all I ever needed and I loved her completely with every part of me.

That morning felt somehow new, but I guess every dawn does in its own way. It was a new day and a new opportunity to be better than the day before. The gentle, rhythmic sound of the waves was punctuated by the seagull's banter.

I glided along the pavement and the early morning clarity that had built over recent months sat happily in my heart.

As I watched the sun come up over the water, I said the words in my mind. I forgive you Dad and I love you. My heart however, heard something different. I forgive myself and I love myself. That was the true awakening. I had myself and my God to answer to. No one else, not even Tess.

I didn't have to impress anyone or prove myself to them. Not the kids from my childhood or the players on my team. Not the colleagues at work or even my family. The broken ten-year-old inside of me had always felt that, somehow, I wasn't good enough and that the relenting standards circling me every day just might make me good enough to be accepted, to be liked and to be loved.

But as the dull grey of the sky slowly morphed into pink blankets of light, I felt good enough. I felt that I deserved to be loved. The acceptance and love that I had been aching for all along had always been there. I just couldn't see it, feel it. But I could see it clearly now and I breathed it in with the crisp morning air. I spun the ring on my left hand as I ran and smiled.

The End

Ingram Content Group UK Ltd.
Milton Keynes UK
UKHW021810130723
425097UK00007B/248